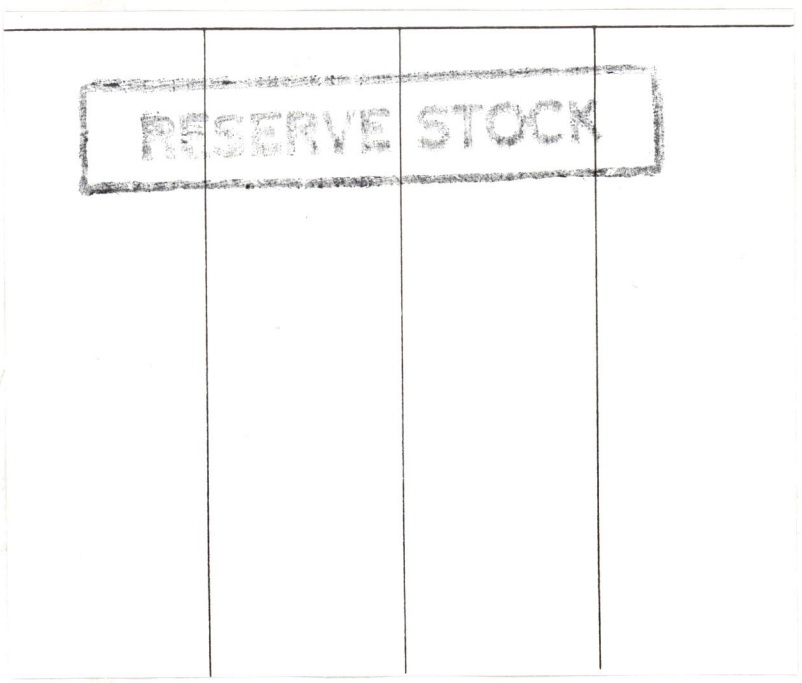

دون

Cavalier 1975-77 Autobook

By Kenneth Ball
Associate Member, Guild of Motoring Writers
and the Autobooks Team of Technical Writers

Vauxhall Cavalier L 1975-77
Vauxhall Cavalier GL 1975-77
Vauxhall Cavalier Coupé GL, GLS 1975-77

Autobooks Ltd. Golden Lane Brighton BN1 2QJ England

The AUTOBOOK series of Workshop Manuals is the largest in the world and covers the majority of British and Continental motor cars, as well as the majority of Japanese and Australian models.

Whilst every care has been taken to ensure correctness of information it is obviously not possible to guarantee complete freedom from errors or to accept liability arising from such errors or omissions.

CONTENTS

Acknowledgement

Introduction

ISBN 0 85147 649 X

First Edition   1977

© Autobooks Ltd 1977

884

Printed and bound in Brighton England for Autobooks Ltd by G. Beard & Son Ltd   A

ACKNOWLEDGEMENT

My thanks are due to Vauxhall Motors Ltd for their unstinted co-operation and also for supplying data and illustrations.

Considerable assistance has also been given by owners, who have discussed their cars in detail, and I would like to express my gratitude for this invaluable advice and help.

Kenneth Ball
Associate Member, Guild of Motoring Writers
Ditchling Sussex England.

INTRODUCTION

This do-it-yourself Workshop Manual has been specially written for the owner who wishes to maintain his vehicle in first class condition and to carry out the bulk of his own servicing and repairs. Considerable savings on garage charges can be made, and one can drive in safety and confidence knowing the work has been done properly.

Comprehensive step-by-step instructions and illustrations are given on most dismantling, overhauling and assembling operations. Certain assemblies require the use of expensive special tools, the purchase of which would be unjustified. In these cases information is included but the reader is recommended to hand the unit to the agent for attention.

Throughout the Manual hints and tips are included which will be found invaluable, and there is an easy to follow fault diagnosis at the end of each chapter.

Whilst every care has been taken to ensure correctness of information it is obviously not possible to guarantee complete freedom from errors or omissions or to accept liability arising from such errors or omissions.

Instructions may refer to the righthand or lefthand sides of the vehicle or the components. These are the same as the righthand or lefthand of an observer standing behind the vehicle and looking forward.

CHAPTER 1

THE ENGINE

1:1 Description

The engine is an in-line four cylinder overhead valve unit of either 1.6 or 1.9 litre capacity, the engine types being designated 16, 16S or 19S. Sections through the engine assembly are shown in **FIGS 1:1** and **1:2**. All engines have the same stroke measurement and differ only in cylinder bore size and compression ratio. Details of engine types and capacities are given in **Technical Data** at the end of this manual, together with further technical information.

The cast iron cylinder block is integral with the upper half of the crankcase, the lower half of which is formed by the pressed steel sump. Valves operated by rockers and short tappets are set in line along the cast iron cylinder head. The camshaft is also mounted in the cylinder head, supported by three bearings in 16 and 16S engines or four bearings in 19S engines. Camshaft drive is by means of a roller chain connecting crankshaft and camshaft sprockets. An automatic adjuster is fitted to control chain tension.

The light alloy pistons have solid skirts and offset gudgeon pins which are an interference fit in the connecting rods.

The distributor and oil pump are driven from a gear on the front of the crankshaft. The oil pump draws oil from the engine sump and delivers it under pressure to a full flow oil filter. Through drilled passages the oil then passes to the main, big-end and camshaft bearings and to the timing chain tensioner and valve gear. The lubrication system incorporates a relief valve which operates should oil pressure become too high, and a bypass valve which operates should the oil filter become clogged. In the latter case, high pressure on the outlet side of the pump will cause the valve to open and allow oil to bypass the filter and pass directly to the engine lubrication points.

1:2 Removing and refitting the engine

The normal operations of decarbonising and cylinder head servicing can be carried out without the need for engine removal. A major overhaul, however, can only be satisfactorily carried out with the engine removed and transferred to the bench. Note that, in the case of an engine needing major overhaul work and, possibly, cylinder reboring, it may well prove to be more economical to fit a complete reconditioned engine. This procedure requires that the original engine is removed, the ancillary

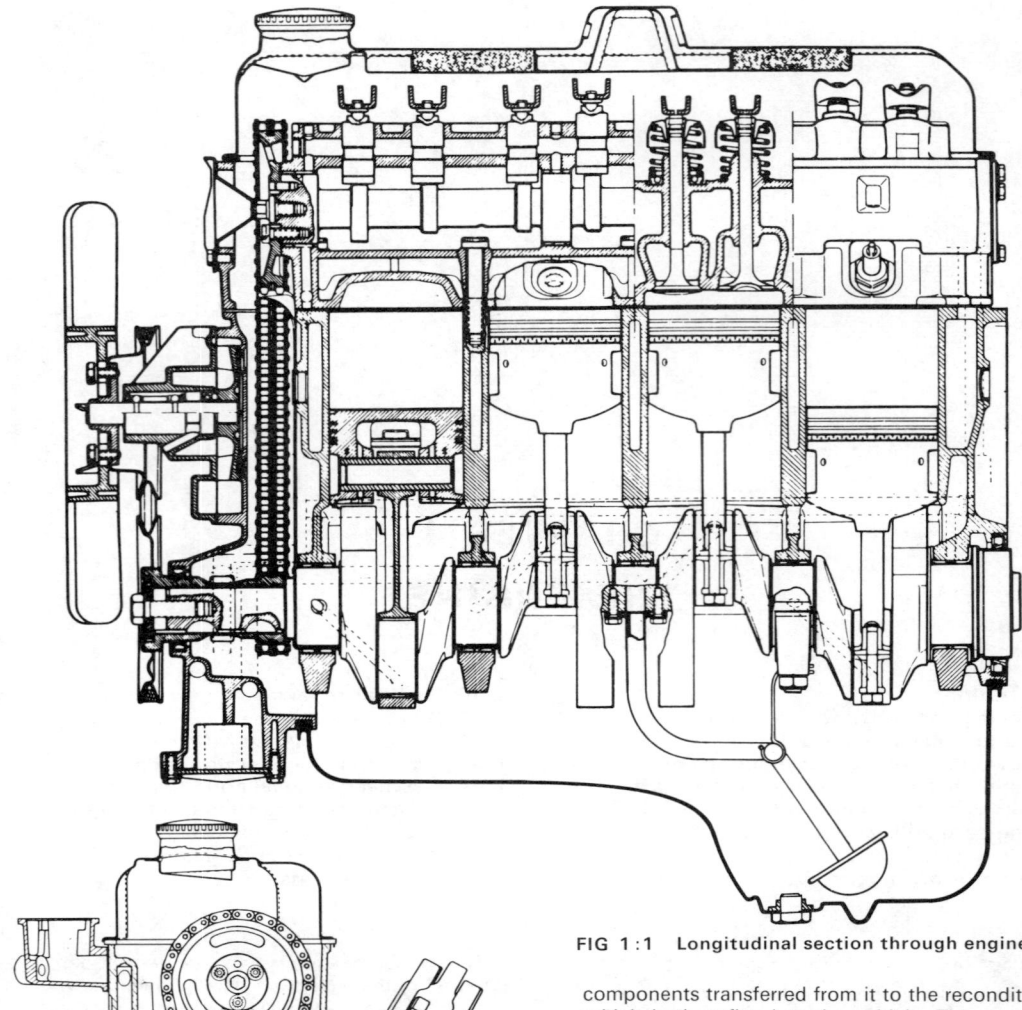

FIG 1:1 Longitudinal section through engine assembly

components transferred from it to the reconditioned unit, which is then fitted to the vehicle. This procedure will effect a great saving in labour time and guarantees engine performance.

If the owner is not a skilled motor engineer, it is suggested that he will find much useful information in **Hints on Maintenance and Overhaul** at the end of this manual and that he read it before starting work. It must be stressed that all lifting equipment should be sound and firmly based and not likely to collapse under the weight imposed.

For some overhaul work, certain special tools are essential and the owner would be well advised to check on the availability of these tools or suitable substitutes before tackling the items involved. Note that the bolts securing certain components, such as the cylinder head, must be turned using a special tri-square wrench of the correct size. A set of suitable wrenches is available as part number VR 2238.

The engine and transmission are removed as an assembly, the two units being separated later if necessary for access to engine components.

FIG 1:2 Engine cross section showing timing gear

Removal:

Drain the engine oil. Where fitted, disconnect the oil cooler at the transmission as described in **Chapter 7**. Remove the bonnet which is fixed by two set screws at each hinge. Drain the cooling system and remove the radiator as described in **Chapter 4**. Refer to **Chapter 2** and remove the air cleaner and the controls, pipes and connections from the carburetter. Disconnect all pipes, wires and controls connected between the engine and bodywork or ancillary components.

Refer to **FIG 1:3** and remove the nuts and washers securing the mounting brackets on the engine to the mounting blocks on each side, Refer to **Chapter 8** and disconnect the propeller shaft from the transmission. Unscrew the exhaust pipe bracket at the transmission and disconnect the exhaust pipe from the exhaust manifold. Refer to **Chapter 6** or **Chapter 7** and remove the manual transmission gearlever or disconnect the automatic transmission selector linkages. On manual transmission models, disconnect the clutch control cable from the release lever as described in **Chapter 5**. Disconnect the speedometer cable and the wires connected to the reversing light switch at the transmission.

Connect suitable lifting equipment to the engine using a 1.5m (60in) long cable at the front and a 2m (70in) long cable at the rear. Refer to **FIG 1:3** and disconnect the crossmember securing the transmission to the underbody. Make a final check to ensure that all connections between the engine and car body are free, then carefully lift out the engine and transmission, guiding the assembly carefully to avoid component damage. If necessary, refer to **Chapter 6** or **Chapter 7** and remove the transmission from the engine.

Refitting:

This is a reversal of the removal procedure, observing the appropriate torque wrench settings given in the **Appendix**. When installing the transmission support crossmember, make sure that the mounting rubber is not twisted when the retaining nuts are tightened. Refill the sump with the recommended grade of engine oil. If drained, refill the transmission with the recommended grade of oil or fluid, as described in **Chapter 6** or **Chapter 7**. Refill the cooling system as described in **Chapter 4**. Start the engine and run it until normal working temperature is reached, then check engine idle and adjust the carburetter if necessary as described in **Chapter 2**.

1:3 Inlet and exhaust manifolds

The inlet and exhaust manifolds are bolted together at their centre to provide a hot spot for the fuel/air mixture. Gaskets are used to seal the joint between inlet and exhaust manifolds and the joint between manifolds and cylinder head (see **FIG 1:4**). The manifolds should be removed as an assembly by removing the bolts securing them to the cylinder head. If the inlet and exhaust manifolds are separated for any reason, it is necessary to ensure that the manifolds assume their correct relative positions when attached to the cylinder head. This is achieved by loosely bolting the manifolds together with joint gasket installed, then temporarily installing the manifolds to the cylinder head without a gasket. With the

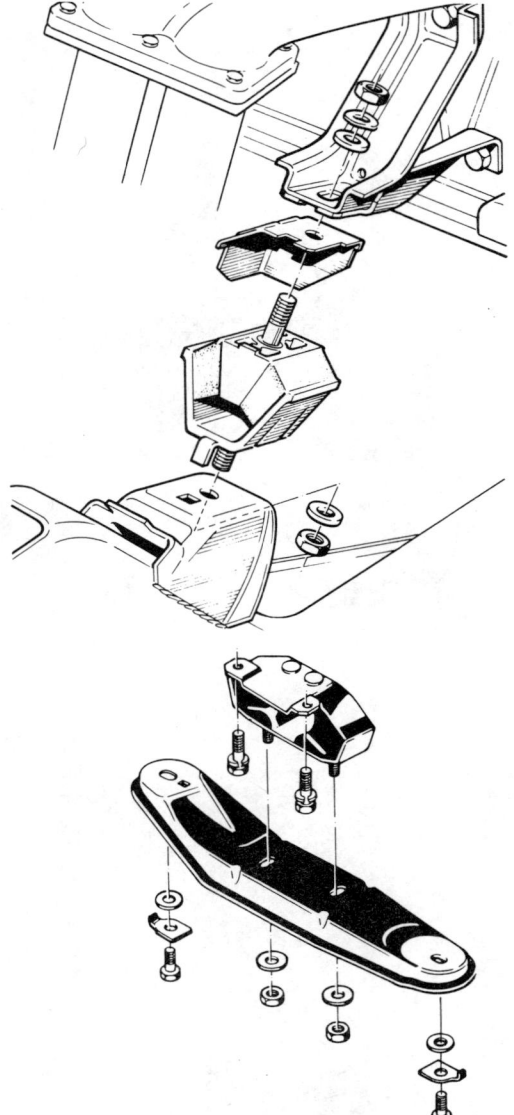

FIG 1:3 Engine mountings (above) and transmission mounting (below)

manifolds in this position, tighten the four bolts securing the manifolds together to the specified torque, then remove the assembly and reinstall to the cylinder head with a new flange gasket. Finally tighten the manifold to cylinder head bolts to the specified torque.

When attaching the exhaust pipe flange to the exhaust manifold, insert the front bolts through the gasket and partially thread into manifold flange (see **FIG 1:5**). Hook slotted hole side of pipe flange over partially installed bolts to support the pipes while locating the remaining bolts. Tighten the centre bolts of the flange evenly, then the four outer bolts. Finally, check tightness of centre bolts.

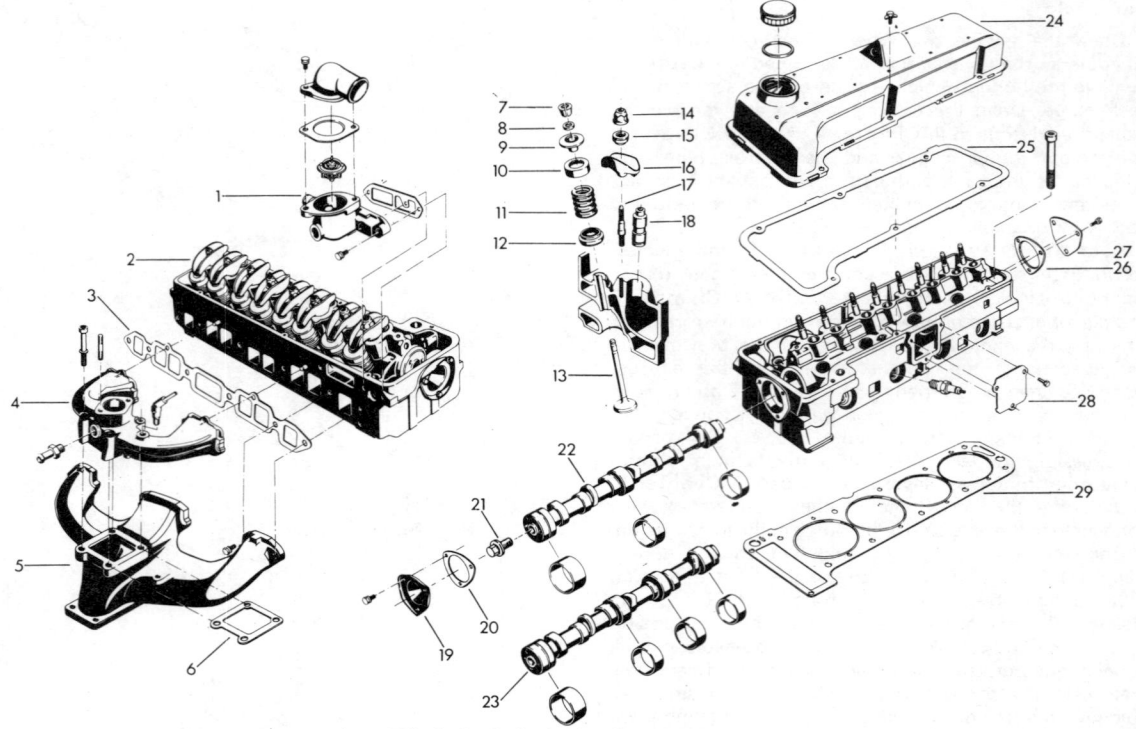

FIG 1:4   Cylinder head components

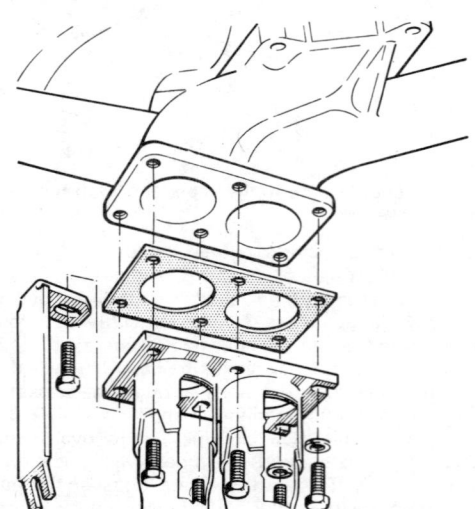

FIG 1:5   Exhaust pipe to manifold connections

1:4 Removing and refitting cylinder head

The cylinder head must be removed in order to service the valve gear, camshaft or both, but note that the rocker gear and tappets can be removed with the cylinder head installed, after detaching the rocker cover.

Removal:

Disconnect the battery earth cable. Drain the cooling system as described in **Chapter 4**, collecting the coolant in a clean container if it is to be re-used. Remove the air cleaner and carburetter as described in **Chapter 2**, then remove the inlet and exhaust manifolds as described in **Section 1:3**. Disconnect all hoses, pipes and wiring connected between cylinder head and bodywork or ancillary components. Remove the sparking plugs.

Refer to **FIG 1:4** and remove rocker cover 24 and gasket 25. Turn the engine until the camshaft recesses shown in **FIG 1:6** are vertical to allow the removal of the lefthand side cylinder head bolts.

Refer to **FIG 1:7** and unscrew the plug arrowed to remove timing chain tensioner from timing case. Refer to **FIG 1:4** and remove plate 19 and gasket 20. Use an 8mm tri-square wrench to remove the three camshaft sprocket to camshaft securing bolts shown in **FIG 1:8**. Slide the

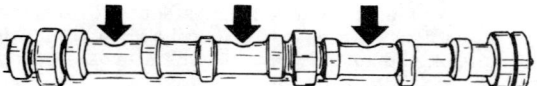

FIG 1:6 Access grooves in camshaft

sprocket off the camshaft, keeping the sprocket teeth firmly engaged in the chain and the chain tight, then allow the sprocket to rest on the support bracket which is bolted to the cylinder block. Do not allow the chain to slip on either the camshaft or crankshaft sprocket, otherwise the engine will have to be further dismantled and retimed according to the instructions in **Section 1:8**.

Using a suitable Allen key, remove the two screws arrowed in **FIG 1:9** which secure the timing cover. Using a 12mm tri-square wrench, slacken the cylinder head bolts in the reverse order to that shown in **FIG 1:10**. Remove the bolts and detach the cylinder head, tapping the head carefully with a soft-faced hammer if it sticks in position. Remove and discard the cylinder head gasket and collect the 'O' ring which is fitted between the cylinder head and the upper face of the timing cover.

When the valves are fully opened they protrude below the level of the cylinder head joint face, so the cylinder head should be supported on the bench by a wooden block at each end to prevent valve stem distortion caused by valves contacting the work surface.

Refitting:

If the engine has been turned while the cylinder head was removed and the timing setting lost, support the camshaft sprocket by suitable means to prevent the sprocket teeth from damaging the support bolted to the engine, then turn the engine until the front and rear pistons are at the tops of their bores and the distributor rotor arm is pointing in a direction diametrically opposite to that shown in **FIGS 3:8** or **3:9**. This brings the engine to the firing point for number four cylinder which ensures correct alignment of the camshaft sprocket when the camshaft is turned to allow for installation of the lefthand side cylinder head bolts.

Before installing the cylinder head, slacken the rocker securing bolts so that all valves are fully closed. This prevents any possibility of valves contacting pistons when the engine is turned for correct alignment. Leave the rocker nuts loose until assembly is complete and the valve clearances checked as described later.

Carefully clean the mating surfaces of cylinder head and cylinder block, avoiding the use of sharp tools which could scratch the surfaces. Before fitting the cylinder head gasket, which must be installed dry, make sure that the rubber 'O' ring is located in the timing cover counterbore and apply two 3mm (0.12in) beads of Silastic 732 RTV sealer over the joint between timing cover and cylinder block (see arrows in **FIG 1:11**). Note that the sealer hardens quickly, so the cylinder head should be installed within five minutes of application.

Fit a new head gasket to the cylinder block, making sure that the gasket is the correct way up by checking that each hole in the gasket matches the appropriate bore in the cylinder block surface. Turn the camshaft until the grooves are correctly located for access to cylinder head bolt holes as shown in **FIG 1:6**, then install the cylinder

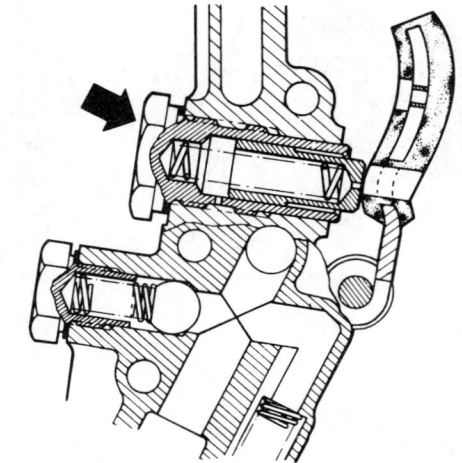

FIG 1:7 Timing chain tensioner location

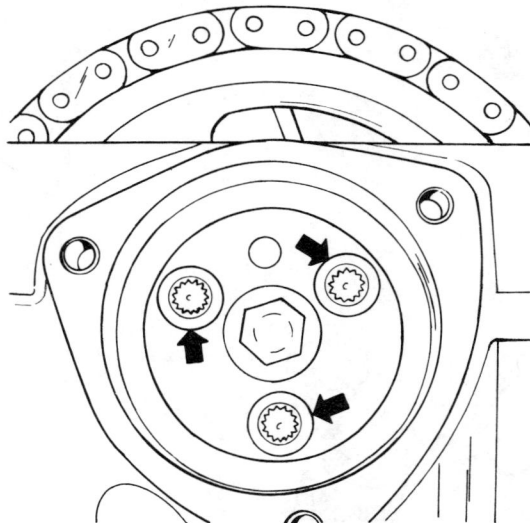

FIG 1:8 Camshaft sprocket securing bolts

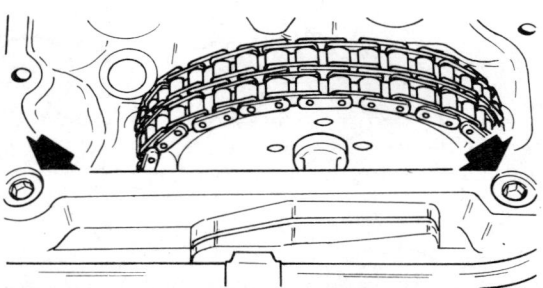

FIG 1:9 Cylinder head to timing cover screws

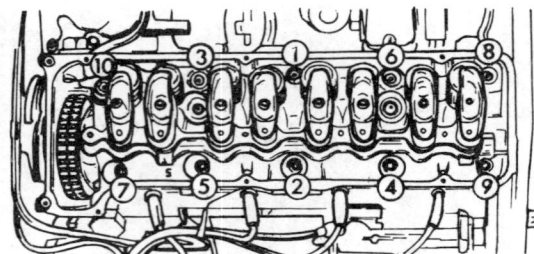

FIG 1:10 Cylinder head bolt tightening sequence

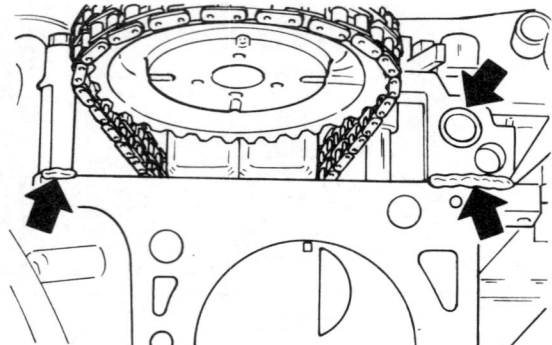

FIG 1:11 'O' ring and sealant bead locations

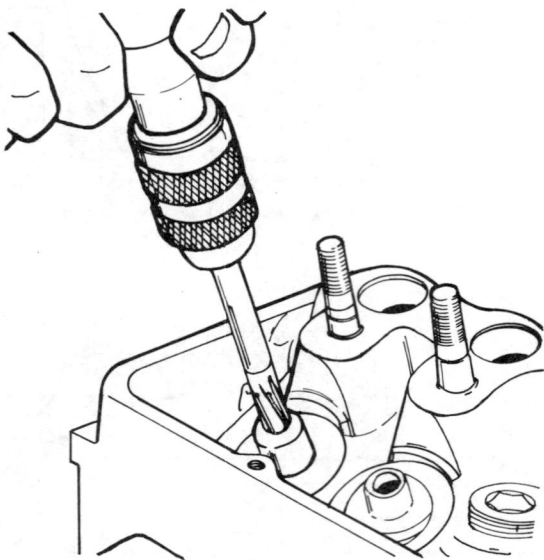

FIG 1:12 Reaming valve guide bores to accept valves with oversize stems

head and fit the retaining bolts finger tight. Now tighten the bolts a little at a time in the order shown in **FIG 1:10** to the specified torque figure. Fit the screws securing cylinder head to timing cover.

Keeping the chain firmly wrapped around the sprocket, slide the camshaft sprocket on to the camshaft and align with the guide pin. If necessary, keep the sprocket supported while turning the engine slightly to align the guide pin. Fit and tighten the sprocket to camshaft securing bolts. Temporarily install the gasket and cover plate, then push the camshaft fully rearwards and check end float between cover 19 and head of bolt 21 (see **FIG 1:4**) using feeling gauges. Clearance should be between 0.10 and 0.20mm (0.004 and 0.008in). Excess clearance can be eliminated by carefully adjusting the cover with a suitable drift. Insufficient clearance can be rectified by removing the cover and carefully tapping with a hammer at the point closest to the camshaft bolt. When finally installing the cover, use a new gasket unless the original is in perfect condition and smear the plate retaining bolts with Loctite 270 (AVV) before installation.

Refit the remaining components in the reverse order of removal, with the exception of the rocker cover. Refer to **Section 1:6** and make an initial adjustment of valve clearances, then install the rocker cover, refill the cooling system and run the engine until it reaches normal operating temperature. Remove the rocker cover and make final adjustments to valve clearances. On completion, finally install the rocker cover using a new gasket unless the original is in perfect condition.

After the vehicle has been driven for a distance of about 1000km (600 miles), the cylinder head bolts must be retightened. This can be carried out with the engine either hot or cold. Remove the rocker cover then slacken each bolt slightly before retightening to the specified torque figure, in the order shown in **FIG 1:10**. On completion, recheck valve clearances as described in **Section 1:6**.

1:5 Servicing head, valve gear and camshaft

FIG 1:4 shows cylinder head components and camshaft installation. Note that the camshaft for 16 and 16S engines is provided with three bearings, that for 19S engines with four bearings.

Dismantling:

It is important to store or mark all components carefully so that they can be refitted in their original positions if they are not to be renewed.

If necessary, remove the thermostat housing assembly 1 complete with gasket (see **FIG 1:4**). Remove nuts 14 and rocker balls 15, then remove rocker arms 16 and tappets 18.

If a camshaft is to be removed, it must be withdrawn through the front of the cylinder head. Remove plate 28 so that the fingers can be inserted in the side aperture to support the camshaft as it is removed, to prevent damage to the journals and cam lobes.

Using a suitable valve spring compressor tool, compress each valve spring in turn and remove the split taper collets 7. Release the spring compressor and remove the seal 8, cap 9, seat 10, spring 11, seal 12 and valve 13.

Servicing:

Valves:

When the valves have been cleaned of carbon deposits they must be inspected for serviceability. Valves with bent stems or badly burned heads must be renewed. Valves that are too pitted to clean up on grinding to their seats may be refaced at a garage, but the amount of metal that can be removed in this operation is limited and new valves will be required if refacing cannot be successfully carried out. Check valve stems for wear or scoring. If replacement valves with oversize stems have been fitted as replacements, these can be indentified by the marking 1, 2 and A on the stem, which represents 0.075, 0.150 and 0.300mm oversizes respectively. When new valves are fitted they must have the same marking as the originals, unless the valve guide is reamed as described later, when a valve having a stem of the next higher oversize must be fitted.

Valve springs:

Test the valve springs by comparison with the figures given in **Technical Data**, or compare their efficiency with that of new springs. To compare with a new spring, insert both the old and new springs end to end with a metal plate between them into the jaws of a vice or under a press. If the old spring is weakened it will close up first when pressure is applied. Make sure that the load is applied squarely to prevent the springs from flying out under pressure. If any spring is shorter or weaker than standard it must be renewed. Note that exhaust valves have tapered springs, intake valves having longer plain springs. Exhaust valve springs must be installed with the narrow tapered end away from the cylinder.

Valve guides:

No separate valve guides are used, the valves operating directly in bores machined in the cylinder head. Guide bores that are worn or scored must be reamed to accept new valves with suitable oversize stems, as described previously. The correct reamers are tools S1183, 1130 or S1131 for valve stem oversizes 1, 2 and A respectively. To ensure an accurate bore at the valve port, reaming should be carried out from the top of the cylinder head as shown in **FIG 1:12**.

Valve seats:

Valve seats in the cylinder head that are too pitted to clean up on grinding to the valves may be refaced at a service station, to the correct angle of 45°.

Rockers and studs:

Inspect the rockers for wear or damage and renew any found to be unserviceable. Damaged threads on rocker studs can be cleaned up by using a suitable die nut. Check that the rocker balls are a free fit on the stud shanks. The balls must be fitted with the spherical face towards the rocker and the threads and shank of the studs should be smeared with hypoid gear oil to prevent excessive friction. Check that the tappet contact foot in each rocker is free to move in its seating (see **FIG 1:13**).

Inspect the rocker studs to check that none are loose in the cylinder head. Check the fit of the self-locking

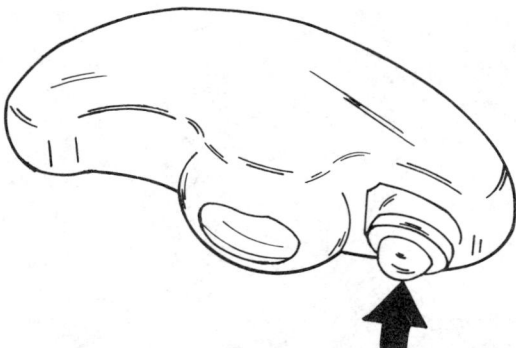

FIG 1:13   Tappet contact foot on rocker

nuts on the threads. Lubricate the thread with hypoid gear oil and test for a minimum reading with a torque wrench of 4Nm (3lb ft) to turn the nut, when the nut is fully engaged on the thread. If a lower reading is obtained, the nut is too slack and it may loosen in service. If the stud is in good condition then the fitting of a new nut may overcome the trouble, but if this still gives a reading that is too low the stud must be renewed as well.

To renew a rocker stud, screw two suitable flat nuts on to the threaded part of the stud and lock the nuts together with two spanners. Use a spanner on the lower nut to unscrew the stud. Lock a pair of nuts on to the new stud, then screw into place until the taper just contacts the cylinder head. Now strike the end of the stud with a soft-faced hammer to seat the taper as shown in **FIG 1:14**, then tighten to the specified torque. Unlock and remove the nuts used for installation.

Camshaft and tappets:

Check the bearing surfaces of the tappets for pitting or scoring and renew if faults are found. Check the tappet bores in the cylinder head for wear or damage. Pitted or lightly scored bores can be smoothed with very fine emerycloth, making sure that all particles of metal are cleaned away afterwards. Excessively worn or damaged bores will dictate cylinder head renewal.

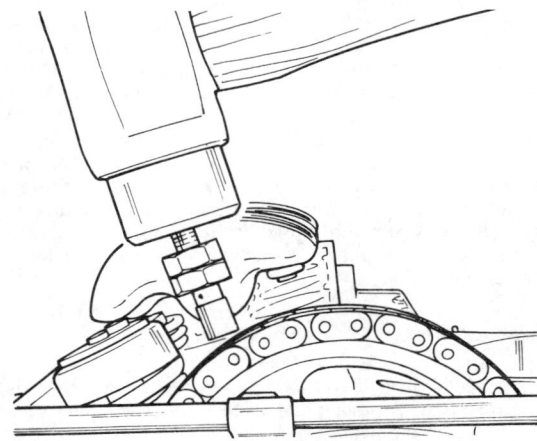

FIG 1:14   Seating rocker stud taper

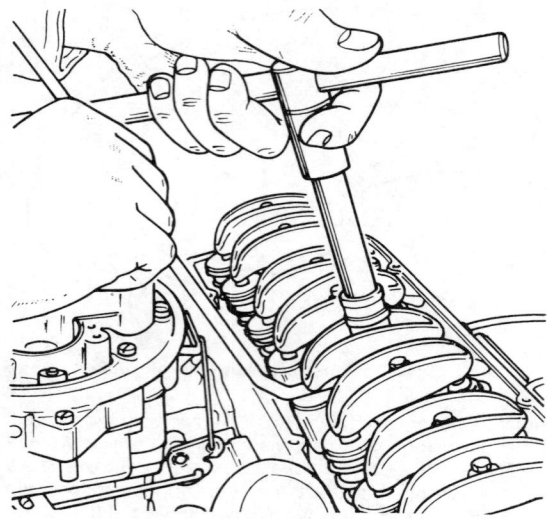

FIG 1:15   Valve clearance adjustment

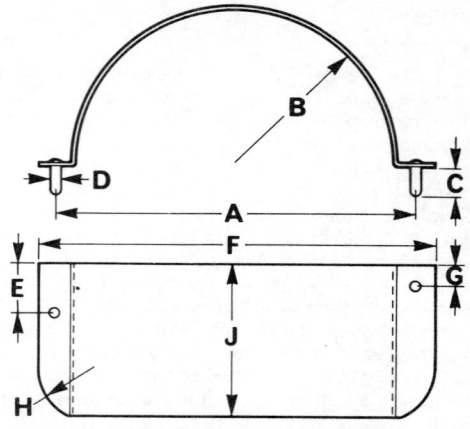

FIG 1:16   Oil deflector dimensions

Key to Fig 1:16   A 168mm (6.61in)   B 75mm (2.95in)
C 12mm (0.47in)   D 4.8mm (0.19in)   E 23mm (0.91in)
F 180mm (7.09in)   G 10mm (0.40in)   H 25mm (0.98in)
J 70mm (2.76in)

Examine the camshaft lobes and journals for wear, scoring or other damage and renew the camshaft if necessary. Check the camshaft bearings in the cylinder head bores. If bearings are worn ·or damaged, or if excessive clearance between camshaft journal and bearing exists, new bearings must be fitted. Due to the need for special in-line reaming equipment, the work should be carried out by a fully equipped service station.

Decarbonising and valve grinding:

Using suitable tools which will not scratch the surfaces, remove all traces of carbon from the combustion chambers, inlet and exhaust ports and joint faces. Plug the water and oil passages in the top surface of the cylinder block with pieces of clean rag to prevent the entry of dirt, then carefully clean the carbon from the piston crowns. Take care not to damage the light alloy piston surfaces during this operation.

Grind the valves to their seats, starting with coarse grade and finishing with fine grade carborundum paste, unless the seats are in very good condition when fine grade paste can be used alone. Use a suction type valve grinding tool and work with a semi-rotary movement, lifting the valve clear of its seat occasionally and turning to a different position before continuing. When the seats of both valve and cylinder head show a smooth matt grey finish on their matching faces, grinding is complete. When the work is finished, clean away every trace of grinding paste from the cylinder head, valves and guides.

Reassembly:

This is a reversal of the dismantling procedure. Use hypoid gear oil to lubricate the rocker stud threads, engine oil for all moving parts. Always use new inlet valve seals, which are available in kit form. If inlet valves with oversize stems are fitted, make sure that the correct valve stem oil seals are used. Seals are identified by the colour of circlip around base of seal, oversizes 1, 2 and A being identified by white, yellow or black circlip colour respectively. After fitting the inlet valve to the cylinder head, locate the protective sleeve, which is included in the seal kit, over the valve stem. Smear sleeve, valve stem and seal with engine oil and carefully slide seal over the valve stem until it is fully located over the boss on the cylinder head.

When valve spring upper seats and caps have been fitted, make sure that the seal shown at 8 in **FIG 1:4** is installed before the split taper collets 7.

When the tappets and rocker assemblies have been installed, fit the rocker securing nuts by a few turns only, so that no valves are held open by the camshaft. This will ensure that the valves cannot contact the pistons when the cylinder head is installed. Refit the cylinder head as described in **Section 1:4**.

1:6 Valve clearance adjustment

Final adjustment of valve clearances must be carried out with the engine at normal operating temperature and running at slow idle speed. If the rocker assembly has been removed and replaced, however, the clearance should first be adjusted in the following manner, in order that the engine can be started and run up to normal operating temperature.

Work on one pair of valves at a time. Start by turning the engine until the timing marks and distributor rotor arm are aligned to set the engine to the firing point for number one (front) cylinder as described in **Chapter 3**. Now adjust valve clearances at number one cylinder as shown in **FIG 1:15**. Using a feeler gauge between the rocker and valve stem, adjust both inlet and exhaust valve clearances to 0.3mm (0.012in). Turn the adjusting nut clockwise to reduce the clearance, anticlockwise to increase the clearance. The adjusting nuts are self-locking. Now turn the engine in the normal forward direction of rotation by half a turn, then repeat the adjustment procedure on the inlet and exhaust valves for cylinder number three. Repeat the adjustment procedure for the valves at cylinder numbers two and four, turning the engine through half a turn each time. This adjustment is only a temporary measure and final adjustment must be carried out as follows:

With the rocker cover installed, run the engine to warm it up to normal operating temperature, then switch off and remove the rocker cover. To prevent oil splashing from the timing chain into the engine compartment, an oil deflector made to the dimensions shown in **FIG 1:16** should be fitted over the exposed part of the camshaft sprocket with the legs engaging in the two rocker cover screw holes. The deflector should preferably be fabricated from 18 or 20swg mild steel, but a temporary item made of card or plastic and retained by two rocker cover screws can be used as a simple alternative and discarded after use.

Start the engine and leave it running at a slow idle. Insert the feeler gauge as described previously and turn the adjusting nut until the clearance is correct, then remove the spanner and recheck. Leave the feeler between rocker and valve stem while the rocker is operating and, during the short period that the valve is closed check that the feeler moves in the gap with a slight drag, being neither tight nor loose. The correct final running clearance for both exhaust and inlet valves is 0.3mm (0.012in).

On completion refit the rocker cover, using a new gasket unless the original is in perfect condition.

1:7 Timing case oil seal

The timing case oil seal can be renewed without disturbing the timing case. Remove the drive belt as described in **Chapter 4**, then remove the crankshaft pulley and prise the seal from the timing case as shown in **FIG 1:17**.

Smear the lip of the new seal with Rocol Anti-scuffing Paste or similar, and the periphery of the seal with Hylomar SQ32/M jointing compound or similar. Using tool S1305 in conjunction with the crankshaft pulley bolt and washer, install the seal open side first as shown in **FIG 1:18**. Remove the bolt, washer and tool, then install the crankshaft pulley and tighten the bolt to the specified torque. Refit and tension the drive belt as described in **Chapter 4**.

1:8 Timing gear

To facilitate removal of the timing gear, the engine and transmission assembly should first be removed as described in **Section 1:2**. However, the valve timing can be checked without the need for engine removal or dismantling.

To check the valve timing, remove the rocker cover and sparking plugs. Refer to **FIG 1:19**. From the centre of notch 1 on crankshaft pulley, mark the pulley rim at a point 129mm (5.1in), measured circumferentially and in an anticlockwise direction. Mount a dial gauge over the inlet valve of No 1 cylinder (second valve front front of engine) so that its button rests on the rocker directly above the tappet. Turn the engine in its normal (clockwise) direction until the gauge shows that the valve is fully

FIG 1:17 Timing case oil seal removal

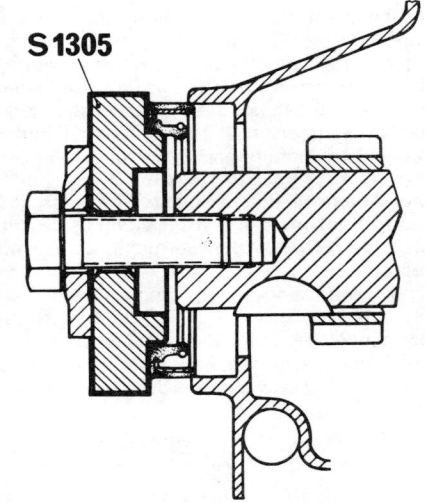

FIG 1:18 Timing case oil seal installation

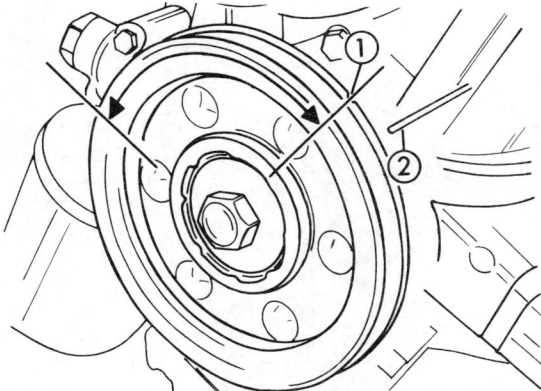

FIG 1:19 Checking valve timing. The method is described in the text

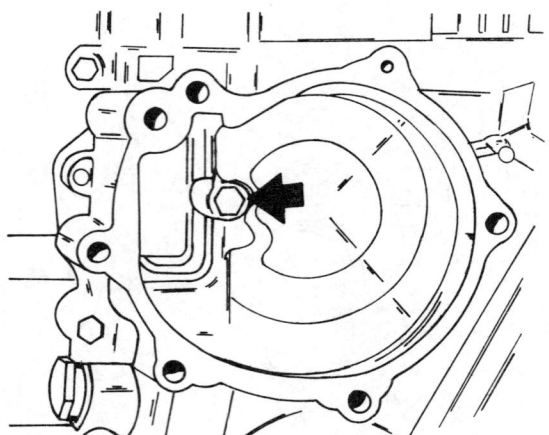

FIG 1:20 Timing case bolt behind water pump

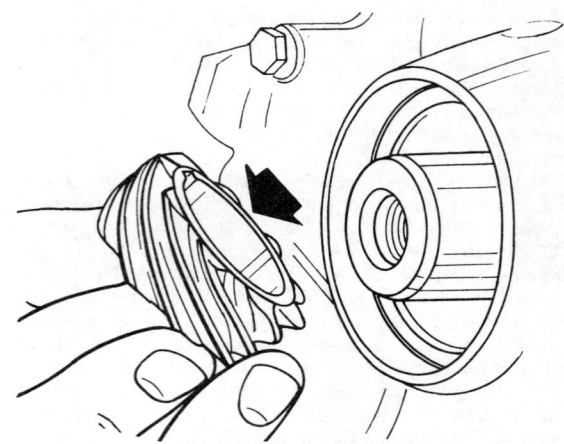

FIG 1:22 Distributor drive gear installation

open. At this point, the mark made on the pulley should be in line with the TDC pointer 2 on the timing case. If incorrect, the timing gear must be removed and reinstalled in the correct position as described later.

To remove the timing gear, remove the engine as described in **Section 1:2**, then refer to **Chapter 12** and remove the alternator and **Chapter 4** to remove the mounting bracket. Refer to **Chapter 3** and remove the distributor. Remove the cylinder head assembly as described in **Section 1:4** and the sump as described in **Section 1:12**. Remove the fuel pump as described in **Chapter 2**.

Unscrew and remove the timing chain tensioner assembly, which is arrowed in **FIG 1:7**. Note that the assembly cannot be dismantled and must be renewed complete if defective in any way. Remove the crankshaft pulley. Remove the water pump as described in **Chapter 4**

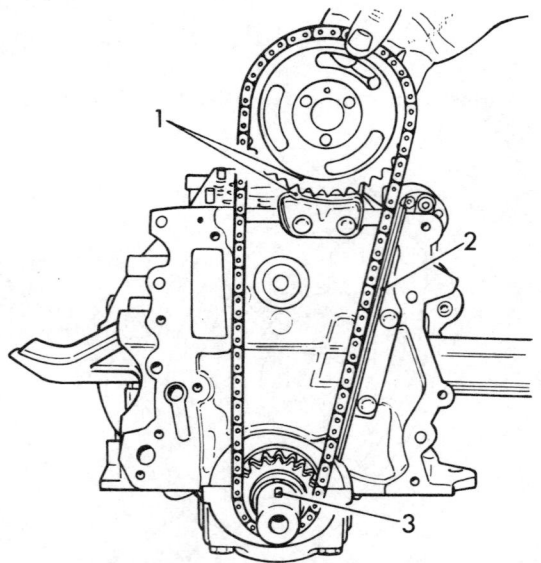

FIG 1:21 Timing chain installation

for access to the timing case bolt arrowed in **FIG 1:20**. Remove this bolt and the remaining securing bolts, then remove the timing case and gaskets. The oil pump and filter can be left in position. Pull off the sprockets and chain complete, collecting the key for the crankshaft sprocket. Mark the front of the chain with a dab of paint for reassembly the same way round if it is not to be renewed.

Clean all parts and inspect them, renewing any that are worn or damaged. Timing chains are supplied either separately or complete with sprockets, it not being permissible to renew sprockets alone.

Reassembly is a reversal of the removal procedure, carrying out the following instructions to obtain correct valve timing. Use new gaskets between timing case and cylinder block.

Turn the crankshaft until key 3 is vertical (see **FIG 1:21**). Install the crankshaft sprocket. Fit the chain around the camshaft sprocket, then offer the assembly into position so that marks 1 on camshaft sprocket and support plate are aligned. Wrap the chain around the crankshaft sprocket, making sure that it does not move from the set position. Key 3 must be vertical and marks 1 must be aligned when the chain is parallel to guide 2. When the setting is correct, allow the camshaft sprocket to rest on the support plate.

Before refitting the engine, check valve timing as described previously as it will be necessary to remove the timing case again and reset the sprocket timing marks if this is incorrect. On completion, check camshaft end float as described in **Section 1:4**.

1:9 Distributor drive gear

The distributor drive gear can be removed without disturbing the timing case. Refer to **Chapter 3** and turn the engine until the distributor is aligned in the position for firing No 1 cylinder (**FIG 3:8** or **3:9**). Remove the crankshaft pulley and timing case oil seal as described in **Section 1:7**.

Turn the distributor rotor anticlockwise and the drive gear will slide from the crankshaft. If the rotor cannot be turned, the drive gear can be removed by using two wire hooks.

Install the drive gear with the raised face, which is arrowed in **FIG 1:22**, towards the crankshaft gear. Locate the gear on the crankshaft key and press into place. Make sure that the distributor returns to the position originally set after the gear is installed. If not, realign the distributor as described in **Chapter 3**. Install a new timing case oil seal and refit the crankshaft pulley as described in **Section 1:7**.

1:10 Oil filter renewal

The oil filter is of the renewable element full flow type, a bypass valve being incorporated in the filter mounting to allow oil to pass directly from the pump to the engine if the filter should become blocked.

The filter is located at the lower righthand side of the timing case (see **FIG 1:23**). Before removal, place an oil tray beneath as some oil will escape even if the sump has been drained. Unscrew the filter, using a strap type tool if it proves difficult to turn by hand. Discard the used cartridge.

Clean the filter mounting face on the timing case then lightly coat the seal on the new filter element with engine oil. Make sure that the seal is correctly fitted, then screw the new filter into place until it just contacts its seating. From this point tighten by hand only. Do not overtighten the filter or oil leaks may result. On completion, start the engine and check for oil leaks around the filter unit. Check and top up the engine oil level to compensate for that used to fill the new filter element.

1:11 Oil pump servicing

The gear type oil pump is driven by the distributor drive shaft, the body of the pump being incorporated in the timing case. A pressure relief valve which operates if oil pressure becomes too high is located above the oil filter unit (see arrow in **FIG 1:24**).

To remove the oil pump gears, remove the pump cover plate from the timing case and withdraw the gears from the housing. Inspect the gears and cover plate for signs of wear, pitting or cracking, which would dictate renewal. Install the gears and use a straightedge and feeler gauge to measure protrusion of gears from pump body, as shown in **FIG 1:25**. Use feeler gauges to measure backlash between gear teeth, as shown in **FIG 1:26**. Check the measurements against the figures given in **Technical Data** and renew parts as necessary if wear limits are exceeded. Note, that some timing cases are manufactured with 0.2mm oversize bores for the gears or shafts, being identified by a 0.2 mark on the lower lefthand side of the timing case adjacent to the pump cover flange. Oversize gears are identified by a 0.2 mark stamped on the lower face.

On completion, install the pump gears together with cover plate and new gasket and evenly tighten the cover retaining screws. Refer to **FIG 1:27** and remove the plug arrowed. Fill the oil pump housing with clean engine oil through the plug hole, filling slowly until oil runs out of the hole. This ensures that the pump is fully primed so that the engine will be supplied with pressure oil immediately it is started. Make sure that the plug is securely refitted.

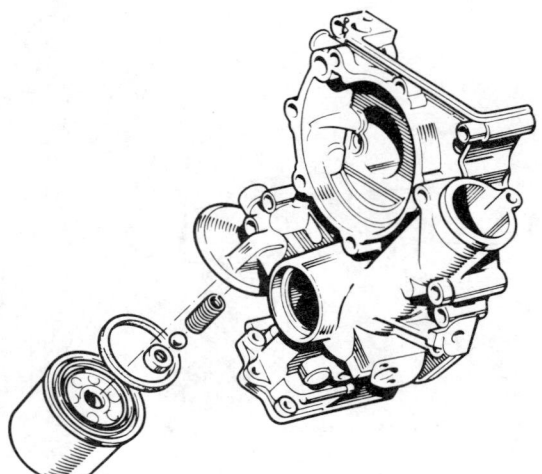

FIG 1:23 Oil filter and seal and bypass valve components

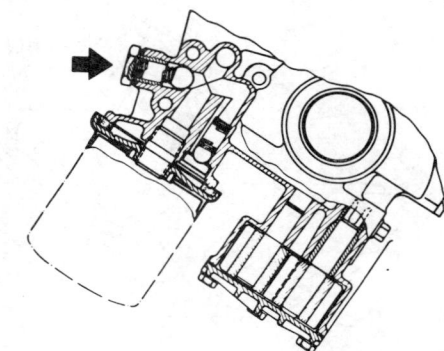

FIG 1:24 Oil pressure relief valve

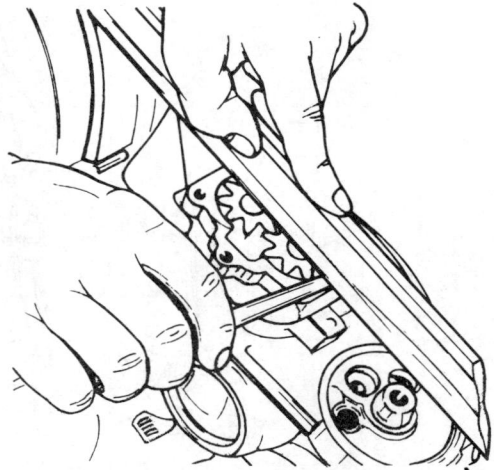

FIG 1:25 Checking pump gear protrusion

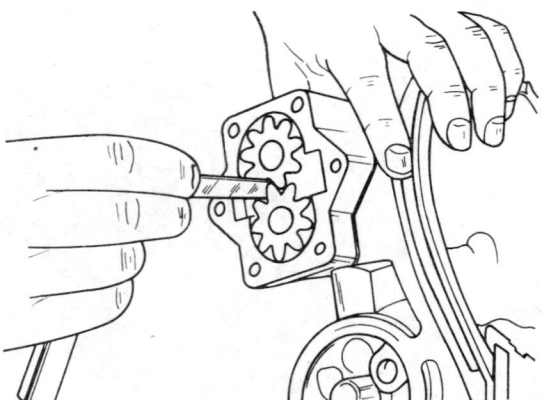

FIG 1:26 Checking pump gear backlash

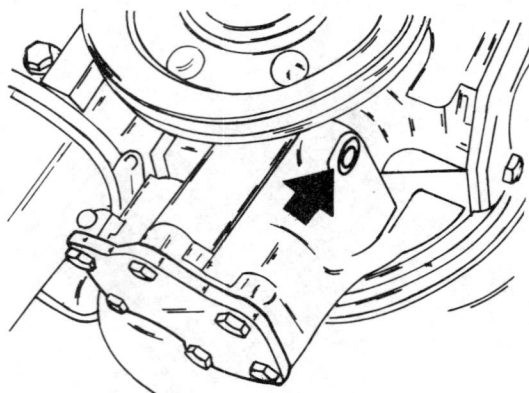

FIG 1:27 Pump oil filler plug

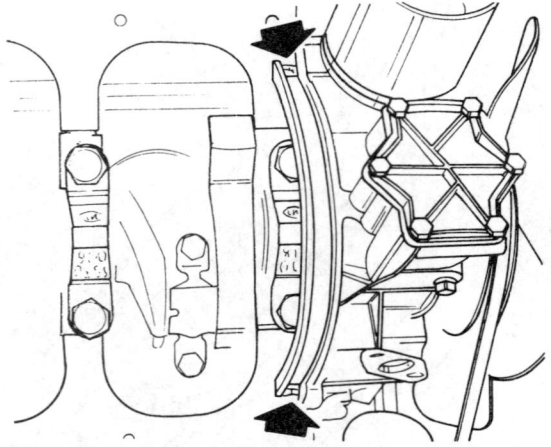

FIG 1:28 Applying sealer to timing case and bearing cap corners

1:12 Sump removal and refitting

In order to remove the sump, the engine mounting nuts must be removed and the engine raised with suitable lifting equipment to provide the necessary clearance. This done, remove the drain plug and allow the oil to drain into a suitable container, then refit the drain plug securely. Remove the fixing bolts and detach the sump, two-piece gasket and semi-circular seals at timing case and rear main bearing cap.

While the sump is removed, examine the oil pick-up strainer and clean if necessary using a suitable solvent, then allow to dry. The strainer and suction pipe is sealed by a gasket at the crankcase inlet port and is supported at the rear intermediate main bearing cap.

Before refitting the sump, inspect the sump contact faces for damage or distortion, then clean all old jointing compound from the sump and crankcase faces. Clean sealer from the timing case and rear main bearing cap. Apply Silastic 732 RTV sealer to the corners formed by the timing case as shown by the arrows in **FIG 1:28**. Apply sealer to the similar corners at the rear bearing cap. Install the new sump gaskets ensuring that gasket ends are fully engaged in bearing cap groove, then apply sealer in the same positions as before so that sealer is both above and below gasket ends. Jointing compound is not used between the gasket and the sump face and both these surfaces should be clean and dry. Install the new front and rear seals to timing case and bearing cap, making sure that each end of the seal is pressed firmly against the ends of the gasket. Apply sealer to the junction of gasket and seal.

Install the sump within five minutes of sealant application, to avoid the possibility of the sealant hardening, making sure that the seals remain correctly seated in their grooves. Tighten the sump bolts alternately and evenly. Lower the engine and refit and tighten the mounting nuts. Refill the engine with fresh oil.

1:13 Pistons and connecting rods

The pistons and connecting rods can be removed with the engine installed, after removing the cylinder head and sump, but if after dismantling it is found that attention to the crankshaft bearing surfaces or to the cylinder bores is required, engine removal will be necessary as described in **Section 1:2**.

Removal:

Remove the cylinder head as described in **Section 1:4** and the sump as described in **Section 1:12**. Remove the engine oil dipstick.

FIG 1:29 shows a piston and connecting rod assembly. Before dismantling the big-ends, mark each piston and connecting rod assembly and its cap with the cylinder number, using paint. Do not use a file or punch as such marks can lead to fatigue failure. Any numbers or symbols which may be found on the rods and caps indicate matching parts but not cylinder numbers. The piston crown has a notch which must face towards the front.

Unscrew the big-end bolts and remove the caps and bearings. Discard the big-end bolts as new ones must be used during reassembly. Keep all remaining parts in the correct order for reassembling in their original positions if they are not to be renewed. Remove carbon from the top of each bore and withdraw the pistons and connecting rods through the top of the cylinder block.

If there has been a big-end bearing failure, the crankpin must be examined for damage and for transfer of metal to its surface. The oilway in the crankshaft must be checked to ensure that there is no obstruction. Big-end bearing clearance can be checked by the use of Plastigage, which is the trade name for a precisely calibrated plastic filament. The filament is laid along the bearing to be measured for working clearance, the bearing cap fitted and the bolts tightened to the specified torque. The bearing is then dismantled and the width of the flattened filament measured with the scale supplied with the material. The bearing clearance can then be read off the scale. Both main and big-end bearing clearances are measured in a similar manner.

Note, that each main bearing must be measured separately and none of the remaining bearing caps must be fitted during the operation. The bearing surfaces must be clean and free from oil and the crankshaft must not be turned during the measuring procedure. The point at which the measurement is taken must be close to the respective dead centre position and no hammer blows must be applied to the bearing or cap.

Place a length of plastic filament identical to the width of the bearing on the crankshaft journal, then fit the main or big-end bearing cap with liners and tighten to the specified torque.

Remove the bearing cap and measure the width of the flattened filament to obtain the running clearance for that bearing. The correct clearances are given in **Technical Data**. If the bearing running clearance is too high, new bearing shells must be selected by the measurement procedure to bring the running clearance to within specified limits.

If the big-end bearing journals or crankshaft main bearing journals are worn below the limits or are damaged in any way, the journals or bearings must be reground to accept suitable undersize bearing shells, this being a specialist job.

Pistons and rings:

Clean carbon deposits from the piston crowns, then gently ease the rings from their grooves and remove them over the tops of the pistons. Keep all rings in the correct order for refitting in their original positions, if they are not to be renewed. Clean carbon from the piston ring grooves, for which job a piece broken from an old piston ring and ground to a chisel point will prove an ideal tool. Inspect the pistons for score marks or any signs of seizure, which would dictate renewal.

Fit the piston rings one at a time into the bore from which they were removed, pushing them down with the inverted piston to ensure squareness. Measure the gap between the ends of the ring when it is positioned in the bore, using feeler gauges. Remove the ring from the bore and hold it in the piston groove from which it was removed, then measure the side clearance with feeler gauges. Compare the measurements taken with the figures given in **Technical Data**. If the clearance measurement in either test is at or near the wear limit,

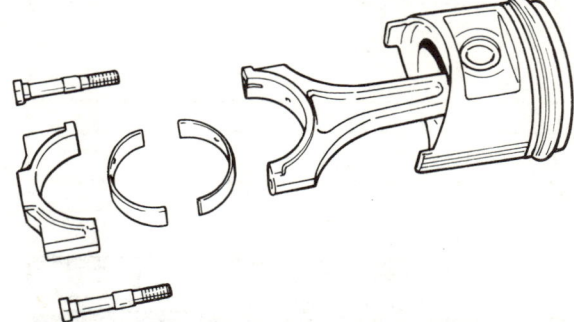

FIG 1:29   Piston and connecting rod assembly

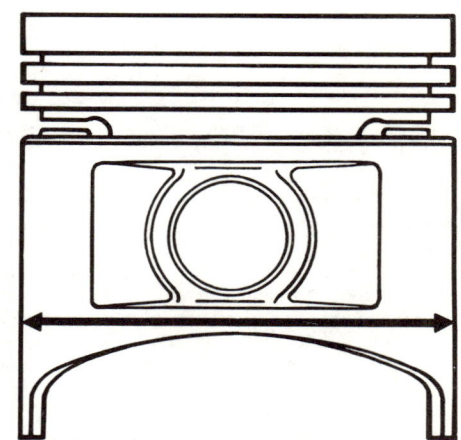

FIG 1:30   Piston diameter must be measured at right angles to the gudgeon pin bore and 22.5mm (0.89in) from the bottom of the skirt

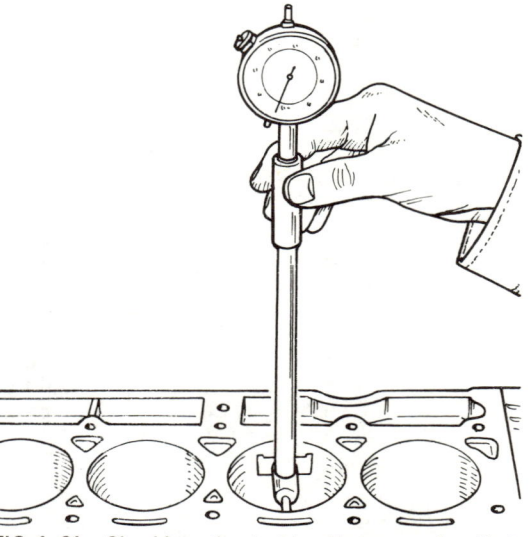

FIG 1:31   Checking the inside diameter of cylinder bores

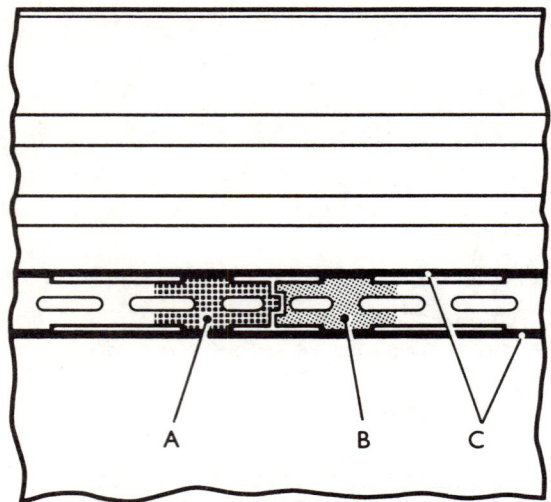

FIG 1:32 The correct assembly of oil scraper rings to the piston is described in the text

new rings must be fitted. Excessive ring clearance can be responsible for high oil consumption and poor engine performance.

Check the cylinder bores for score marks and remove glaze and carbon deposits. Badly scored or worn surfaces will dictate a rebore to accept new pistons. This being a specialist job. The fitting of new pistons to connecting rods must be carried out by a fully equipped service station, due to the need for special tools and press equipment to remove and refit the gudgeon pins.

Check the clearance of each piston in its bore. To do this, measure the outside diameter of the piston and the inside diameter of the bore and compare the two figures. The clearance limits are given in **Technical Data**. As the piston skirt is ground both oval and tapered, it is essential that piston size is measured only at right angles to the gudgeon pin and 22.5mm (0.89in) from the bottom of the skirt, as shown in **FIG 1:30**. The micrometer

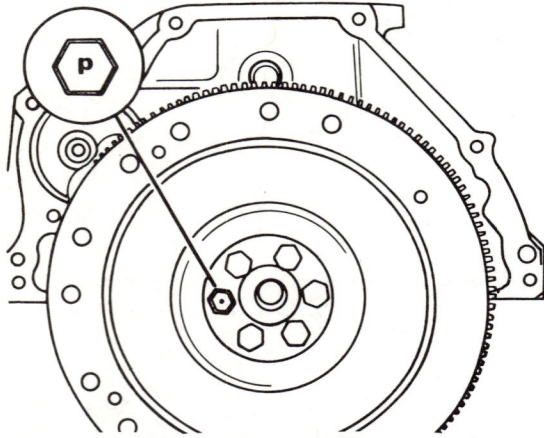

FIG 1:33 Identification of flywheel shouldered bolt

spindle must turn freely so that it can be adjusted to the piston with a very light turning effort. If the micrometer is adjusted too tightly against the piston, it will indicate a dimension significantly smaller than the actual size. For maximum accuracy in checking cylinder bores, it is essential to use a cylinder gauge in conjunction with the same micrometer as used for measuring the piston, as shown in **FIG 1:31**. This avoids any discrepancy between individual micrometers. Excessive clearance will dictate the fitting of new pistons and rings and, possible, reboring of the cylinders. This is a specialist job.

When refitting the rings to the pistons, scraper ring spacers must be assembled to the piston bottom grooves so that ends **A** and **B** do not overlap, but have their ends engaged as shown in **FIG 1:32**. The ends of rails **C** and spacer should be positioned equally around the piston. Install the second ring with the wider face to the bottom of the piston. The top ring can be installed either way up. Space all ring gaps evenly around the piston. Use a piston ring clamp when installing the pistons in the bores. Lubricate pistons and big-end bearings with engine oil.

1:14 Flywheel removal and refitting

Removal:

Remove the clutch from the flywheel as described in **Chapter 5**. Before removing the flywheel, mark the position of the shouldered bolt stamped with letter **P** to ensure correct positioning relative to crankshaft on reassembly (see **FIG 1:33**). Remove the fixing bolts and detach the flywheel from the crankshaft.

Check the clutch pilot bearing in the flywheel as described in **Chapter 5**. Check the surface of the flywheel against which the clutch operates for cracks or deep scoring. Light score marks are unimportant, but deep scoring will necessitate resurfacing at a service station. The starter ring gear should be renewed if it is badly worn or if broken teeth are found. The ring gear is shrunk on to the flywheel and renewal is a specialist job, so the work should be carried out by a fully equipped service station.

Refitting:

This is a reversal of the removal procedure, fitting the shouldered bolt marked **P** in the correct position as noted during removal. Tighten flywheel securing bolts alternately and evenly to specified torque.

1:15 Drive plate removal and refitting

On models with automatic transmission, a drive plate 4 (see **FIG 1:34**) is bolted to crankshaft flange to provide drive through torque converter 2 to the transmission. A distance plate 1 is interposed between the crankshaft end and drive plate to ensure correct location. The converter is attached to the drive plate by three bolts 3.

Removal:

Remove the automatic transmission as described in **Chapter 7**. Mark the position of the bolt stamped with letter **P** on the drive plate. This is a shouldered bolt and locates in a smaller diameter hole to ensure correct positioning relative to crankshaft. Check the drive plate for wear or damage. Note, that the starter ring gear is welded to the drive plate, so if the gear is worn or damaged the drive plate must be renewed.

Refitting:

Install the drive plate making sure that the starter ring gear offset is towards crankshaft and bolt stamped with letter **P** is installed in correct position. Tighten the fixing bolts alternately and evenly to the specified torque.

1:16 Crankshaft rear oil seal

The crankshaft rear oil seal can be renewed without disturbing the sump or rear main bearing cap. Remove the flywheel or drive plate as described previously to gain access to the seal.

Pierce the seal with a pointed tool, then screw in a suitable self-tapping screw. Use pincers on the screw to lever out the seal, as shown in **FIG 1:35**.

Before installing the new seal, smear the lip of seal and crankshaft land with Rocol Anti-scuffing Paste or similar, then locate seal over protector tool S1296/3 as shown in **FIG 1:36**. Use the protector to guide the lip of seal, open side first, over the crankshaft land. The seal may then be driven in flush with crankcase and bearing cap face using suitable driver tools such as installers S1296/1 and S1296/2.

On completion, refit the flywheel or drive plate as described in **Section 1:14** or **1:15**.

1:17 Crankshaft and main bearings
Removal:

Remove the engine and transmission assembly as described in **Section 1:2**, then separate the transmission from the engine. Remove the flywheel or drive plate as described in **Section 1:14** or **1:15**. Invert the engine and remove the sump as described in **Section 1:12**. Refer to **Section 1:13** and remove the big-end bearing caps, then push the pistons up into their bores until the connecting rods are clear of the crankshaft.

Before removing the crankshaft, check that crankshaft end float is between 0.043 and 0.156mm (0.0017 and 0.0061in). If end float is excessive, new rear main bearing shells must be fitted. If the crankshaft is being reground to accept undersize bearings, these flanged rear main bearing shells must be ground on their flanged faces to provide the correct crankshaft end float. This is a specialist job.

Mark the main bearing caps with paint to ensure that they will be refitted in their original positions. Remove the main bearing bolts and caps, keeping each bearing shell with its respective cap. Lift out the crankshaft and discard the oil seals. Remove the bearing shells from the crankcase, again keeping them in the correct order.

If there has been a main bearing failure, the crankshaft journal must be checked for damage and for transfer of metal to its surface. The oilways in the crankshaft must be checked to ensure that there is no obstruction. Main

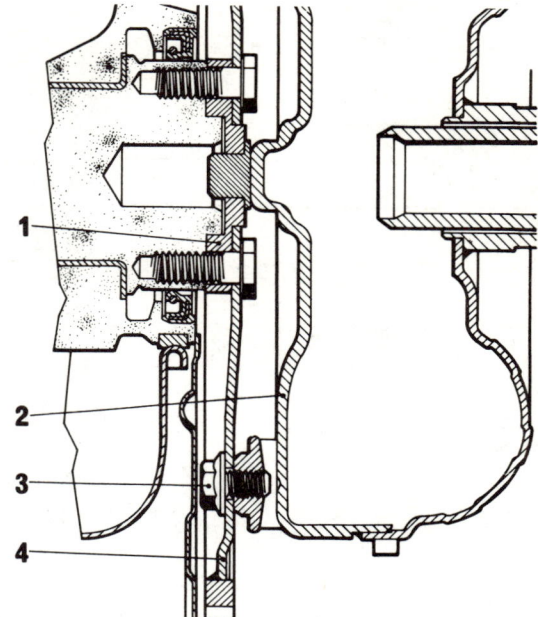

FIG 1:34   Drive plate installation

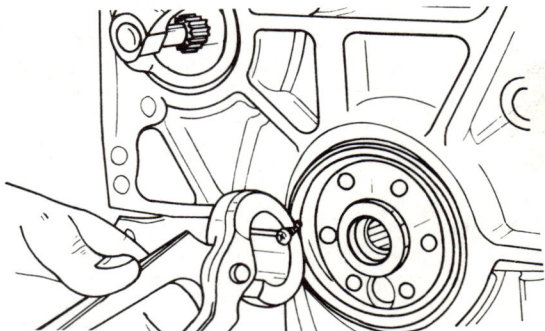

FIG 1:35   Crankshaft rear seal removal

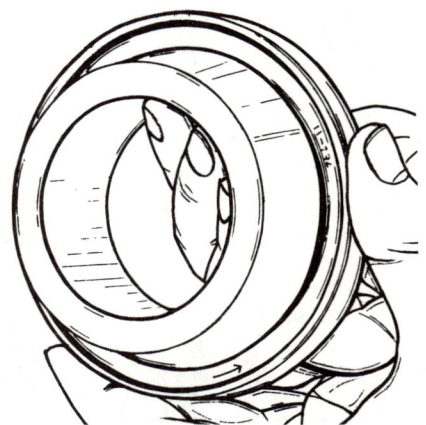

FIG 1:36   Crankshaft rear seal protector

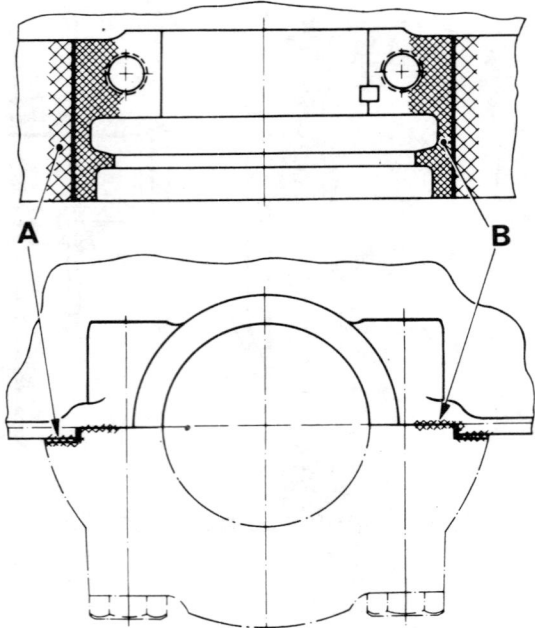

FIG 1:37   Rear main bearing cap installation

bearing clearance can be checked by the use of Plastigage, in the manner described in **Section 1:13** for big-end bearings, the procedure being the same. If there is any doubt about the condition of the crankshaft it should be taken to a specialist for more detailed checks.

Refitting:

This is a reversal of the removal procedure. Fit the upper shell bearings into the crankcase locations and lubricate with engine oil. Install the crankshaft then lubricate the lower shell bearings and install with caps, making sure that the caps are refitted in their original locations. Fit the cap bolts and tighten to the specified torque. Before installing rear bearing cap, apply a small quantity of Silastic 732 RTV sealer or similar to areas **A** and **B** of cap joint face, as shown in **FIG 1:37**. Make sure that the face of the cap is clean and free from oil before applying sealant. Install the bearing cap within five minutes as the sealer hardens quickly.

Reassemble the remaining components in the reverse order of dismantling. Install new crankshaft oil seals as described in **Sections 1:7** and **1:16**.

1:18 Fault diagnosis

(a) Engine will not start

1 Defective coil
2 Faulty distributor capacitor
3 Dirty, pitted or incorrectly set contact points
4 Ignition wires loose or insulation faulty
5 Water on spark plug leads
6 Battery discharged, corrosion of terminals
7 Faulty or jammed starter
8 Sparking plug leads wrongly connected
9 Vapour lock in fuel pipes
10 Defective fuel pump
11 Overchoking or underchoking
12 Blocked fuel filter or carburetter jet
13 Leaking valves
14 Sticking valves
15 Valve timing incorrect
16 Ignition timing incorrect

(b) Engine stalls

1 Check 1, 2, 3, 4, 5, 10, 11, 12, 13 and 14 in (a)
2 Sparking plugs defective or gaps incorrect
3 Retarded ignition
4 Mixture too weak
5 Water in fuel system
6 Petrol tank vent blocked
7 Incorrect valve clearances

(c) Engine idles badly

1 Check 2 and 7 in (b)
2 Air leak at manifold joints
3 Carburetter adjustment wrong
4 Air leak in carburetter
5 Over-rich mixture
6 Worn piston rings
7 Worn valve stems or guides
8 Weak exhaust valve springs

(d) Engine misfires

1 Check 1, 2, 3, 4, 5, 8, 10, 12, 13, 14, 15 and 16 in (a)
2 Weak or broken valve springs

(e) Engine overheats (see **Chapter 4**)

(f) Compression low

1 Check 13 and 14 in (a); 6 and 7 in (c); and 2 in (d)
2 Worn piston ring grooves
3 Scored or worn cylinder bores

(g) Engine lacks power

1 Check 3, 10, 11, 12, 13, 14, 15 and 16 in (a); 2, 3, 4 and 7 in (b); 6 and 7 in (c); and 2 in (d). Also check (e) and (f)
2 Leaking joint washers or gaskets
3 Fouled sparking plugs
4 Automatic advance not working

(h) Burned valves or seats

1 Check 13 and 14 in (a); 7 in (b); and 2 in (d). Also check (e)
2 Excessive carbon round valve seats and head

(j) Sticking valves

1 Check 2 in (d)
2 Bent valve stem
3 Scored valve stem or guide
4 Incorrect valve clearances

(k) Excessive cylinder wear

1 Check 11 in (a)
2 Lack of oil
3 Dirty oil
4 Piston rings gummed up or broken
5 Badly fitting piston rings
6 Connecting rod bent

(l) Excessive oil consumption

1 Check 6 and 7 in (c) ; and check (k)
2 Ring gaps too wide
3 Oil return holes in piston choked with carbon
4 Scored cylinders
5 Oil level too high
6 External oil leaks

(m) Crankshaft and connecting rod bearing failure

1 Check 2 in (k)
2 Restricted oilways
3 Worn journals or crankpins
4 Loose bearing caps
5 Extremely low oil pressure
6 Bent connecting rod

(n) Engine vibration

1 Loose alternator or other belt driven component
2 Engine mountings loose or defective
3 Misfiring due to mixture, ignition or mechanical faults

NOTES

CHAPTER 2
THE FUEL SYSTEM

2:1 Description

Models fitted with standard 16 engines are provided with Solex 35 PDSI single barrel carburetters equipped with manual choke units. 16S and 19S engines are fitted respectively with Solex 32/32 DIDTA and Zenith 35/40 INAT dual barrel carburetters which are provided with electrically operated automatic choke units. In all cases, the carburetter is supplied with fuel from the rear mounted tank by means of a mechanical type fuel pump operated by a special eccentric on the distributor drive shaft.

Models with 16S engines are fitted with pleated paper type air cleaner assemblies, attached to the carburetter intake by means of a worm drive clip. Similar air filter units are fitted to 19S engines, but attachment to the carburetter intake is by means of a centrally located screw.

2:2 Routine maintenance

At the intervals recommended in the manufacturer's service schedule, the air cleaner element should be renewed and the fuel pump filter removed and cleaned.

The fuel tank vent pipe must be checked occasionally to ensure that it is clear, as the fuel pump cannot function correctly unless there is atmospheric pressure on the fuel in the tank. The fuel tank is situated in the luggage compartment immediately behind the rear seat and the vent pipe is secured by clips with its outlet protruding through the luggage compartment floor.

2:3 Air cleaner

To renew the air filter element, release the spring clips securing the cover to the body and, on 19S models, remove the central securing screw. Lift off the cover and remove and discard the element (see FIG 2:1). Wipe the inside of the casing and cover to remove oil and dirt, then reassemble using a new filter element. Check the condition and seating of the seal around the cover, as shown by the arrow in FIG 2:1.

To remove the air cleaner assembly complete, remove the worm drive clip on 16 and 16S models, or the central screw on 19S models. Disconnect the pipes attached to the air cleaner assembly, if fitted, then lift the unit from the carburetter. Refitting is a reversal of the removal procedure. When installing the air cleaner on 19S models, make sure that the metal support washer beneath the insulator rubber is correctly positioned with the locating tangs situated as shown in FIG 2:2.

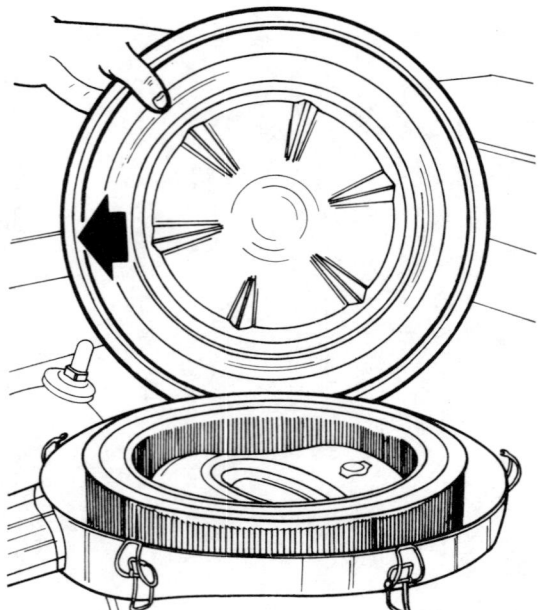

FIG 2:1   Air filter element removal

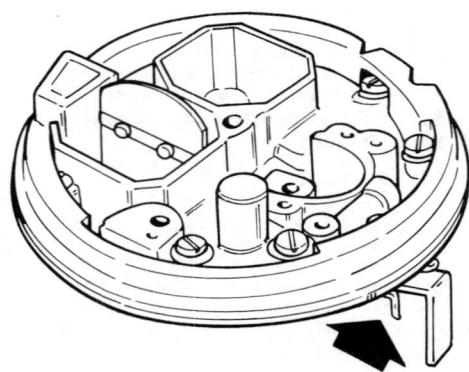

FIG 2:2   Support washer location on 19S models

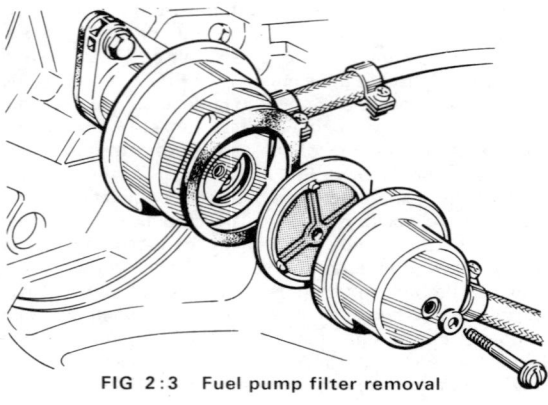

FIG 2:3   Fuel pump filter removal

Some models are provided with a hot air intake for the air cleaner assembly, which should be switched into operation during winter by moving the lever provided on the air intake to the winter position. If no hot air shroud is provided, the intake flap should be left in the summer position permanently.

Some 19S models are fitted with an air cleaner assembly provided with an automatically controlled air inlet system. When the engine is cold, the system operates to provide pre-heated air from the region of the exhaust manifold to the carburetter. As the engine warms up, a thermal switch operates to gradually close the warm air intake and open the cold air intake. If operational faults are suspected, the car should be taken to a service station for detailed checks to be carried out.

2:4 Fuel pump

The fuel pump is a sealed assembly which cannot be dismantled for overhaul, only the filter unit being accessible for cleaning as described later. If the pump is found to be defective, it must be renewed.

Testing:

Before testing the pump, ensure that the fuel tank vent system is not blocked, as described in **Section 2:2**. If it is suspected that fuel is not reaching the carburetter, disconnect the carburetter feed pipe and hold a suitable container under the end of the pipe. Turn the engine over a few times with the starter and watch for fuel squirting from the end of the pipe, which indicates that the pump is working. If so, check the float needle in the carburetter for possible sticking.

Reduced fuel flow can be caused by blocked fuel pipes or a clogged filter. If an obstructed pipeline appears to be the cause of the trouble, it may be cleared with compressed air. Disconnect the pipeline at the pump and carburetter. **Do not pass compressed air through the pump or the valves will be damaged.** If there is an obstruction between the pump and the tank, remove the tank filler cap before blowing the pipe through from the pump end.

If the pump delivers insufficient fuel, suspect an air leak between the pump and the tank, dirt under the pump valves or faulty valve seatings. If no fuel is delivered, a sticking valve or faulty pump diaphragm are likely causes. Faults of this type will dictate pump renewal.

Filter cleaning:

Remove the single screw and detach the pump cover, filter and gasket, as shown in **FIG 2:3**.

Wash the filter and the inside of the pump cover and sediment chamber with clean petrol, using a small brush to remove stubborn deposits. If the filter is damaged or will not clean up properly it should be renewed. On completion, refit the filter and cover using a new gasket. Start the engine and check for leaks around the pump cover.

Removing and refitting pump:

To remove the pump, disconnect the two hoses from the pump, plugging the inlet hose to prevent leakage.

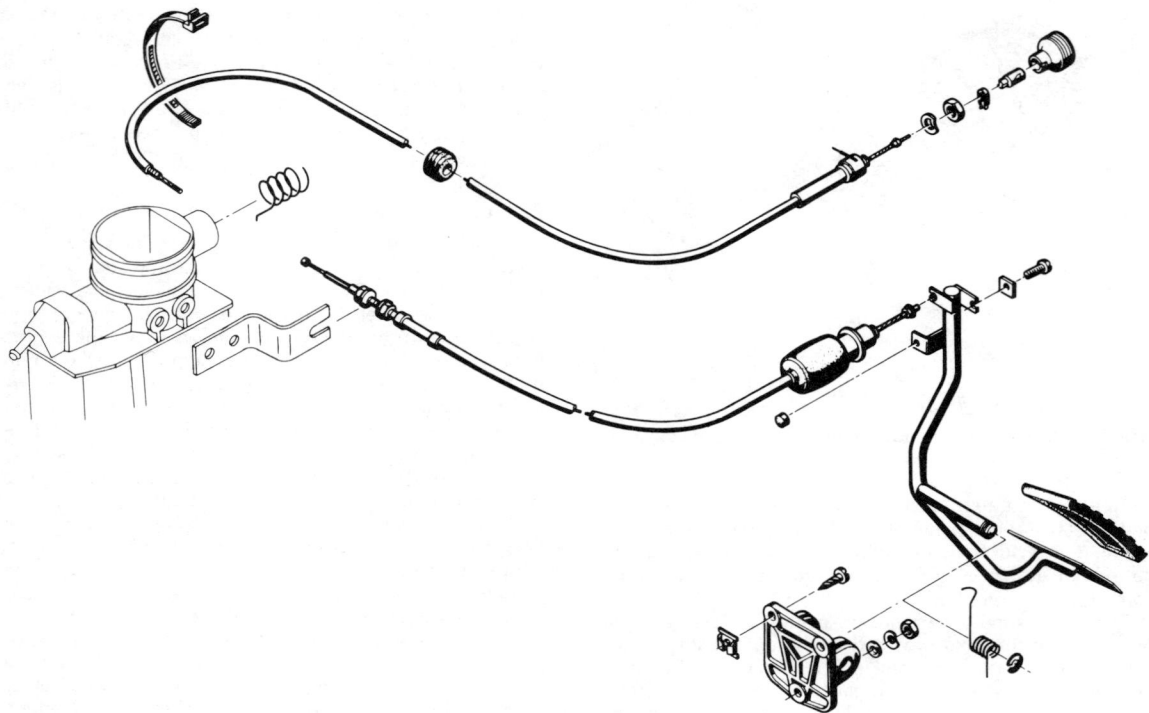

FIG 2:4   Choke and throttle control linkages, 16 models

Undo the two bolts holding the pump to the crankcase
and remove the pump and insulator. In some cases, a
gasket will also be fitted each side of the insulator.

Refit the pump in the reverse order of removal.
Use a new insulator unless the original is in perfect
condition. Renew the two gaskets, if fitted. Tighten the
fixing bolts alternately and evenly to avoid distortion of
the mounting flange.

2:5 Control linkages

Choke control cable:

The control cable for the manual choke unit, on models
fitted with Solex 35 PDSI carburetters only, is shown in
FIG 2:4. The cable should be adjusted so that, when the
choke is fully off, a small amount of free play exists in the
cable.

Throttle control linkage:

The throttle cable connection to the accelerator pedal
is shown in **FIG 2:5**. The inner cable ball 2 seats in a bush
located in a bracket on the pedal shaft lever. The return
position of the accelerator pedal is controlled by an
adjustable stop 3. On cars with automatic transmission, a
detent valve operating cable 1 is connected to an
additional bracket on the pedal shaft lever. The throttle
cable outer cover at the pedal end connects to a spring
loaded override plunger in a casing, as shown in **FIG
2:6**. The casing is a push fit into a sleeve in the dash
panel.

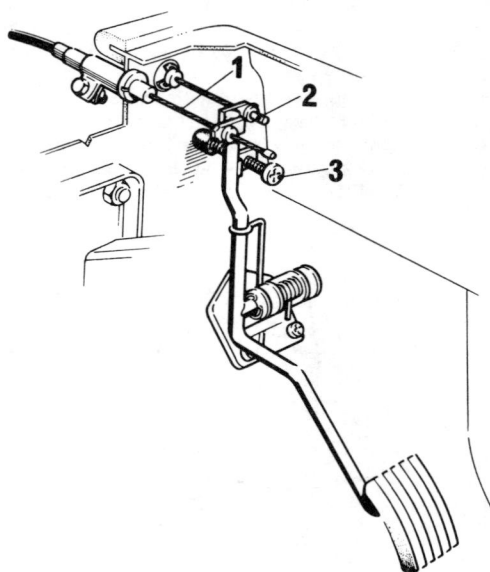

FIG 2:5   Cable connections at accelerator pedal

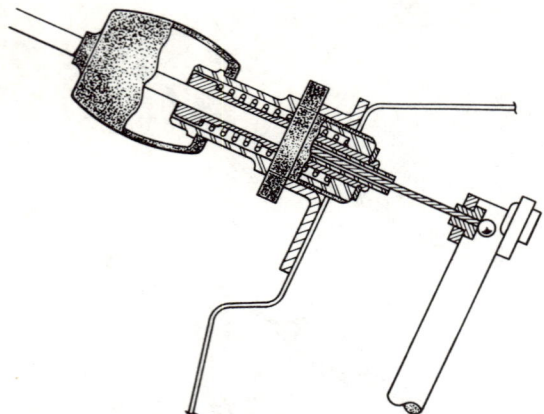

FIG 2:6 Throttle cable outer cover and override spring

To adjust the throttle cable, first check that accelerator pedal shaft to floor panel clearance is correct, as shown in **FIG 2:7**. With the pedal fully back, distance **A** should be 50mm (2in). If not, adjust the pedal stop until correct.

The cable should be adjusted at the carburetter end by means of the nuts provided at the outer cable connection to the mounting bracket. The choke must be fully off, whether manual or automatic, so that the throttle stop screw on the carburetter linkage is contacting its abutment. Under these conditions, slacken and adjust the nuts to provide a small amount of slackness in the inner cable when accelerator pedal is fully back against its stop. Tighten the nuts to secure the adjustment and recheck.

On models fitted with an adjustable accelerator control rod, check that the distance between ball joints is 76mm (3in), as shown at **A** in **FIG 2:8**. If not, pull the rod from the linkage connections, slacken the locknuts and turn the sleeves as necessary. Tighten the locknuts and refit the rod.

On models fitted with automatic transmission, the detent cable should be adjusted after carrying out throttle cable adjustments as described previously. Fit a 10mm (0.4in) wood block between pedal shaft and floor panel, as shown at **A** in **FIG 2:9**. Have an assistant fully depress

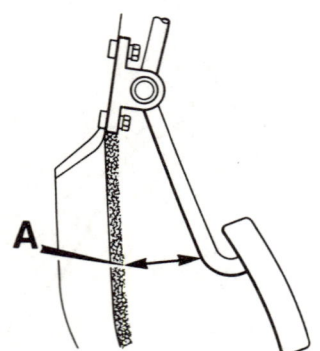

FIG 2:7 Pedal shaft to floor panel clearance

the pedal against the block and hold in this position. The carburetter throttle flap should fully open. Refer to **FIG 2:10** and loosen clamp 2. Pull sleeve 1 through the clamp until resistance of the inner cable ball is felt against the sleeve in the accelerator shaft bracket. Hold in this position, tighten the clamp, then release the accelerator pedal and remove the wood block.

2:6 Idling adjustments

In all cases, carburetter adjustment screws are precisely set at the factory then the throttle stop screw is sealed by means of a plastic cap. Normal service adjustments, if necessary, are carried out by making fine adjustments to the idle mixture screws to set the engine to the correct idling speed and ensure that CO (carbon monoxide) emissions are within specified limits. Tachometer equipment will be needed to accurately set the idle speed and exhaust gas analysing equipment will be necessary to check CO level. If a satisfactory idle setting cannot be obtained by this means, or if the carburetter has been reassembled after overhaul, adjustments to the throttle stop screw will be necessary. In this case, accurate setting can only be achieved if suitable vacuum gauge equipment is available. If not, CO content of the exhaust gas and the setting of throttle stop screw should be carried out at a fully equipped service station.

Note that idle speed adjustments will only be effective if the sparking plugs, contact points and ignition system are in good order. The engine must be at normal operating temperature before starting the adjustment procedure. The air filter must be in position.

If carburetter faults are suspected as the cause of poor engine performance at higher speeds, or if automatic choke operation is incorrect on DIDTA or INAT carburetters, the appropriate additional carburetter adjustment procedures should be carried out as described in **Section 2:7**, **2:8** or **2:9**. The idle speed setting should then be rechecked.

Carburetter adjustment procedures which require the engine to be run for checking purposes should be carried out with the gearlever in the neutral position for manual transmission, or in the **N** position for automatic transmission, with the handbrake fully applied.

Solex 35 PDSI carburetter:

Refer to **FIG 2:11**. Adjust additional idle mixture screw **A** a little at a time to obtain an engine idling speed of 800 to 850rev/min. Volume control screw **B** should now be adjusted to obtain the smoothest possible idle while retaining a CO content in the exhaust of 1.5 to 2.5 per cent by volume. When correct, readjust screw **A** if necessary to correct the idle speed.

If the correct CO content at the idle speed stated cannot be obtained, pull the distributor vacuum pipe from the fitting on the carburetter and connect a suitable vacuum gauge to the fitting. Check vacuum while the engine is idling, which should be between 1 and 15mm Hg. If the vacuum is outside the limit stated, refer to **FIG 2:12** and slacken fast idle screw **D** until there is a clearance between the screw and lever. Now remove the plastic cap from throttle stop screw **C** and adjust the screw until the desired vacuum is obtained. Aim for a vacuum midway between the limits.

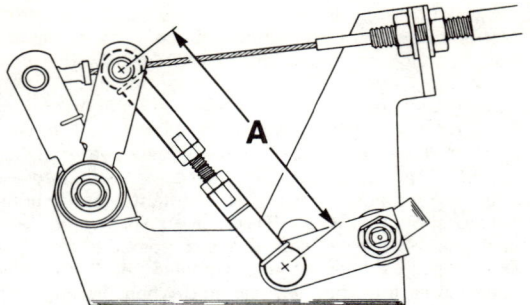

FIG 2:8 Accelerator control rod adjustment

With the vacuum setting correct, repeat the adjustments at screw **B** (see **FIG 2:11**) to correct the CO content, then finally adjust mixture screw **A** if necessary to correct the idle speed. Do not forget to refit the distributor vacuum pipe to the carburetter fitting. On completion, turn fast-idle screw **D** (see **FIG 2:12**) until it just touches the lever. Fit the red plastic cap to seal throttle stop screw **C**.

Solex 32/32 DIDTA carburetter:

Slow-idle adjustment:

Refer to **FIG 2:13**. Air volume screw 3 should be adjusted in conjunction with mixture control screw 2 to achieve an idle speed of 800 to 850rev/min and a CO content in the exhaust gas of between 1.5 and 2.5 per cent by volume. Make adjustments to the two screws alternately and by small amounts.

If correct idle speed or CO content is difficult to achieve, it indicates that the throttle valve is incorrectly

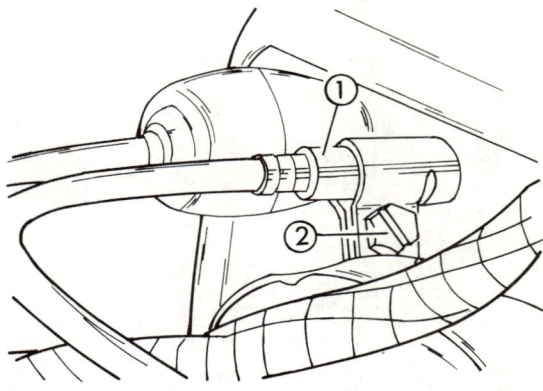

FIG 2:10 Detent cable sleeve 1 and clamp 2

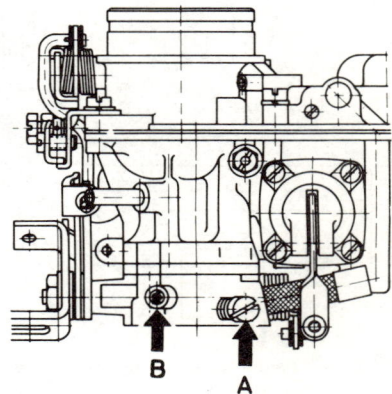

FIG 2:11 Mixture and volume control screws on PDSI carburetter

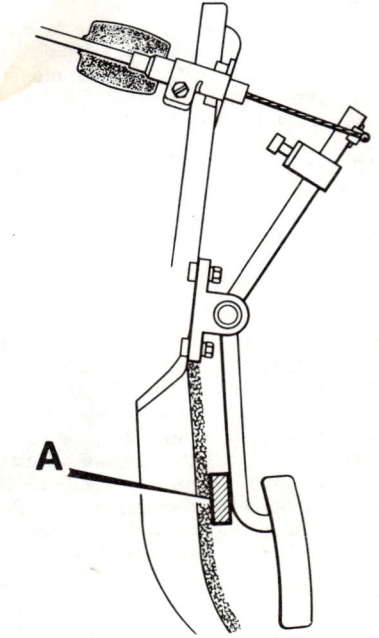

FIG 2:9 Setting accelerator pedal for detent cable adjustment

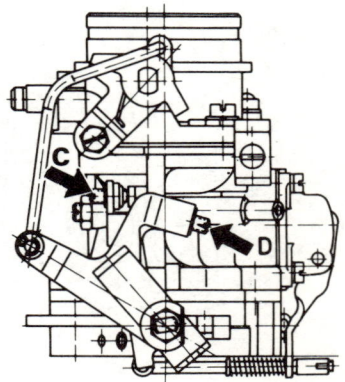

FIG 2:12 Throttle stop screw C and fast-idle screw D

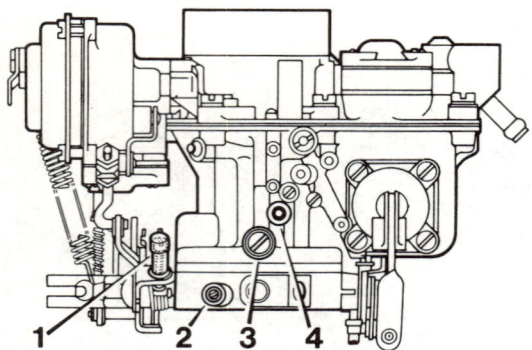

FIG 2:13 Idle adjustment screws and vacuum connection, DIDTA carburetter

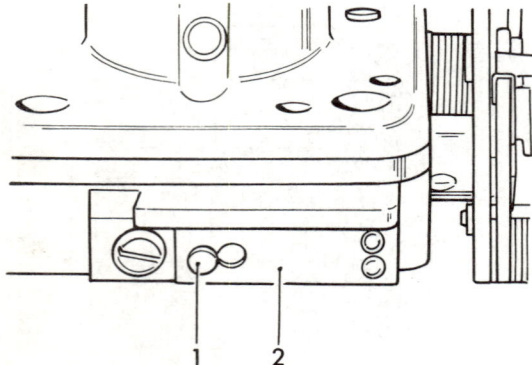

FIG 2:14 Temperature compensator valve

FIG 2:15 Setting choke before fast-idle adjustment, DIDTA carburetter

positioned. If so, pull the distributor vacuum pipe from the fitting on the carburetter and connect a suitable vacuum gauge to the fitting, which is shown at 4 in **FIG 2:13**. Remove the plastic cap from throttle stop screw 1 and adjust the screw until a vacuum of 1 to 15mm Hg is obtained at specified idling speed. Ideally, adjust to a vacuum value midway between specified limits. If difficulty is still experienced in obtaining the correct conditions, check that the temperature compensator shown in **FIG 2:14** is not open. The compensator consists of a bi-metal blade 2 and a tapered plug 1. The valve is set to open at approximately 90°C to allow additional air into the inlet manifold when the engine is hot. If the valve is open, either allow the engine to cool down slightly before repeating the adjustments, or hold the valve lightly against its seat with a finger.

When the correct vacuum value is achieved, readjust the air volume and mixture control screws to obtain the correct idle speed and CO content, not forgetting to reconnect the distributor vacuum pipe. On completion, refit the plastic cap to the throttle stop screw. Note that difficulty in correctly adjusting idling speed could be due to an excessive secondary barrel throttle clearance in the return position. This should be checked and if necessary adjusted as described in **Section 2:8**, before repeating the idling adjustments given in this section.

Fast-idle adjustment:

Before checking fast-idle adjustment, ensure that the engine is at normal operating temperature and that the slow-idle speed adjustments have been correctly carried out as described previously.

Switch off the engine and remove the air cleaner assembly (see **Section 2:3**). Note the setting of the automatic choke unit then remove the thermostat cover (see **Section 2:8**).

Refer to **FIG 2:15**. Open the throttle fully and close the choke flap by hand to position fast-idle lever 2 on top step of fast-idle cam 1. Close the throttle to retain the cam in this position. Start the engine without touching the accelerator pedal and check that the engine speed is 3200rev/min. If adjustment is necessary, refer to **FIG 2:16**, and reposition nuts 2 on throttle link rod to move rod through operating link swivel 1. On completion, refit the thermostat cover making sure that alignment is correct.

Zenith 35/40 INAT carburetter:

Slow-idle adjustment:

Slow-idle adjustment for INAT carburetters is carried out in the same manner as that previously described for DIDTA carburetters, referring to **FIG 2:17** for locations of idle adjustment screws and vacuum connection. Note, however, that throttle stop screw 1 may not be fitted with a plastic cap and that the temperature compensator is installed the opposite way around with plug 1 (see **FIG 2:14**) on the right and blade 2 on the left. Secondary barrel throttle clearance in the return position for INAT carburetters is described in **Section 2:9**.

Fast-idle adjustment:

Before checking fast-idle speed it is necessary to ensure that the engine is at normal operating temperature and that slow-idle settings are correct.

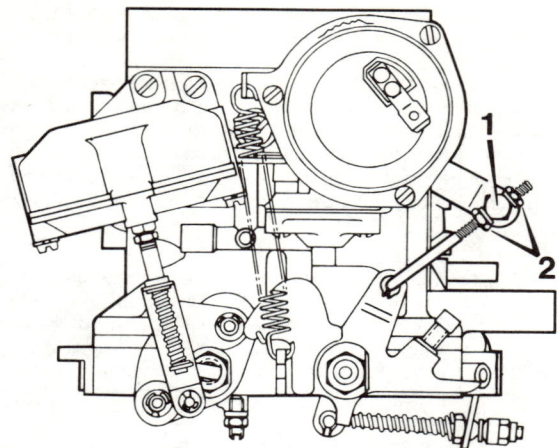

FIG 2:16   Fast-idle adjustment nuts

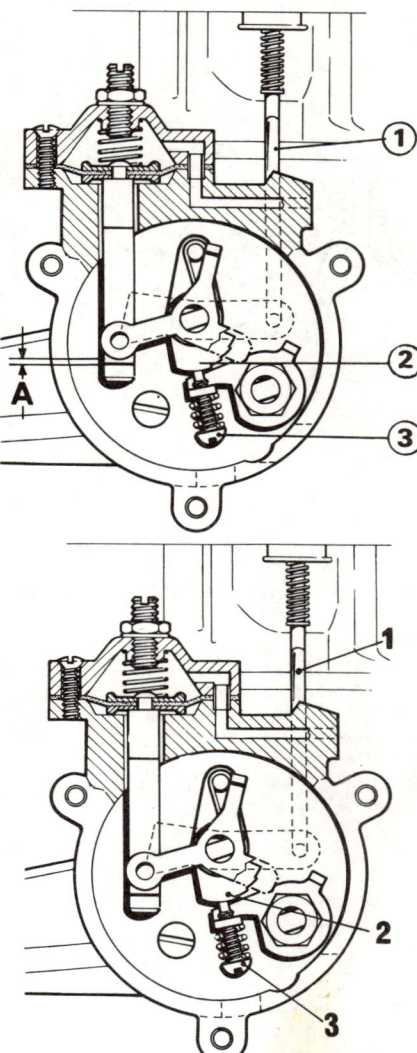

FIG 2:18   Setting choke before fast-idle adjustment, INAT carburetter

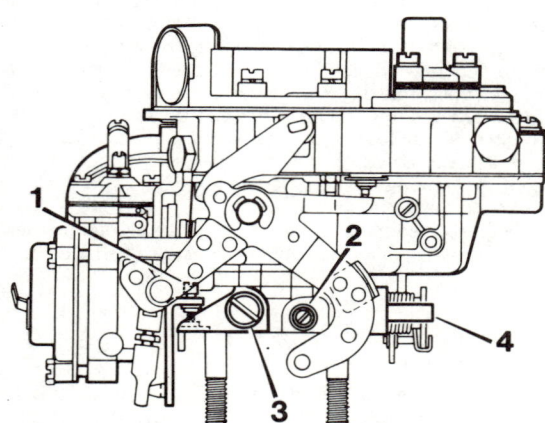

FIG 2:17   Idle adjustment screws and vacuum connection, INAT carburetter

Switch off the engine and remove the air cleaner assembly (see **Section 2:3**). Note the position of the automatic choke unit, then remove the thermostat cover (see **Section 2:9**).

Refer to **FIG 2:18**. Open the throttle and raise rod 1 fully to close the choke in order to set fast-idle screw 3 on step 2 of cam. Close the throttle to retain the cam in this position. Start the engine without touching the accelerator pedal and check that engine speed is 2700rev/min.

To adjust fast-idling speed, switch off the engine and open the throttle fully to expose the stop screw through a hole in the automatic choke housing (see arrow in **FIG 2:19**). Turn the screw clockwise to increase engine speed, anticlockwise to decrease. Make adjustments a

little at a time, resetting the screw on the cam as described previously and checking engine speed after each adjustment. On completion, refit the thermostat cover with the choke correctly aligned.

2:7 Solex 35 PDSI carburetter

Carburetter removal:

Remove the air cleaner assembly as described in **Section 2:3**, then remove the fuel pipe and distributor vacuum advance pipe from the fittings on the carburetter. Unhook the return spring at the air inlet, then unhook the choke and throttle control cables from the carburetter (see **FIG 2:20**). Remove the fixing screws and detach the carburetter and gasket from the inlet manifold.

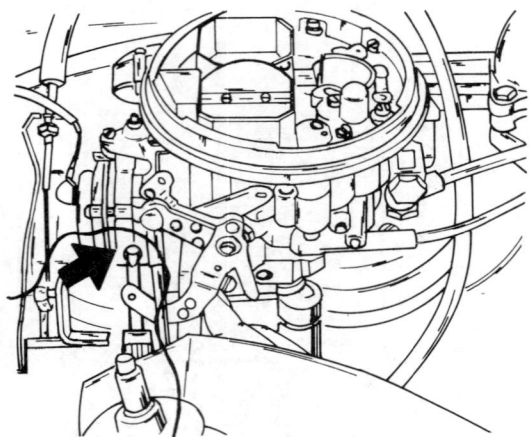

FIG 2:19 Fast-idle adjustment screw

Refitting:

This is a reversal of the removal procedure, using a new gasket. On completion, check and if necessary adjust engine idle as described in **Section 2:6**.

Dismantling:

Refer to **FIG 2:21**. Remove circlip 1 and detach rod 2 from linkage 3. Remove screws 4 and detach top cover 5 and gasket 6. Remove screw 7 and filler pin 8. Unscrew needle valve assembly 9, collecting sealing washer 10. Unscrew plug 11.

Remove spring 12 and lift float 13 with hinge pin 14 from carburetter body 15.

Remove air correction jet 16 and pump passage 17. Unscrew the enrichment valve from the float chamber, as shown by the arrow in **FIG 2:22**. If the valve needle shows signs of wear or damage or if the spring does not fully shut the valve needle, the entire valve must be renewed.

Refer to **FIG 2:21**. Remove plug 18 with sealing washer then unscrew main jet 19. Remove circlip 20

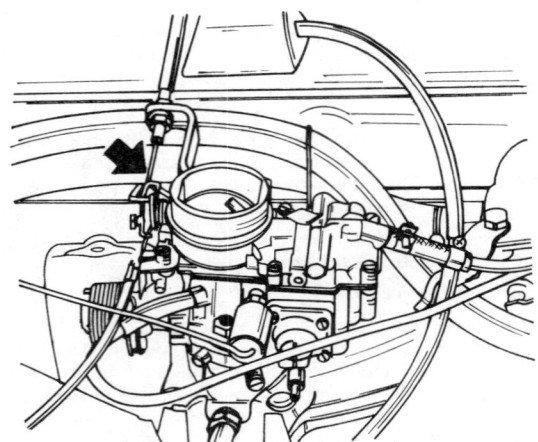

FIG 2:20 PDSI carburetter removal

and four screws 21, then remove accelerator pump cover 22 complete with rod 23. Remove diaphragm 24 and spring 25.

Remove screws 26 and detach throttle body 27 and gasket 28. Remove volume control screw with 'O' ring 29 and idle mixture screw with spring 30.

The carburetter will now be dismantled sufficiently for cleaning and inspection, which should be carried out as described in **Section 2:10**.

Reassembly:

Reassemble the carburetter in the reverse order of dismantling, using new gaskets. On completion, refit the carburetter as described previously but do not install the air cleaner. Run the engine briefly to fill the float chamber with fuel, then check accelerator pump injection rate as described next.

Accelerator pump injection rate adjustment:

Fit a suitable piece of tube to the injector nozzle, which is shown at 31 in **FIG 2:21**. Operate the throttle lever gently until fuel flows through the tube, then put the end of the tube into an accurately calibrated measuring cylinder. Now move the throttle lever slowly at first then quickly to the end of its stroke. Carry out this operation a total of five times. The correct quantity of fuel injected for a single stroke is 0.7cc, so the quantity injected into the measuring cylinder during the test should be 3.5cc. Measuring the quantity delivered from five strokes gives a more accurate indication than attempting to measure a single stroke only. If the injection rate is incorrect, refer to **FIG 2:23** and turn the brass nut on the operating linkage to alter the amount of fuel delivered. Turn clockwise to increase the amount, anticlockwise to decrease. When correct, compress the brass nut with pliers to lock in position.

On completion refit the air cleaner assembly then carry out the idling adjustments described in **Section 2:6**.

2:8 Solex 32/32 DIDTA carburetter

Carburetter removal:

Remove the air cleaner assembly as described in **Section 2:3**. Refer to **FIG 2:24**. Remove the fuel pipe and distributor vacuum advance pipe from the fittings on the carburetter. Remove the spring clip then press the ball socket of the disc pivot off the ball end of throttle valve spindle. Disconnect the wire from the automatic choke thermostat cover. Remove the carburetter fixing nuts and lift the carburetter and gasket from the inlet manifold.

Refitting:

Refit the carburetter in the reverse order of removal, using a new gasket. Check engine idle and, if necessary, carry out the adjustment procedures described in **Section 2:6**.

Dismantling:

Refer to **FIG 2:25**. Remove circlip 1 then withdraw rod 2 from throttle lever. Remove circlip 3 then prise pull rod 4 from lever pin. Disconnect return spring 5. Remove the fixing screws and detach top cover 6 and gasket 7.

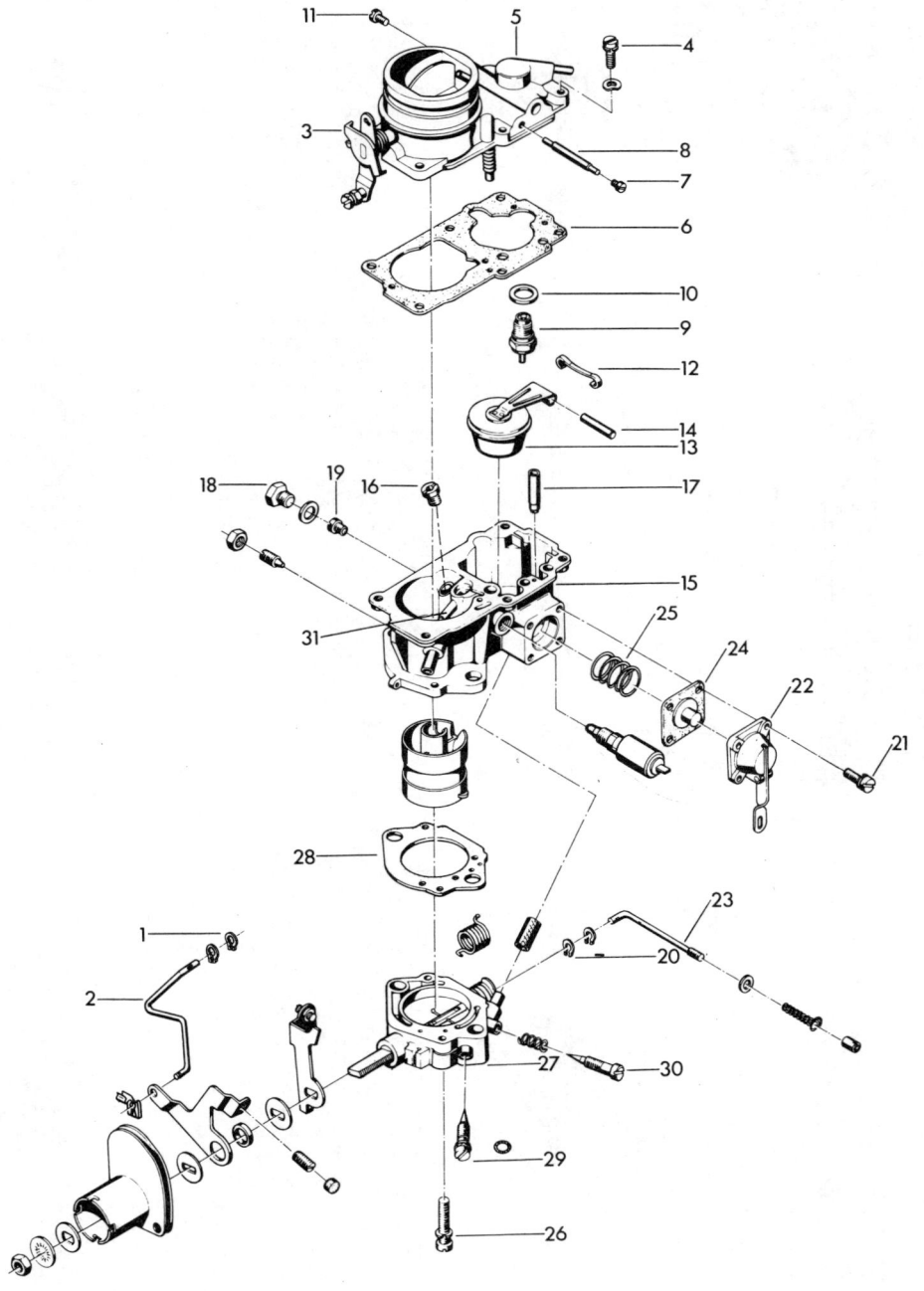

FIG 2:21 Typical Solex 35 PDSI carburetter components. The numbers are referred to in the text

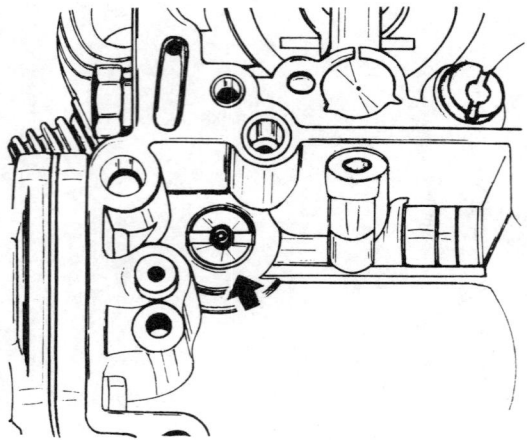

FIG 2:22   Enrichment valve location

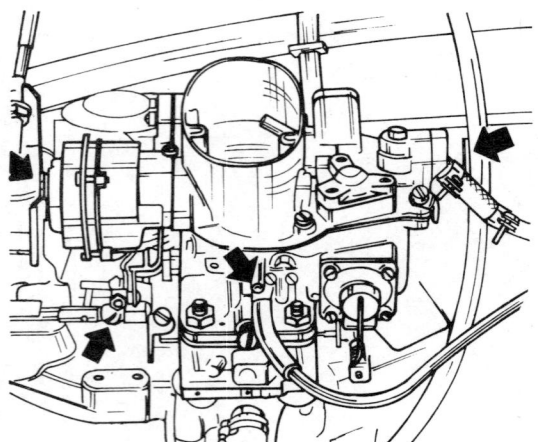

FIG 2:23   Accelerator pump adjustment nut

FIG 2:24   DIDTA carburetter removal

Remove needle valve assembly 8, collecting sealing washer 9. Remove the three screws and lift off enrichment device cover 10, then dismantle the gasket, diaphragm and spring. Remove the similar cover on the opposite side for access to the automatic choke override unit diaphragm. Take care not to mix the components between the two assemblies.

Remove spring 11 and lift out float 12 with hinge pin 13. Remove circlip 14 and separate rod 15 from the lever. Remove the fixing screws and detach accelerator pump cover 16 complete with rod 15. Remove the accelerator pump diaphragm and spring.

Note that there is no need to separate throttle body 17 from carburetter body 18 unless gasket 19 is faulty or throttle body components are to be renewed. Pull accelerator pump nozzle 20 from the carburetter body, collecting 'O' ring 21. Renew the 'O' ring if not in perfect condition. Remove the jets from the carburetter body as shown in **FIG 2:26**, taking care to note the positions of the jets for correct refitting without mixing parts.

Check the float chamber vent valve and its seating for condition of contact surfaces, as shown in **FIG 2:27**. Renew components as necessary if any faults are found.

Remove the screws 22 (see **FIG 2:25**) and related components 23, 24, 25, 26 and 27 for inspection and access to passages in carburetter body and throttle body. Do not dismantle vacuum unit 28 for secondary throttle unless an internal fault, such as a damaged diaphragm, is suspected. The carburetter will now be dismantled sufficiently for cleaning and inspection, which should be carried out as described in **Section 2:10**.

Reassembly:

Reassemble the carburetter in the reverse order of dismantling, using new gaskets. On completion, check the automatic choke, accelerator pump stroke, float chamber vent valve and secondary barrel throttle settings, then refit the carburetter as described previously and check the automatic choke setting. On automatic transmission models, check the throttle damper setting as described at the end of this section.

Automatic choke setting:

The normal setting of the automatic choke is indicated by a mark 1 (see **FIG 2:28**) on the thermostat cover which aligns with the central pointer 2 on the thermostat housing. At this setting, the choke flap should open fully within three to five minutes of switching on the ignition. Operation of the choke flap can be observed after removing the air cleaner. If the choke flap operates outside the specified time limit, the thermostat cover can be rotated relative to the housing. This will increase or decrease the torque of the bi-metal spring according to direction of rotation. If the original setting was incorrect, re-mark the cover to align with the central pointer after adjustments have been made.

To check that the fast-idle cam is positioned correctly, remove the thermostat cover from the automatic choke unit. Remove the air cleaner. Operate the throttle linkage by hand and fully open the choke flap, then release the throttle linkage to retain this position. The top edge of fast-idle lever 2 should align with the centre of the step on cam 1, as shown in **FIG 2:15**. To adjust cam position,

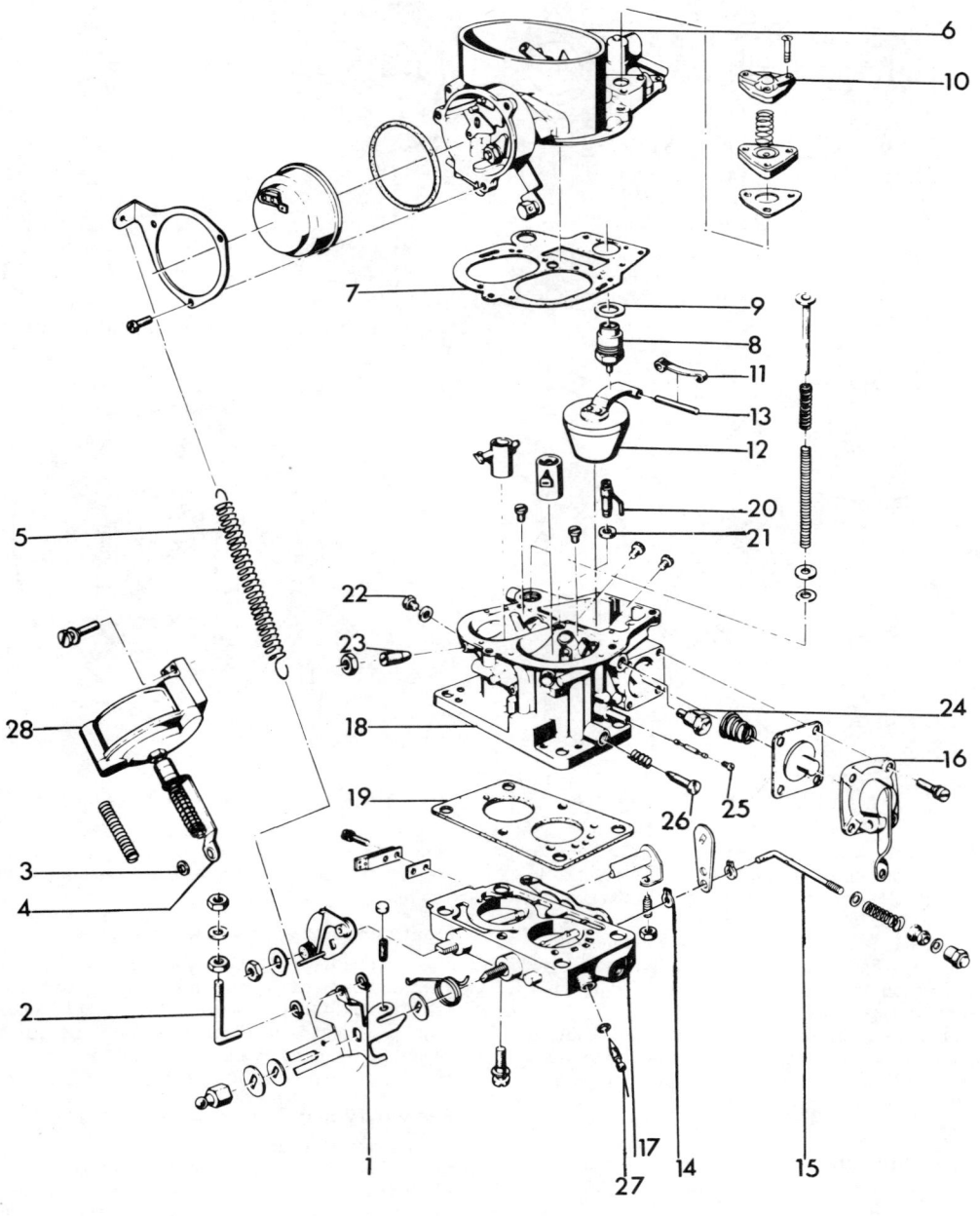

FIG 2:25 Typical Solex 32/32 DIDTA carburetter components. The numbers are referred to in the text

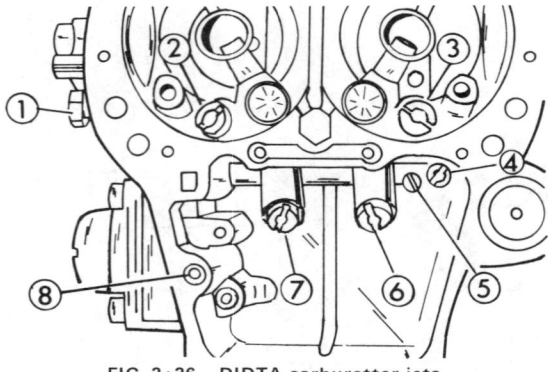

FIG 2:26   DIDTA carburetter jets

Key to Fig 2:26   1 Idle air jet   2 Primary air correction jet
3 Secondary air correction jet   4 Progression air jet
5 Progression jet   6 Secondary main jet   7 Primary main jet
8 Enrichment air jet

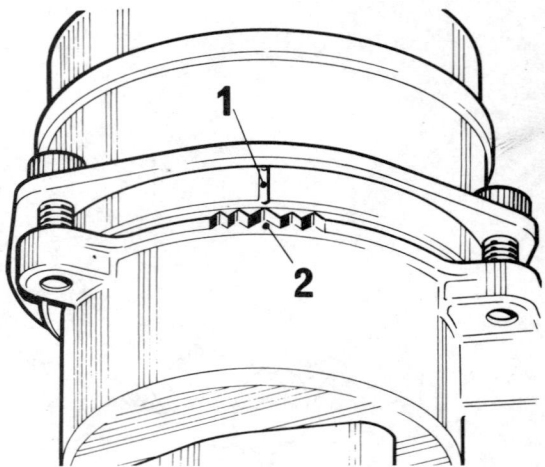

FIG 2:28   Automatic choke alignment, DIDTA carburetter

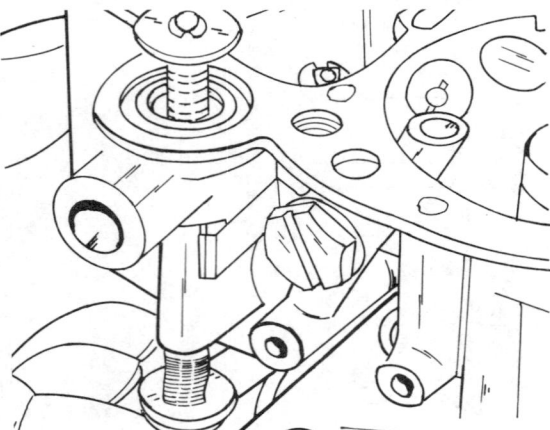

FIG 2:27   Checking float chamber vent valve

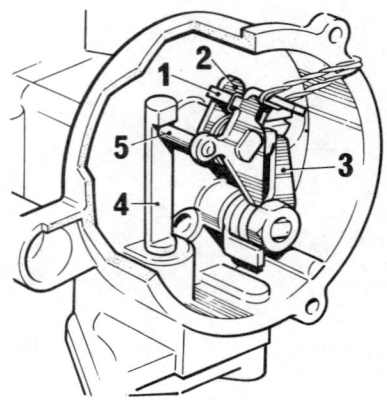

FIG 2:29   Adjusting choke cam position

refer to **FIG 2:29**. Attach an elastic band to the choke
lever plate to hold choke flap closed. Bend lever 1 to
move cam plate 2 in the required direction until correctly
positioned on fast-idle lever 3. Check that a gap of
2.5 to 3.0mm (0.098 to 0.118in) exists between choke
flap edge and the carburetter intake bore, when vacuum
controlled override unit 4 is fully depressed. The gap may
be altered, if necessary, by bending relay pin 5.

On completion, refit the thermostat cover, making
sure that the spring assembly in the cover is correctly
fitted over the lever in the choke unit. Index the alignment
marks and tighten the fixing screws.

Accelerator pump stroke setting:

Refer to **FIG 2:30**. Make sure that the operating
rod is correctly fitted in the upper hole 2 in spindle
lever. Operating rod setting is correct when, with primary
barrel throttle in the idle position, pump lever 1 just
contacts the pump diaphragm without free play. To
adjust, tighten nut 4 to compress spring 3 sufficiently to

produce slack in the pump lever. Now unscrew nut
slowly until spring lengthens just sufficiently to eliminate
free play.

Float chamber vent valve setting:

Refer to **FIG 2:31**. Vent valve setting is correct when
the distance between air vent lever and washer on vent
valve rod is 4.0 to 4.5mm (0.157 to 0.177 inch) with
vent valve and primary barrel throttle closed. Adjust if
necessary by carefully bending the pump lever abutment
bracket on air vent lever, as shown in **FIG 2:32**.

Secondary barrel throttle setting:

To prevent secondary barrel throttle flap jamming in
the closed position, the throttle flap screw shown in
FIG 2:33 should be adjusted to obtain a gap of 0.05mm
(0.002in) between edge of throttle flap and housing bore.
This is approximately a quarter turn inwards of the screw
from the flap closed position. Note that an excessive
secondary throttle flap clearance can adversely affect
engine idle speed adjustment.

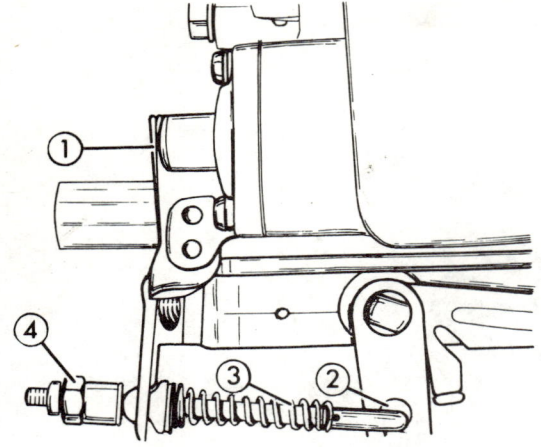

FIG 2:30 Accelerator pump stroke setting

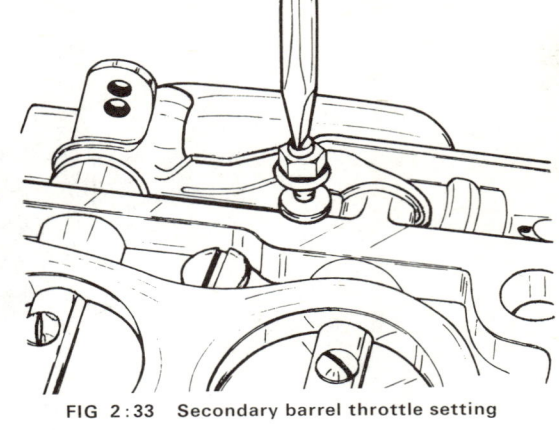

FIG 2:33 Secondary barrel throttle setting

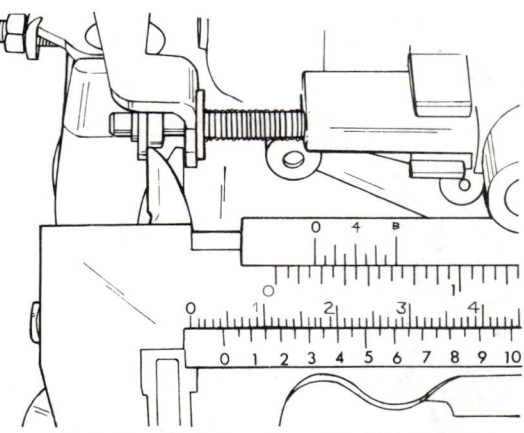

FIG 2:31 Float chamber vent valve setting

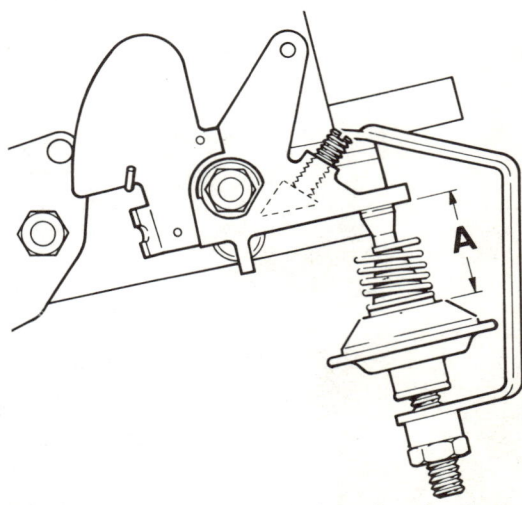

FIG 2:34 Automatic transmission throttle damper adjustment

FIG 2:32 Float chamber vent valve adjustment

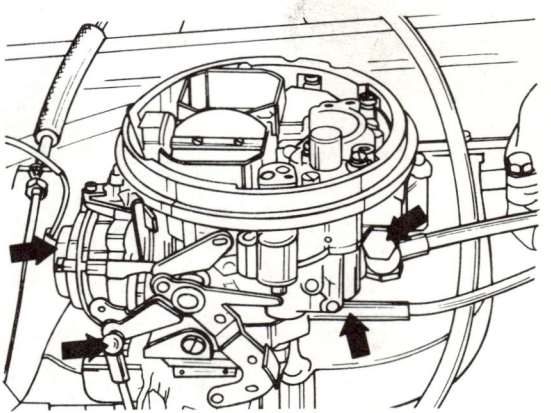

FIG 2:35 INAT carburetter removal

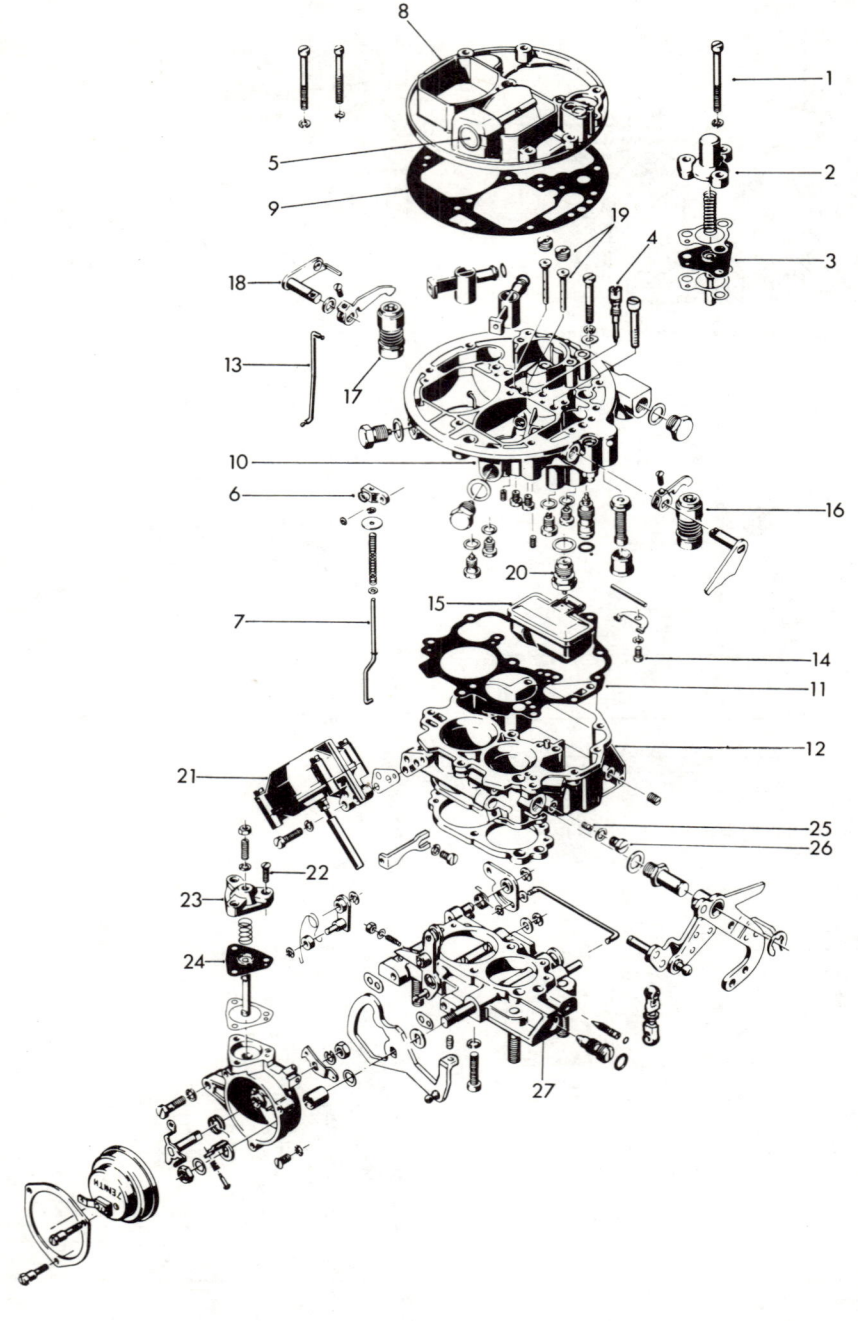

FIG 2:36 Typical Zenith 35/40 INAT carburetter components. The numbers are referred to in the text

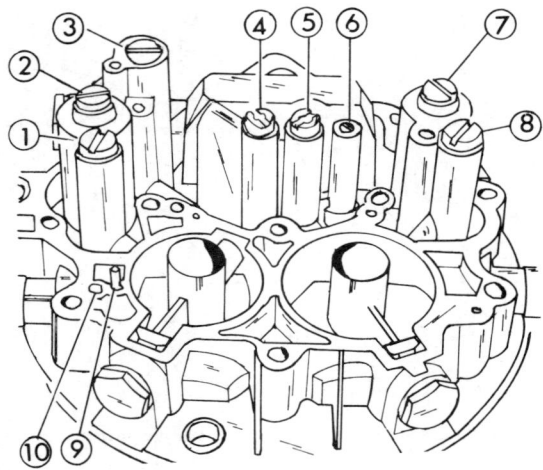

FIG 2:37   INAT carburetter jets and valves

Key to Fig 2:37   1 Primary accelerator pump outlet valve
2 Primary accelerator pump intake valve   3 Enrichment
valve   4 Primary metering jet   5 Secondary metering jet
6 Secondary progression jet   7 Secondary accelerator
pump intake valve   8 Secondary accelerator pump outlet
valve   9 Additional idle mixture air vent   10 Additional
idle mixture jet

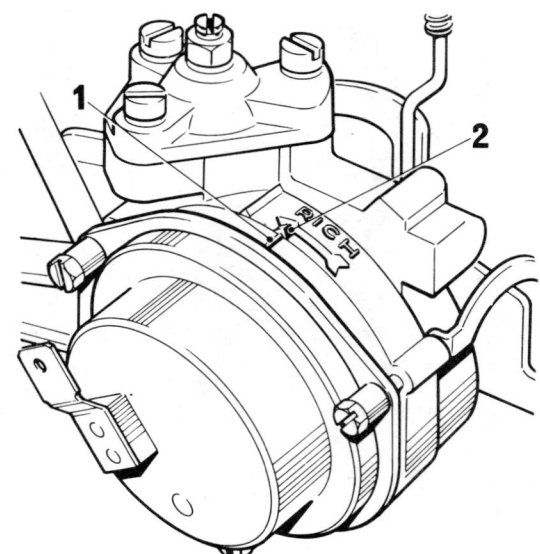

FIG 2:38   Automatic choke adjustment, INAT carburetter

Automatic transmission throttle damper:

On cars with automatic transmission, a throttle damper
is fitted to cushion the last part of throttle closing
movement to prevent engine stalling. Before checking
damper adjustment, the engine must be at normal
operating temperature and the idling adjustments correctly
carried out as described in **Section 2:6**.

Switch off the engine, hold throttle partially open so
that throttle lever just contacts damper plunger, then
measure distance **A** between lever and damper housing
(see **FIG 2:34**). Allow throttle to return fully to the
idling position and again measure distance **A**. The
difference between the two measurements is the plunger
travel, which should be 3.5mm (0.14in). If necessary,
slacken the locknut and rotate the damper until the
correct measurement is obtained. Tighten the locknut to
secure the adjustment.

2:9 Zenith 35/40 INAT carburetter

Carburetter removal:

Remove the air cleaner assembly as described in
Section 2:3. Refer to **FIG 2:35**. Disconnect the fuel
pipe and distributor vacuum pipe from the carburetter
fittings. Remove the spring clip, then remove ball socket
of disc spindle from ball end of control lever. Pull the
wire from the automatic choke connection. Remove the
fixing nuts and lift the carburetter from the inlet manifold,
collecting the gasket.

Refitting:

This is a reversal of the removal procedure, using a new
gasket. On completion, check the engine idle and if
necessary carry out the adjustments described in
Section 2:6.

Dismantling:

Refer to **FIG 2:36**. Remove the three screws 1, then
detach cover 2 and remove enrichment diaphragm and
plunger assembly 3. Unscrew idling jet 4 from the
carburetter top cover.

Detach plastic cap 5 then slacken screw 6 to release
rod 7 from the linkage. Ten screws secure carburetter
cover 8 and gasket 9 to jet housing 10, including a
centrally located small-headed screw situated in the
threaded recess for air filter securing screw. Remove all
10 screws and lift off the cover and gasket.

Detach jet housing 10 and gasket 11 from carburetter
body 12, after disconnecting secondary barrel accelerator
pump linkage 13 and removing the three jet housing
securing screws.

Remove screw 14 from the jet housing and detach
float 15 with pivot assembly. Primary barrel accelerator
pump piston 16 can be removed from jet housing without
removing operating lever. To remove secondary barrel
pump piston 17, remove the fixing screw to detach lever
and shaft assembly 18. Remove air correction jets and
emulsion tubes 19, taking care not to mix the parts as they
are differently calibrated for primary and secondary
barrels. Remove needle valve assembly 20 complete with
sealing washer.

The jets and valves in the jet housing assembly are
shown in **FIG 2:37**. Carefully remove all components,
taking great care to note their positions for correct
refitting.

Refer to **FIG 2:36**. Remove vacuum control unit 21 if
necessary, by removing the fixing screws. Remove three
screws 22 and detach cover 23 and spring and diaphragm
assembly 24 for the automatic choke override unit.
Access to idling fuel jet 25 is gained by removing plug 26.

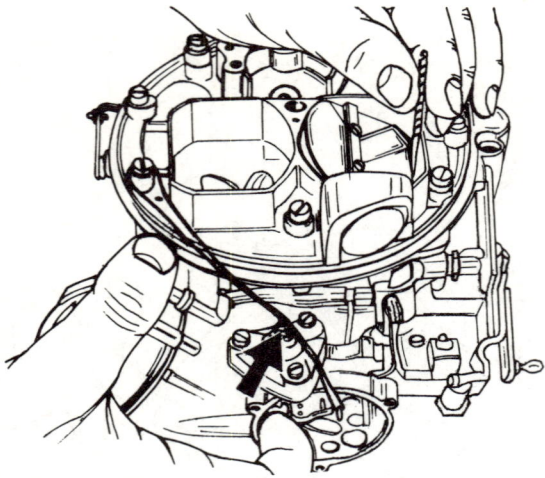

FIG 2:39 Vacuum unit travel stop setting

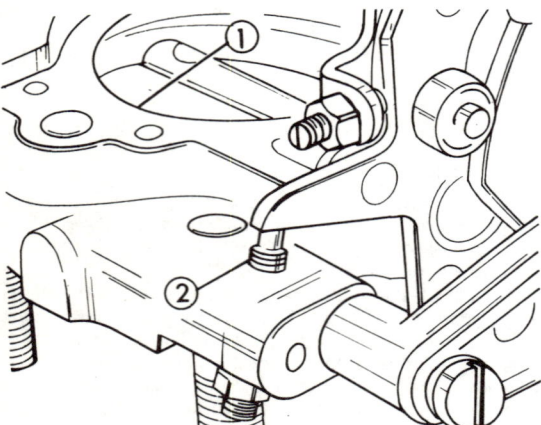

FIG 2:40 Secondary barrel throttle setting

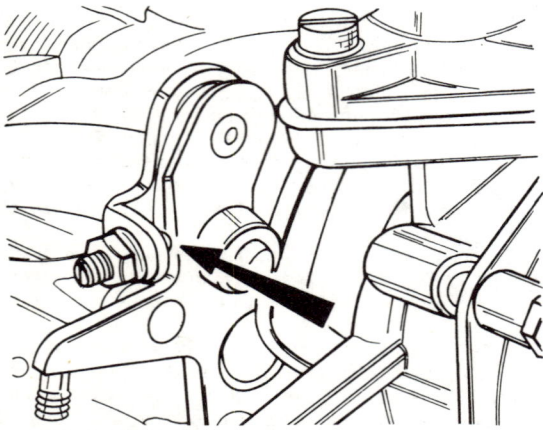

FIG 2:41 Throttle flap link roller adjustment

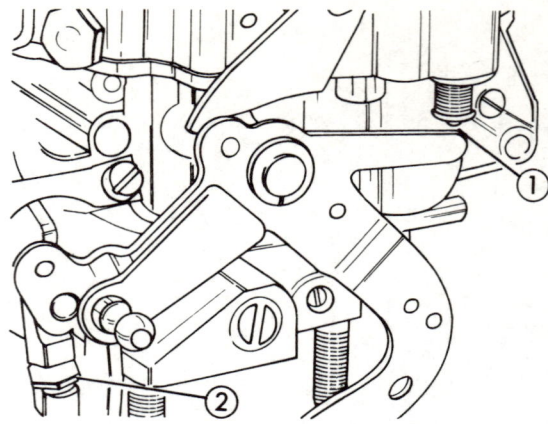

FIG 2:42 Float chamber vent valve setting

The carburetter is now sufficiently dismantled for cleaning and inspection, which should be carried out as described in **Section 2:10**. Do not dismantle the vacuum control unit 21 unless damage to the internal diaphragm is suspected and do not detach throttle body 27 from carburetter body 12 unless component renewal is necessary.

Reassembly:

This is a reversal of the removal procedure, using new gaskets throughout. On completion, carry out those setting and adjustment procedures given in the remainder of this section which can be carried out with the carburetter on the bench. Refit the carburetter as described previously, then carry out the automatic choke setting procedure. On models with automatic transmission, check the throttle damper setting.

Automatic choke setting:

Normal setting of the automatic choke is indicated by mark 1 (see **FIG 2:38**) on thermostat cover which aligns with pointer 2 on the thermostat housing. At this setting, the choke flap should open fully within three to five minutes of switching on the ignition. Remove the air cleaner to observe the operation of the choke flap. If choke operation is outside the limits stated, adjust by rotating the thermostat cover relative to the housing. This will decrease or increase torque of the bi-metal spring according to direction of cover rotation. If original setting was incorrect, re-mark cover to align with the pointer on housing.

To check the travel stop setting of vacuum control override unit, remove the choke thermostat cover then close the choke flap and attach a rubber band to the choke intermediate lever to hold the flap closed (see **FIG 2:39**). Raise the diaphragm pull rod fully and check that a gap of 2.0 to 2.2mm (0.078 to 0.086in) exists between choke flap edge and housing bore. The gap can be altered if necessary by rotating the pull rod stop screw (arrowed) clockwise or anticlockwise to reduce or increase the gap respectively.

To check choke flap rod linkage setting, refer to **FIG 2:18**. Hold the choke flap closed and check the distance between intermediate lever and vacuum diaphragm pull rod boss (dimension **A**) is 0.2 to 1.0mm (0.008 to 0.040in). The distance can be altered if necessary by removing plastic cover 5 (see **FIG 2 : 36**), slackening screw 6 and modifying position of rod 7. Tighten the screw to secure the adjustment and recheck.

Secondary barrel throttle setting :

Refer to **FIG 2 : 40**. To prevent secondary barrel throttle flap 1 jamming in the closed position, throttle flap stop screw 2 should be adjusted to obtain a gap of 0.05mm (0.002in) between flap edge and housing bore. This is approximately a quarter turn in on the stop screw from the flap closed position. Note that an excessive secondary throttle flap clearance can adversely affect engine idling adjustments.

Throttle flap link roller :

Refer to **FIG 2 : 41**. To ensure correct roller contact on primary barrel throttle lever, link lever screw should be adjusted to obtain a gap of 0.1 to 0.2mm (0.004 to 0.008in) between screw and secondary barrel throttle lever, with primary barrel throttle closed.

Float chamber vent valve setting :

Refer to **FIG 2 : 42**. Vent valve setting is correct when a gap of 1.5 to 1.8mm (0.06 to 0.07in) exists between throttle flap stop screw and abutment, with air vent lever just contacting base of vent valve 1. Valve setting can be altered if necessary by adjusting length of intermediate link 2. Note that the throttle stop setting should not be disturbed as this will affect ignition vacuum advance and carburetter primary barrel progression system.

Automatic transmission throttle damper :

Checking and adjustments for automatic transmission throttle damper are carried out in the same manner as that described in **Section 2 : 8** for DIDTA carburetters, noting, however, that damper mounting for INAT carburetter is slightly different to that shown in **FIG 2 : 34**.

2 : 10 Servicing carburetter components

Clean all parts in petrol or an approved carburetter cleaner, then examine them for wear or damage. Renew any faulty parts. Clean jets and passages thoroughly, using compressed air, clean petrol and a small brush.

Do not use cloth for cleaning purposes, as small fibres may remain after cleaning and clog the jets or passages. Never use a wire probe as this will damage or enlarge the jets.

If a jet has a blockage which cannot be cleared with compressed air, use a single bristle from a stiff brush for the purpose. If this method is unsuccessful, renew the jet. When jets are to be renewed, take the old components to the spares department for matching purposes, so that the correct replacement part is obtained.

Make sure that all sediment is cleaned from the float chamber and check the float for damage or leakage. Float leakage can generally be detected by shaking the float and listening for the sound of fuel splash inside. Renew the float if any fault is found.

Check the float needle valve assembly carefully, renewing the assembly if there is any sign of a ridge on the tapered valve seat. A damaged needle valve can lead to flooding by failing to cut off the fuel supply properly when the float chamber is full, or may stick in the closed position and prevent sufficient fuel from reaching the float chamber. Check for correct sealing by blowing through from the feed end. The air flow should be cut off completely when the needle is held on to its seat by gentle finger pressure. Renew the assembly if there is any doubt about its condition. Check the needle valve sealing washer and renew if damaged or distorted. Note that the correct sealing washer must always be installed, as this controls float level.

Examine the tips of the idle control screws and renew them if there is any sign of wear or damage. Check the diaphragms used in carburetter sub-assemblies for splits, tears, deformities and for hardening of the material. Renew any diaphragm that is not in perfect condition.

If shafts, levers or flap valves are to be dismantled for any reason, mark the components so that they can be reassembled in their correct relative positions. Note that excessive wear in shaft bearings will generally dictate renewal of the complete housing assembly.

2 : 11 Fault diagnosis

(a) Leakage or insufficient fuel delivered

1 Air vent to tank obstructed
2 Fuel pipes blocked
3 Air leaks at pipe connections
4 Fuel filter blocked
5 Pump gasket faulty
6 Pump diaphragm defective
7 Pump valves sticking or seating badly

(b) Excessive fuel consumption

1 Carburetter requires adjustment
2 Fuel leakage
3 Sticking choke unit
5 Dirty air cleaner
5 Worn jets in carburetter
6 Excessive engine temperature
7 Idling speed too high

(c) Idling speed too high

1 Rich fuel mixture
2 Throttle control sticking
3 Sticking choke control
4 Worn throttle valve

(d) Noisy fuel pump

1 Loose pump mountings
2 Air leaks on suction side of pump
3 Obstruction in fuel pipeline
4 Clogged fuel filter

(e) No fuel delivery

1 Float needle valve stuck
2 Tank vent system blocked
3 Defective pump diaphragm
4 Pump valve stuck
5 Pipeline obstructed
6 Bad air leak on suction side of pump

NOTES

CHAPTER 3

THE IGNITION SYSTEM

3:1 Description

The ignition system is conventional, comprising an ignition coil, distributor and contact breaker assembly. The distributor incorporates automatic timing control by centrifugal mechanism and a vacuum operated unit. As engine speed increases, the centrifugal action of rotating weights pivoting against the tension of small springs moves the contact breaker cam relative to the distributor drive shaft and progressively advances the ignition. The vacuum control unit is connected by small bore pipe to a fitting on the carburetter. At high degrees of vacuum the unit advances the ignition, but under load, at reduced vacuum, the unit progressively retards the ignition.

The ignition coil is wound as an auto-transformer with the primary and secondary windings connected in series, the common junction being connected to the contact breaker with the positive feed from the battery going to the opposite terminal of the LT windings via the ignition switch. LT current supplied to the coil is via a resistance wire which reduces nominal battery voltage to approximately 6 volts at the coil terminal. This resistance wire is bypassed when the starter is in operation, so that full battery voltage is supplied to the coil. The coil then provides increased voltage to the HT system for maximum

sparking plug efficiency when the engine is being started.

When the contact breaker points are closed, current flows in the coil primary winding, magnetising the core and setting up a fairly strong magnetic field. Each time the contacts open, the battery current is cut off and the magnetic field collapses, inducing a high current in the primary winding and a high voltage in the secondary. The primary current is used to charge the capacitor connected across the contacts and the flow is high and virtually instantaneous. It is this high current peak which induces the surge in the secondary winding to produce the sparking voltage across the plug points. Without the capacitor the current peak would be much smaller and the sparking voltage considerably reduced, in fact to a point where it would be insufficient to fire the mixture in the engine cylinders. The capacitor, therefore, serves the dual purpose of minimising contact breaker points wear and providing the necessary high charging surge to ensure a powerful spark.

3:2 Routine maintenance

Remove the distributor cover as shown in **FIG 3:1**. On some models, the cover is retained by three stud fasteners, which must be released with the aid of a

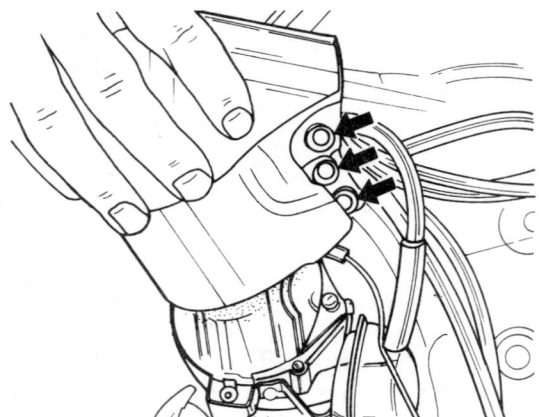

FIG 3:1   Removing distributor cover

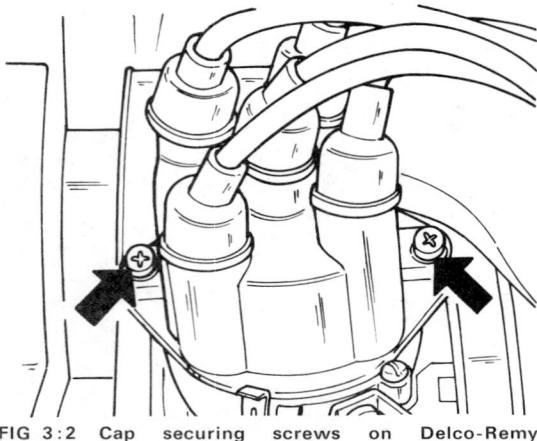

FIG 3:2   Cap securing screws on Delco-Remy distributor

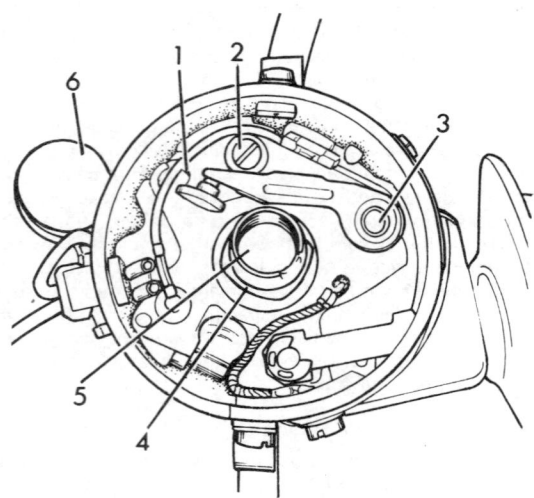

FIG 3:3   Contact points, Bosch distributor

screwdriver. On Bosch distributors, release the two spring clips and remove the distributor cap. On Delco-Remy distributors, remove the two screws arrowed in **FIG 3 : 2** and lift off the distributor cap.

Carefully pull the rotor arm from the top of the distributor shaft, taking care not to damage the brass strip contact on Delco-Remy units. Remove the dust cover.

Refer to **FIG 3 : 3** or **3 : 4**. Apply a single drop of oil to pivot point 3 and apply just enough oil to felt pad 5 to soak it. Apply a thin smear of grease to cam 4. When lubricating the internal parts of the distributor, take great care to avoid oil or grease contaminating the contact breaker points, lubricating sparingly for this reason.

Adjusting the contact breaker points:

Turn the engine until one of the cams has opened the contact breaker points to their fullest extent, then check the gap between the points with clean feeler gauges. The correct gap is 0.50mm (0.020in). To adjust the gap, loosen the fixed contact point clamp screw 2, insert a screwdriver into slot 1, then turn the plate until the correct gap is obtained (see **FIG 3 : 3** or **3 : 4**). Tighten the screw 2 and recheck the gap. If new contact points have been fitted, the gap should be set to 0.55mm (0.022in) to allow for the initial bedding down of the new rubbing block.

Cleaning the contact breaker points:

Use a fine carborundum stone or special contact point file to polish the points if they are dirty or pitted, taking care to keep the faces flat and square. If the points are too worn to clean up in this manner, they should be renewed. On completion of cleaning, wipe away all dust with a cloth moistened in petrol.

Renewing the contact breaker points:
Bosch distributor:

The contact points are of the one-piece type and can be withdrawn after disconnecting the low tension wire and removing the securing screw shown at 2 in **FIG 3 : 3**. Wash the mating faces of the new contact points with methylated spirits to remove the protective coating, then install in the reverse order of removal. On completion, set the points gap as described previously.

Delco-Remy distributor:

Refer to **FIG 3 : 5**. Use a small screwdriver to lever the moving contact spring 5 away from the insulator 2 then pull the moving contact from the pivot post. Detach the wiring connectors 3 and 4 and the insulator 2 from the fixed contact plate. Remove the fixing screw shown at 2 in **FIG 3 : 4**, then lift the fixed contact from the base plate.

Wash the mating faces of the new contact points with methylated spirits to remove the protective coating. Fit the fixed contact point to the base plate and secure with the single screw. Fit the insulator and terminal connectors to the fixed contact plate, making sure that these parts are in the correct order as shown in **FIG 3 : 5**. Apply a drop of oil to the pivot post, then fit the moving contact and ease the spring into position. Set the contact points to the correct gap as described previously.

Checking rotor arm:

Check the rotor arm for cracks and for excessive wear or burning of the brass contact strip. Renew the rotor arm if any faults are found. On Delco-Remy units, make sure that the contact spring on the rotor arm is not damaged or distorted. Spring height must be such that the upper part of the spring firmly contacts the carbon brush in the distributor cap, but without excessive pressure which could cause undue wear.

To check rotor insulation, remove the central HT lead from the distributor cap and hold it about half an inch from the brass strip on the rotor. To avoid shocks, hold the lead well away from the end. With the ignition switched on, flick open the contact points. If a spark jumps the gap the rotor is faulty and must be renewed.

3:3 Ignition faults

If the engine runs unevenly, set it to idle at approximately 1000rev/min and, taking care not to touch any conducting part of the sparking plug leads, remove and replace each lead from its plug in turn. To avoid shocks during this operation it is necessary to wear a pair of thick gloves or to use insulated pliers. Doing this to a plug which is firing correctly will accentuate uneven running but will make no difference if the plug is not firing.

Having by this means located the faulty cylinder, stop the engine and remove the plug lead. Pull back the insulation or remove the connector so that the end of the lead is exposed. Alternatively, use an extension piece, such as a small bar or drill, pushed into the plug connector. Hold the lead carefully to avoid shocks, so that the end is about $\frac{1}{8}$in away from the cylinder head. Crank the engine with the starter with the ignition switched on. A strong, regular spark confirms that the fault lies with the sparking plug which should be removed and cleaned as described in **Section 3:6**, or renewed if defective.

If the spark is weak and irregular, check the condition of the lead and, if it is perished or cracked, renew it and repeat the test. If no improvement results, check that the inside of the distributor cap is clean and dry and that there is no sign of tracking, which can be seen as a thin black line between the electrodes or to some metal part in contact with the cap. Tracking can only be cured by fitting a new cap. On Delco-Remy distributors, check also that the contact in the centre of the rotor arm is set correctly and that the contact button inside the cap is in good condition. On Bosch distributors, check that the carbon brush in the cap is in good condition and free to move in and out against its internal spring. On all models, check the brass segments inside the cap for wear or burning. Renew the cap if any fault is found.

If these checks do not cure a weak HT spark, or if no spark can be obtained at the plug or lead, check the LT circuit as described next.

Testing the low tension circuit:

A 12-volt test lamp can be used to check circuit continuity, but accurate checking of the components requires the use of a voltmeter due to the different voltages supplied to the coil during starting and running.

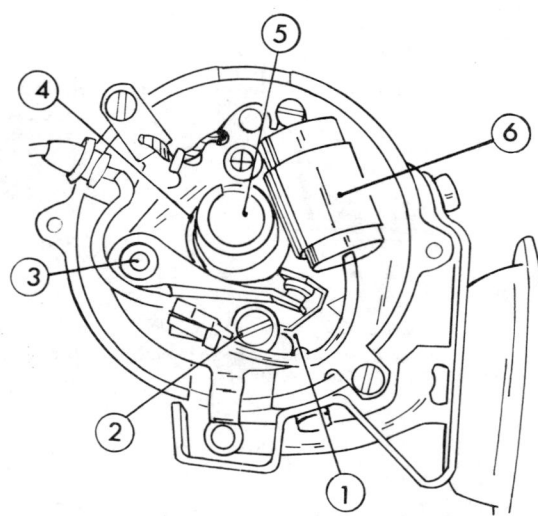

FIG 3:4   Contact points, Delco-Remy distributor

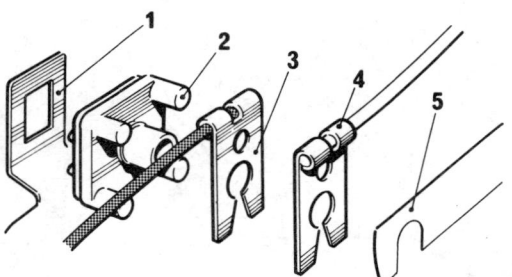

FIG 3:5   Contact breaker wiring and insulator assembly, Delco-Remy distributor

Key to Fig 3:5   1 Fixed contact plate   2 Insulator
3 Capacitor terminal   4 LT terminal   5 Moving contact spring

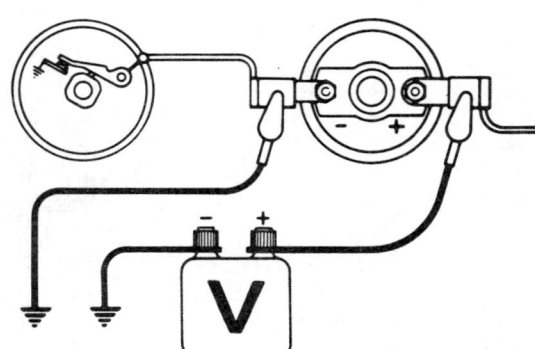

FIG 3:6   Voltmeter connections to test coil current supply

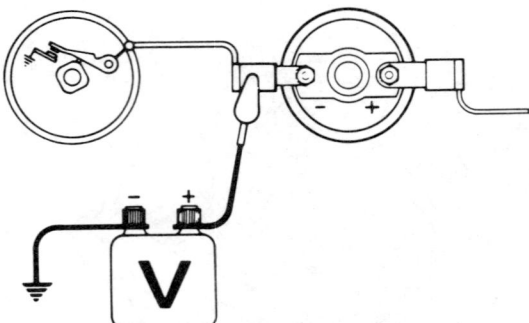

FIG 3:7 Voltmeter connections to check coil windings, contact breaker and capacitor

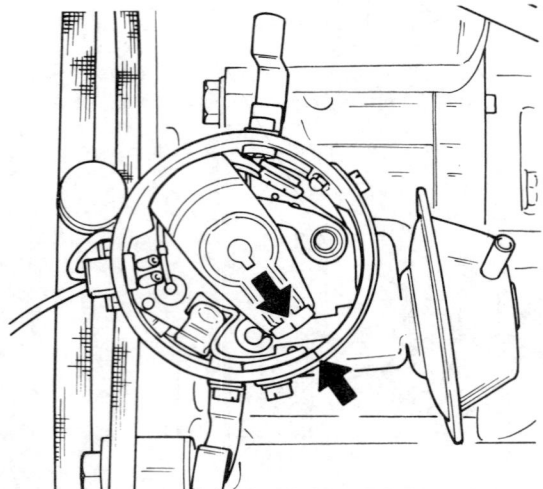

FIG 3:8 Bosch distributor alignment

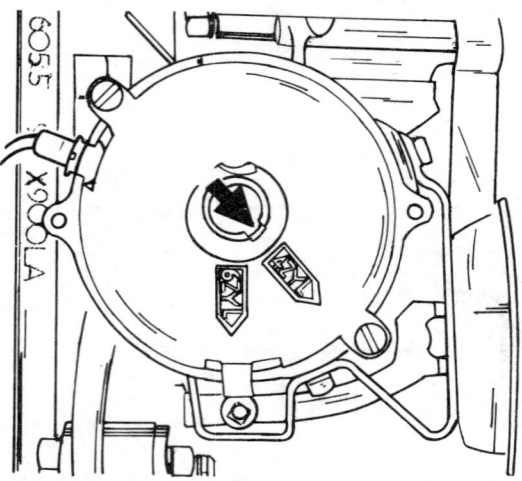

FIG 3:9 Delco-Remy distributor alignment

Checking coil current supply:

Connect the voltmeter positive to the coil positive terminal and the voltmeter negative to a good earth on the car engine or body, then connect a jumper lead from the coil negative to a good earth (see FIG 3:6).

To check the starting supply to the coil, turn the ignition switch to the start position and crank the engine. While the engine is turning on the starter, the voltmeter should register at least 8 volts. A low or zero reading may be due to faulty contacts in the starter solenoid switch or to defective wiring. To check the running supply to the coil through the resistance wire, switch on the ignition without operating the starter, when the voltmeter should register 4.5 to 6 volts. A voltmeter reading outside the limits stated indicates a fault in the resistance wire. Note that this wire cannot be serviced separately from the wiring harness.

Primary winding, contact breaker and capacitor check:

This check involves turning the engine, which should be carried out using a spanner of the correct size on the crankshaft pulley mounting bolt. The engine will be easier to turn if all of the sparking plugs are removed first. Connect the voltmeter positive to the coil negative terminal, and the voltmeter negative to a good earth on the engine or body as shown in FIG 3:7.

Remove the distributor cap as described in Section 3:2 and position it to one side. Turn the engine until the contact points are open, then switch on the ignition. The voltmeter should register battery voltage (11.5 to 12 volts). If there is no reading, there is a break in the coil primary winding or there is a shortcircuit in either the contact breaker connection or in the capacitor. The capacitor is shown at 6 in FIG 3:3 or 3:4.

Turn the engine until the contact breaker points are closed, then switch on the ignition. The voltmeter reading should be zero to 0.2 volt. If over 0.2 volt, the contact points are dirty, the contact breaker plate and/or the distributor housing earth is faulty, or the green wire has a break in it.

3:4 Removing and dismantling distributor

Removal:

Remove the fuel pump as described in Chapter 2, to allow the distributor to be withdrawn.

Remove the distributor cap as described in Section 3:2 and position it to one side. On Bosch units, turn the engine until the mark on the rotor arm aligns with the mark on the distributor housing as shown in FIG 3:8. On Delco-Remy units, remove the rotor arm then turn the engine until the slot in the distributor drive shaft aligns with the 4ZYL mark on the dust cover as shown in FIG 3:9. Disconnect the green lead at the coil and pull off the vacuum pipe which is attached to a fitting on the distributor vacuum unit.

Remove the fixing bolt and washer and the mounting plate shown in FIG 3:10, then lift the distributor from the engine. Place a rag over the distributor mounting hole to prevent foreign matter from entering the engine. Distributor installation will be facilitated if the engine is not turned while the distributor is removed.

Refitting :

If the engine has not been turned, rotate the distributor drive shaft slightly so that the notch in the shaft on Delco-Remy units is positioned between the 4ZYL and 6ZYL marks on the dust cover, or turn the rotor arm clockwise by a similar amount on Bosch units. This will allow for the slight rotation of the shaft as the distributor drive gear is engaged.

Install the distributor and press it down into position. As the drive gear engages, the distributor shaft will turn anticlockwise slightly. When the distributor is fully installed and the drive tongue engaged with the slot in the oil pump drive, alignment should be as shown in **FIG 3:8** or **3:9**. The distributor body can be rotated slightly to set the alignment exactly, but if the alignment is out by several degrees, the distributor should be removed again, the shaft turned to a new position, then the distributor installed as described previously. When the drive tongue is fully engaged and the distributor alignment correct, install the distributor clamp plate and bolt loosely. Refit the remaining components, then check and adjust ignition timing as described in **Section 3:5**.

If the engine has been turned with the distributor removed and the timing setting lost, set the engine to the firing point for number one cylinder as described in **Section 3:5** before installing the distributor as described previously.

Dismantling Bosch distributor :

Remove the distributor as described previously. Remove the rotor arm, cover and contact breaker points as described in **Section 3:2**.

Refer to **FIG 3:11**. Use a small screwdriver to press off circlip 11, then remove the fixing screws and detach vacuum unit 8. Remove capacitor 4. Remove the screws securing fixing clips 1 on each side, then withdraw contact breaker plate 12. For access to centrifugal advance mechanism 2, drive out the pin securing drive gear 6 to the shaft, then remove circlip 5 and slide the shaft from the housing. To avoid damaging the bearing bushes, remove any burrs from the circlip groove before removing the main shaft.

Clean the internal parts with petrol and allow them to dry. Inspect all parts for wear or damage. Note that parts are not serviced individually for the centrifugal advance mechanism, distributor shaft or drive gear, so if any of these parts is found to be worn or damaged, the distributor assembly must be renewed.

Reassembly :

This is a reversal of the removal procedure. If distributor shaft end float is excessive, a thrust washer of greater thickness should be fitted between circlip 5 and housing 3 (see **FIG 3:11**). Lubricate the centrifugal advance mechanism sparingly with grease. On completion, lubricate the upper distributor components and set the contact points gap as described in **Section 3:2**.

Dismantling Delco-Remy distributor :

Remove the distributor as described previously. Remove the rotor arm, cover and contact breaker points as described in **Section 3:2**.

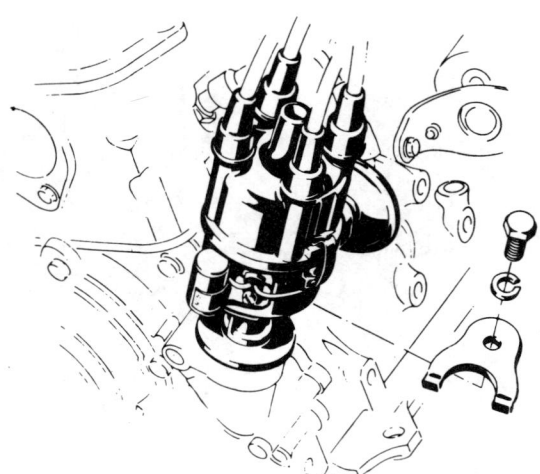

FIG 3:10 **Distributor mounting details**

Refer to **FIG 3:12**. Remove the fixing screws and detach vacuum unit 5, unhooking the arm from the pin on the contact breaker plate. Remove the two screws and detach contact breaker plate 10. If necessary, detach detach capacitor 6 from the plate.

For access to the centrifugal advance mechanism 1, detach the distributor drive gear by driving out the retaining pin, then remove circlip 3 and withdraw the drive shaft from housing 2. To avoid damage to the bearing bushes, remove any burrs from the circlip grooves before sliding the main shaft from the body.

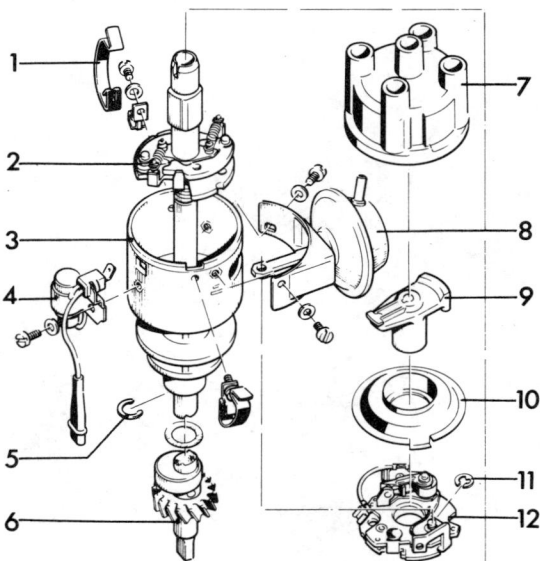

FIG 3:11 **Bosch distributor components**

Key to Fig 3:11   1 Spring clip   2 Centrifugal advance mechanism   3 Distributor housing   4 Capacitor   5 Circlip   6 Drive gear   7 Cap   8 Vacuum unit   9 Rotor arm   10 Dust cover   11 Circlip   12 Contact breaker plate assembly

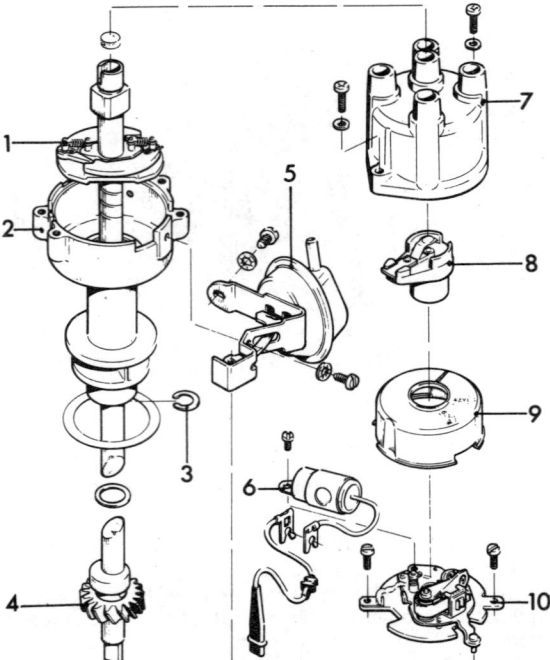

FIG 3:12 Delco-Remy distributor components

Key to Fig 3:12   1 Centrifugal advance mechanism
2 Distributor housing   3 Circlip   4 Drive gear   5 Vacuum
unit   6 Capacitor   7 Cap   8 Rotor arm   9 Dust cover
10 Contact breaker plate assembly

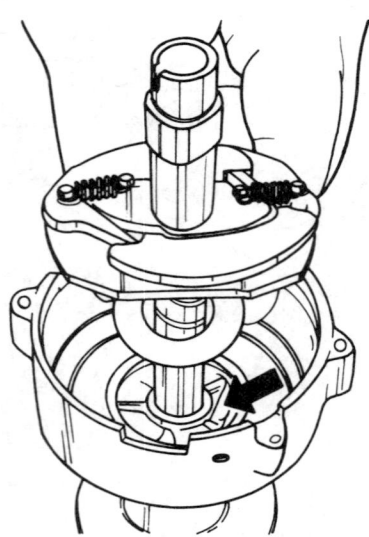

FIG 3:13 Lubricant pockets on Delco-Remy distributor

Clean all internal parts in petrol and allow to dry, then examine for wear or damage and renew parts as necessary. Note that parts are not serviced individually for the centrifugal advance mechanism, drive shaft or drive gear, so if any of these parts are worn or damaged a new distributor should be fitted.

Reassembly:

Reassemble the distributor in the reverse order of dismantling. Lubricate the centrifugal advance mechanism sparingly with grease. Before fully installing the distributor shaft, lift up the plastic washer and fill lubricant pockets 2 with clean engine oil (see **FIG 3:13**). If distributor shaft end play is excessive, a thrust washer of greater thickness should be installed between circlip 3 and housing 2 (see **FIG 3:12**). On completion, lubricate upper distributor components and set contact points gap as described in **Section 3:2**.

3:5 Timing the ignition

Checking the ignition timing involves turning the engine, which should be carried out using a spanner of the correct size on the crankshaft pulley mounting bolt. The engine will be easier to turn if all of the sparking plugs are removed first.

If the distributor is correctly installed, remove the distributor cap as described in **Section 3:2** and, on Delco-Remy units, remove the rotor arm. Turn the engine until the distributor is aligned as shown in **FIG 3:8** or **3:9**.

If the engine has been turned after distributor removal and the timing setting lost, the engine must be first set to the firing point for No 1 (front) cylinder. To do this, either remove the rocker cover and turn the engine until both valves for No 1 cylinder are closed (springs fully extended), or turn the engine until pressure can be felt by a thumb placed over No 1 cylinder plug hole.

Some models have a timing mark on the crankshaft pulley which must be aligned with a mark on the timing cover as shown in **FIG 3:14**. Other models have a steel ball embedded in the flywheel which must be aligned with a pointer as shown in **FIG 3:15**, access to these timing marks being through a hole in the flywheel cover at the rear of the engine.

With the engine set on the firing stroke for No 1 cylinder as described previously, turn the engine a little more as necessary until the timing marks are exactly aligned as shown in **FIG 3:14** or **3:15**. This sets the engine to the firing point for No 1 cylinder. Install the distributor if it was removed. Set the contact breaker points gap as described in **Section 3:2**.

Connect a suitable test lamp in parallel with the contacts. One lead will go to the terminal on the side of the distributor and one to earth. Slacken the distributor clamp bolt shown in **FIG 3:10** just enough to allow the distributor body to be rotated by hand. Turn the distributor body clockwise as far as possible to ensure that the contact points are fully closed. Now switch on the ignition and turn the distributor body very slowly in an anticlockwise direction until the lamp just lights up, which indicates that the contact points are just opening. Without moving the distributor from this position, tighten the mounting bolt.

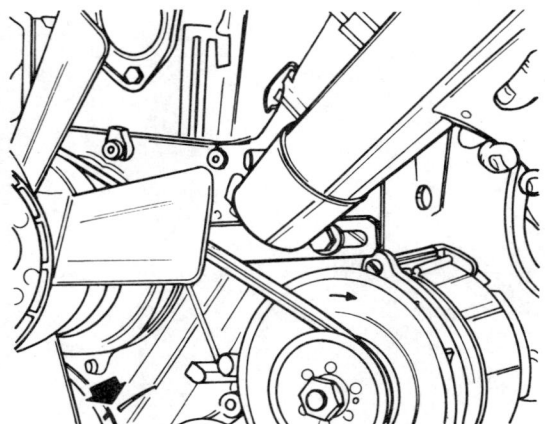

FIG 3:14 Timing marks on crankshaft pulley and timing cover

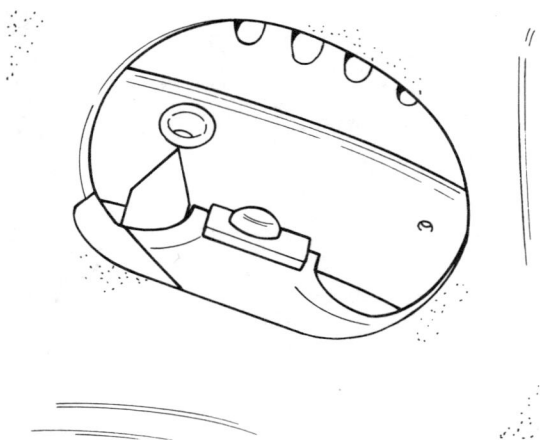

FIG 3:15 Timing marks on flywheel and housing

Stroboscopic timing:

If this method of timing is used, the engine must be run at cranking speed only, as a higher speed will cause the distributor advance mechanism to operate and give a false reading. Connect the stroboscopic lamp equipment equipment according to the manufacturer's instructions, into the ignition circuit for No 1 cylinder. Remove the sparking plug leads from Nos 2, 3 and 4 cylinders to prevent the engine from running during the operation. Slacken the distributor mounting bolt shown in **FIG 3:10**, then have an assistant operate the starter motor to turn the engine. While the engine is turning, shine the stroboscopic lamp on to the timing marks and turn the distributor until they appear in correct·alignment as shown in **FIG 3:14** or **3:15**. Tighten the distributor mounting bolt, switch off the ignition and remove the stroboscopic equipment. Reconnect the sparking plug leads previously removed.

3:6 Sparking plugs

Sparking plugs should be of the recommended type, details of which are given in **Technical Data**. The gaps should be set to 0.75mm (0.030in) by bending the outer electrode only. Have sparking plugs cleaned on an abrasive-blasting machine and tested under pressure with the electrode gaps correctly set. Any plug which fails the test should be renewed. As a general rule, plugs should be cleaned and tested at about 6000 mile intervals and renewed at about 12,000 mile intervals, or before if badly worn.

The HT leads from the distributor to sparking plugs and coil should be examined for cracks and defective insulation. Renew any lead found to be defective in any way. The leads are of the suppressor type with a non-metallic graphited core. Replacement leads are supplied to the correct lengths and are complete with end connectors.

3:7 Fault diagnosis

(a) Engine will not fire

1 Battery discharged
2 Contact breaker points dirty, pitted or maladjusted
3 Distributor cap dirty, cracked or tracking
4 Rotor contact not touching carbon brush in cap
5 Faulty cable or loose connection in low tension circuit
6 Distributor rotor arm cracked
7 Faulty coil
8 Broken contact breaker spring
9 Contact points stuck open

(b) Engine misfires

1 Check 2, 3, 5 and 7 in (a)
2 Weak contact breaker spring
3 HT plug or coil lead cracked or perished
4 Loose sparking plug
5 Sparking plug insulation cracked
6 Sparking plug gap incorrect
7 Ignition timing too far advanced

(c) Poor acceleration

1 Ignition retarded
2 Centrifugal advance weights seized
3 Centrifugal advance springs weak, broken or disconnected
4 Loose distributor mounting
5 Excessive contact points gap
6 Worn sparking plugs
7 Faulty vacuum unit or leaking pipe

NOTES

CHAPTER 4

THE COOLING SYSTEM

4:1 Description

The cooling system is pressurised and thermostatically controlled. Water circulation is assisted by a centrifugal pump which is mounted at the front of the cylinder block. The cooling fan, which draws air through the radiator, is fitted to the same shaft as the pump impeller. The pump and fan and the alternator are driven from a pulley on the crankshaft by an endless belt. The tension of this belt is adjustable at the alternator mountings.

The pump takes coolant from the bottom of the and delivers it to the cylinder block from which it rises to the cylinder head. At normal operating temperatures the thermostat is open and the coolant returns from the head to the top of the radiator. At lower temperatures, the thermostat valve is closed and the coolant bypasses the radiator and returns to the pump inlet to provide a rapid warm-up.

4:2 Maintenance

The pump bearing is a permanently sealed and lubricated assembly and requires no maintenance.

The cooling system should be filled with an inhibited, year-round ethylene glycol coolant solution, formulated to withstand two years of normal operation without draining. **Alcohol base coolants or plain water must not be used in the cooling system.** If for any reason water only is used as a coolant in an emergency, the system must be drained and refilled with the correct solution as soon as possible. The cooling system should be completely drained and refilled with a new coolant solution of the recommended type every two years.

The cooling system should be checked regularly for correct coolant level when the engine is cool. If it is essential to remove the radiator filler cap when the engine is hot, hold the cap with a large piece of rag. Turn the cap anticlockwise and wait a few moments for the pressure to release, before turning the cap further anticlockwise and lifting off. Topping up should be carried out with an antifreeze solution of appropriate strength to avoid weakening the solution in the system.

Periodically, check that the clips are tight on all hoses and that the radiator pressure cap is in good condition and sealing effectively. Loss of system pressure due to a leaking filler cap can be a cause of overheating.

Regular checks should be made on the condition and tension of the drive belt, as described in **Section 4:4**.

Draining the system:

Place the heater temperature control in the car to the maximum heat position. Make sure that the system is

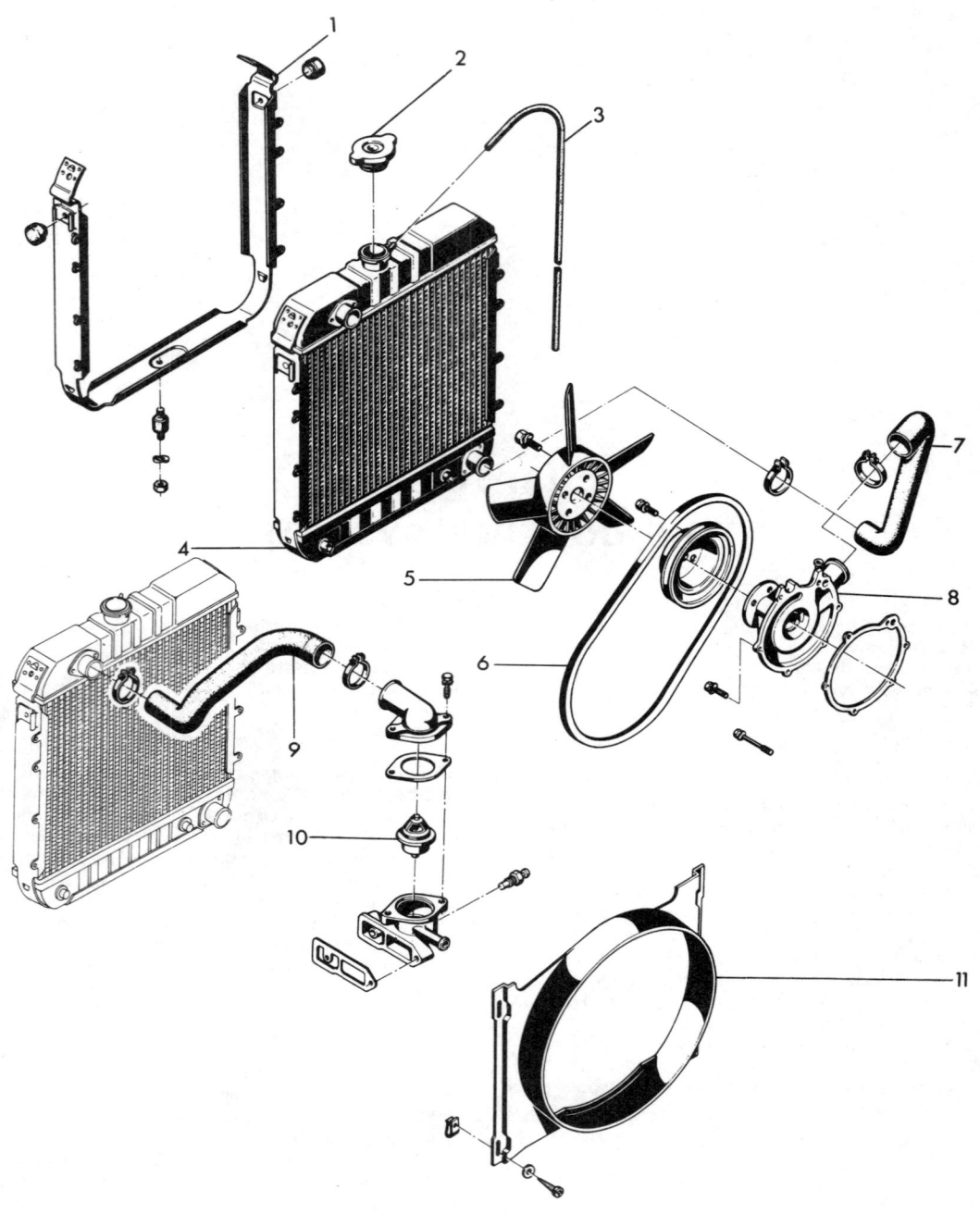

FIG 4:1 Cooling system components

Key to Fig 4:1   1 Mounting strap   2 Filler cap   3 Overflow pipe   4 Radiator   5 Cooling fan   6 Drive belt   7 Bottom hose   8 Water pump   9 Top hose   10 Thermostat   11 Fan cowl

cool, then remove the radiator cap. Slacken the clip and remove the bottom hose 7 from the radiator (see **FIG 4:1**). Remove the square-headed drain plug which is located on the righthand side of the engine cylinder block.

Flushing:

When all old coolant has drained, reconnect the bottom hose and refit the drain plug temporarily. Fill the system with clean water and run the engine until the top radiator hose feels warm, which indicates that the thermostat has opened for complete circulation. Now completely drain the system again before the sediment has time to settle.

Filling:

Check that the drain plug is properly fitted and that the hose clips are tight. Note that the drain plug threads should be smeared with a non-setting sealant. Prepare the new antifreeze mixture according to the manufacturer's instructions. If the system is still warm, allow it to cool down as adding the cold liquid when the system is warm may crack the engine cylinder block. Fill the system to a level about 1in from the bottom of the filler neck. Check the coolant level after running the engine for some time and top up if necessary.

4:3 Removing the radiator

Drain the radiator as described in **Section 4:2**. Refer to **FIG 4:1** and remove top and bottom hoses 9 and 7 from the radiator. On vehicles with automatic transmission, remove the fluid pipes from the angled connectors on the oil cooler mounted at the bottom of the radiator. Plug the pipes to prevent fluid loss. **It is essential that no dirt enters the fluid lines.**

Remove the nut from the lower rubber mounting and lift the radiator from the side support panels. On models fitted with a cooling fan cowl, shown at 11 in **FIG 4:1**, take out the four fixing screws to detach the cowl, then hang the cowl over the fan assembly until the radiator is removed, then remove the cowl.

Refitting:

Refitting is a reversal of the removal procedure, but check the condition of the radiator mounting rubber pads and renew them if necessary. On completion, refill the cooling system as described previously and, on models fitted with automatic transmission, check and if necessary, top up the transmission fluid as described in **Chapter 7**.

4:4 Adjusting drive belt

A tight drive belt will cause rapid wear of the alternator and water pump bearings, a loose belt will slip and wear excessively with the consequent possibility of engine overheating, reduced alternator output and, possibly, a squealing noise. The tension is correct when the belt can be deflected approximately 8mm (0.32in) for a used belt or 5mm (0.20in) for a new belt, by firm hand pressure applied midway between alternator and water pump pulleys.

Adjustment is carried out by slackening the alternator mounting bolts shown in **FIG 4:2** and pivoting the alternator away from the engine. If a lever is used to move the alternator, it must be applied at the front mounting

FIG 4:2 Alternator mounting details

bracket only. **Never lever against the alternator body**. When belt tension is correct, the alternator mountings must be tightened.

The alternator mounting bracket is provided with rubber bushes to allow the alternator to be fitted to the engine without imposing side loads on the mounting bracket lugs. For this reason, it is essential to tighten the mountings in the order 1, 2 and 3, as shown in **FIG 4:2**. On completion, recheck belt tension.

If the drive belt is worn or damaged, it must be renewed. To do this, loosen the alternator mounting as just described and push the alternator towards the engine until the belt can be removed from the crankshaft and alternator pulleys, then withdrawn over the fan. Fit the new belt, then set to the correct tension as described previously. The tension of a new belt should be adjusted after approximately 1600km (1000 miles) of service, to take up the initial stretch.

4:5 The water pump

Removal:

The water pump and fan can be removed as an assembly, with the radiator in position, but removal will be facilitated on models fitted with a fan cowl if the four fixing screws are removed so that the cowl is freed from the radiator.

Drain the cooling system and remove the drive belt as described previously. Refer to **FIG 4:1** and disconnect the radiator hose 7 from water pump 8. Remove the bolts securing the pump to the engine, then lift off the pump and fan assembly. Remove and discard the pump gasket. If necessary, remove the fan and pulley from the pump assembly.

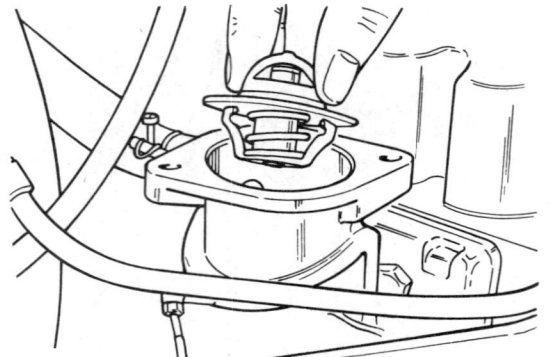

FIG 4:3 Thermostat installation

Check the pump shaft bearing for end play or roughness in operation. If the bearings are not in serviceable condition, or if any other part of the pump is worn or damaged, the water pump assembly must be renewed complete.

Refitting:

Refitting is a reversal of the removal procedure, making sure that the joint faces of the pump and engine are clean. Use a new water pump gasket, smearing the gasket lightly with a suitable sealing compound. Tighten the water pump mounting bolts alternately and evenly to avoid distortion of the mounting flange.

4:6 The thermostat

The thermostat is located in a housing mounted on the cylinder head as can be seen at 10 in **FIG 4:1**.

Removal:

Drain sufficient coolant so that the level is below the thermostat housing, then disconnect the top hose from the housing. Refer to **FIG 4:3** and lift out the thermostat.

Testing:

Clean the thermostat and immerse it in a container of cold water together with a zero to 100°C thermometer. Heat the water, keeping it stirred and observe the operation of the valve. As the temperature rises the valve should begin to open at 87°C. At around 95°C the valve should be almost fully open. Complete opening takes place with the thermostat installed and the cooling system under pressure, at approximately 102°C. If the thermostat does not operate correctly it must be renewed.

Refitting:

Renew the thermostat flange gasket. Make sure that the thermostat is correctly installed with the spring downwards, as shown in **FIG 4:3**, and that it is seated correctly in the housing. On completion, refill the cooling system to the correct level as described previously.

4:7 Frost precautions

With the correct coolant solution in use as described in **Section 4:2**, no additional frost precautions should be necessary. However, it is advisable to have the solution tested at intervals during the winter to make certain that it has not weakened. A hydrometer calibrated to read both specific gravity and temperature for the type of coolant in the system must be used for testing, most garages having such equipment. Always ensure that the antifreeze mixture used for filling the system is of sufficient strength to provide protection against freezing, according to the manufacturer's instructions.

4:8 Fault diagnosis

(a) Internal water leakage

1 Cracked cylinder wall
2 Loose cylinder head bolts
3 Cracked cylinder head
4 Faulty head gasket

(b) Poor circulation

1 Radiator core blocked
2 Engine coolant passages restricted
3 Low coolant level
4 Loose drive belt
5 Defective thermostat
6 Perished or collapsed radiator hoses

(c) Corrosion

1 Impurities in the coolant
2 Infrequent draining and flushing

(d) Overheating

1 Check (b)
2 Sludge in crankcase
3 Faulty ignition timing
4 Low oil level in sump
5 Tight engine
6 Choked exhaust system
7 Binding brakes
8 Slipping clutch
9 Incorrect valve timing
10 Weak fuel mixture

CHAPTER 5

THE CLUTCH

5:1 Description

The clutch is a single dry plate unit of diaphragm spring type. The main components are the driven plate, pressure plate assembly and release bearing, these being shown in **FIG 5:1**.

The driven plate consists of a resilient steel disc attached to a hub which slides on the splined gearbox input shaft. Friction linings are riveted to both sides of the disc.

The pressure plate assembly consists of the pressure plate, diaphragm spring and housing, the assembly being bolted to the engine flywheel. The release bearing is a ballbearing of special construction with an elongated outer ring which presses directly against the diaphragm spring when the clutch pedal is operated. The bearing is mounted on a guide sleeve and operated by a release lever and pivot, journaled in the clutch housing.

Clutch pedal movement is transmitted to the release bearing by a sheathed steel cable attached to the clutch release lever.

When the clutch is fully engaged, the driven plate is nipped between the pressure plate and the engine flywheel and transmits torque to the gearbox through the splined input shaft. When the clutch pedal is depressed, the pressure plate is withdrawn from the driven plate by force transmitted through the cable and the driven plate ceases to transmit torque to the gearbox.

5:2 Clutch cable adjustment

Clutch cable adjustment should be checked regularly as normal wear of the driven plate linings will alter the adjustment in service. The design of the clutch is such that the release bearing is always in contact with the clutch diaphragm spring fingers. As there is no free travel at the clutch release lever, wear of the driven disc linings causes the pedal to move progressively upwards. On models fitted with a handbrake warning light, this light also serves to indicate the need for clutch cable adjustment, as upward movement of the pedal contacts the plunger of the warning switch which is mounted at the pedal bracket. If the cable is adjusted too tightly it will tend to prevent the clutch from engaging properly, causing slip and rapid clutch plate wear. If the cable is too slack, the clutch will not release properly, causing drag and consequent poor gear change quality and difficulty in engaging gears from rest.

The clutch adjustment point on the bellhousing beneath the car is shown in **FIG 5:2**. When the clutch

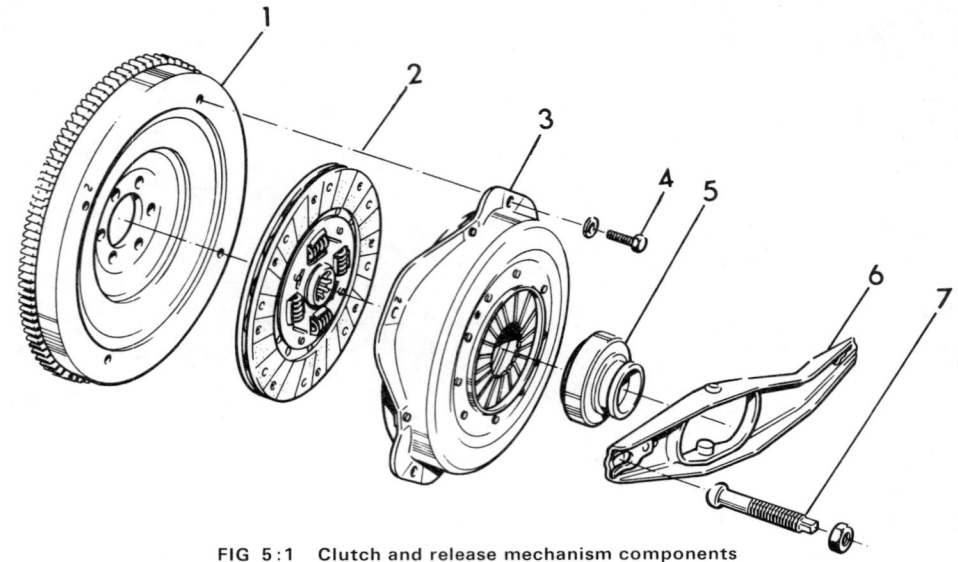

FIG 5:1   Clutch and release mechanism components

Key to Fig 5:1   1 Flywheel   2 Driven plate   3 Pressure plate assembly   4 Attachment bolt   5 Release bearing   6 Release lever
7 Ball stud bolt

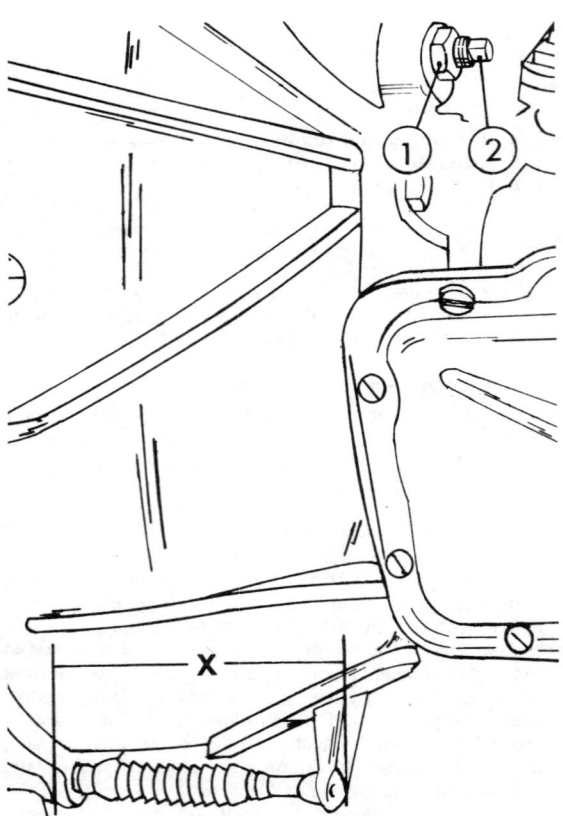

FIG 5:2   Release lever adjustment locknut 1 and bolt 2

release lever is pressed lightly towards the cable to take up free play, distance **X** between the end of the release lever and the front of the bellhousing should be 109mm (4.29in). If the dimension is incorrect, slacken locknut 1 and turn ball stud bolt 2 until the setting is correct, making sure that the engagement lever is kept lightly pressed in a forward direction to take up free play between the release bearing and diaphragm spring. When the setting is correct, firmly tighten locknut 1 to secure. Clutch pedal travel should now be checked in the following manner:

Locate the clutch cable upper adjustment point in the engine compartment, as shown in **FIG 5:3**. With the clutch cable connected to the release lever and correctly adjusted as described previously, initially position the outer cable by pulling it from the steel damper until the clutch pedal moves upward to just contact the warning switch plunger or the stop. Hold the outer cable in this position and locate the circlip shown in **FIG 5:3** so that there are three grooves between it and the washer (dimension **A**). Slide the outer cable back into the steel damper until the circlip contacts the washer. Depress the clutch pedal several times to settle the cable.

Refer to **FIG 5:4** and measure the distance **B** from the centre of clutch pedal pad to outer edge of steering wheel. This should be between 570 and 610mm (22.4 and 24.0in). Now depress the clutch pedal with the foot against the edge of the pad and repeat the measurement procedure with the pedal against the floor. This measurement should be at least 150mm (5.9in) more than the previous measurement **B**, this being the minimum distance which will ensure sufficient release lever travel to fully disengage the clutch. If either of the measurements is incorrect, adjust by repositioning the circlip on the outer cable grooves until the correct settings are obtained (see **FIG 5:3**).

5:3 Clutch cable renewal

Refer to **FIG 5:5**. Remove the nylon lockwasher arrowed to enable the cable to be disengaged from the clutch release lever beneath the car. Pull the cable assembly through the locating hole in the bellhousing and into the engine compartment.

From inside the car, release the inner cable loop from the hook at the upper end of the clutch pedal. Pull the upper end of the cable assembly through the bulkhead and into the engine compartment, noting the locations of the steel damper sleeve and rubber grommets for correct installation.

Install the new clutch cable in the reverse order of removal, making sure that the damper sleeve and rubber grommets are correctly fitted. On completion, adjust the cable as described in **Section 5:2**.

5:4 Removing and dismantling clutch

Remove the gearbox as described in **Chapter 6**, then remove the clutch housing from the engine crankcase. Check for matching numbers on the clutch cover flange and the flywheel which serve as alignment marks to ensure correct refitting. If none can be found, punch or scribe mark the two components so that they will be refitted correctly to retain the original balance of the assembly. Loosen the clutch cover retaining bolts 4 (see **FIG 5:1**) alternately and evenly until clutch spring pressure has been released, then remove the bolts completely. Lift off the clutch pressure plate and driven plate, taking care not to contaminate the driven plate friction linings with grease or oil. To remove the release lever and bearing from the transmission bellhousing, lift the ball socket and pull off the lever in the direction of the arrows, as shown in **FIG 5:6**. The lever and bearing can then be removed from the input shaft. The ball stud bolt on which the lever pivots can be removed if worn or damaged, after slackening the locknut shown at 1 in **FIG 5:2**. Count the number of turns used to remove the bolt, so that the new bolt can be fitted by the same number of turns to provide a basic setting for clutch adjustment.

Servicing:

Thoroughly clean all parts in a suitable solvent, with the exception of the driven plate linings and the release bearing. The release bearing must not be cleaned with solvent as this would wash the internal lubricant from the bearing.

The clutch cover, spring and pressure plate assembly is an integral unit and must not be dismantled. If any part is defective, the assembly must be renewed complete.

Inspect the surface of the flywheel where the driven plate makes contact. Light scoring on the surface is unimportant, but if there are any deep scratches the flywheel should be machined smooth or renewed. Check the pressure plate for scoring or damage and that the operating surface is flat and true. Check the diaphragm spring for cracks or other damage and the release bearing for any roughness when it is pressed and turned by hand. Any parts which are worn or damaged must be renewed.

Check the driven plate for loose rivets and broken or very loose torsional springs. The friction linings should be well proud of the rivets and have a light colour

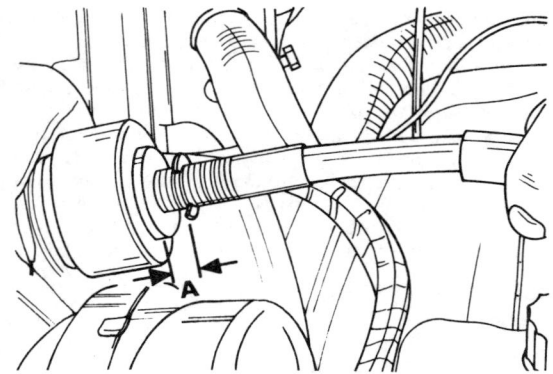

FIG 5:3 Cable upper adjustment point

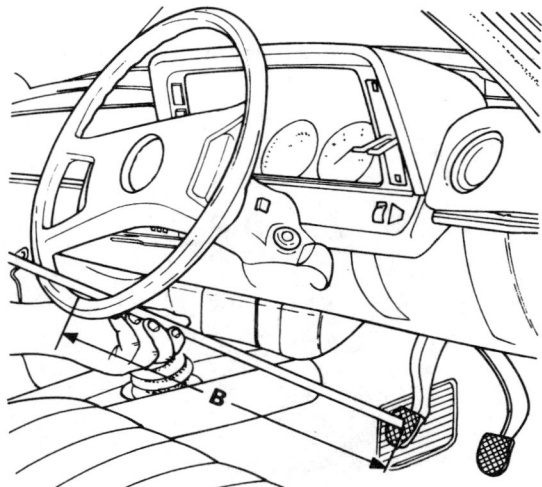

FIG 5:4 Checking clutch pedal height

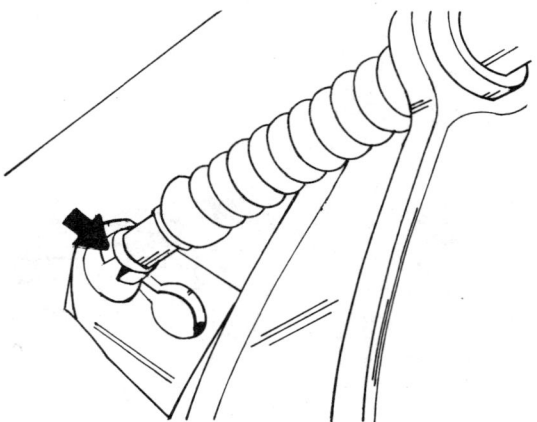

FIG 5:5 Nylon retaining washer

with a polished glaze through which the grain of the material is clearly visible. A dark, glazed deposit indicates oil on the facings and, as this condition cannot be rectified, a new or reconditioned driven plate will be required. Any sign of oil in the clutch should be investigated as to the cause and rectified to prevent recurrence of the problem. A slightly twisted driven plate can usually be corrected by mounting it on the splined shaft and using hand pressure to straighten it. Check the driven plate hub for a smooth, sliding fit on the splined input shaft, removing any burrs on the shaft or in the hub.

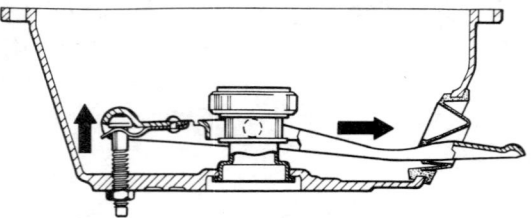

FIG 5:6   Removing release lever and bearing

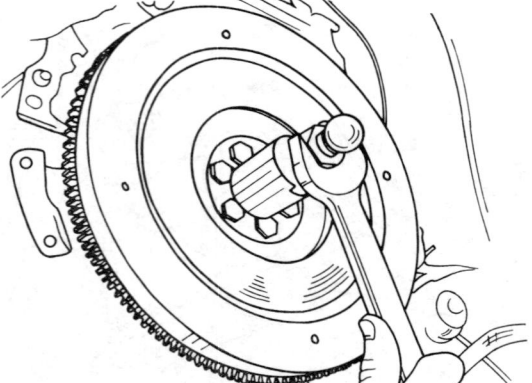

FIG 5:7   Pilot bearing removal

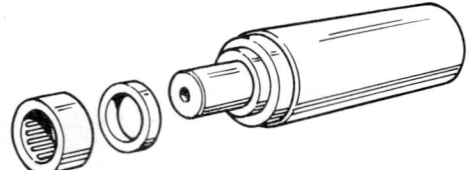

FIG 5:8   Pilot bearing and installation tools

FIG 5:9   Longer side of driven plate hub must face away from flywheel

Check the pilot bearing in the rear of the crankshaft for wear or damage. If a new bearing is required, the worn bearing must be withdrawn with special tool Z8527, as shown in **FIG 5:7**. Installation of the new bush should be carried out using the tools shown in **FIG 5:8**, driving the bearing in until the installer tool contacts the crankshaft face.

5:5 Assembling and refitting clutch

Reassembly is a reversal of the dismantling instructions. The hub of the driven plate must be centralised with the hub of the flywheel during assembly, using a spare gearbox input shaft or other suitable alignment tool. Make sure that the clutch driven plate is installed with the longer side of the centre hub away from the flywheel (see **FIG 5:9**).

Place the driven plate correctly on the pressure plate and insert the alignment tool through both. Hold the complete assembly against the flywheel while inserting the end of the tool into the pilot bearing in the crankshaft. Index the alignment marks on pressure plate and flywheel and install the clutch cover to flywheel attachment bolts finger tight. Complete tightening of the bolts alternately and evenly to a final torque of 45Nm (32lb ft), then remove the alignment tool. Lubricate the release lever pivot ball, release bearing guide sleeve in the transmission bellhousing, the input shaft splines and the pilot bearing sparingly with an approved grade of grease. Install the clutch housing, then refit the gearbox as described in **Chapter 6** and adjust the clutch cable as described in **Section 5:2**.

5:6 Fault diagnosis

(a) Drag or spin

1 Oil or grease on driven plate linings
2 Clutch cable binding
3 Distorted driven plate
4 Warped or damaged pressure plate
5 Broken driven plate linings
6 Excessive clutch free play

(b) Fierceness or snatch

1 Check 1, 2, 3 and 4 in (a)
2 Worn driven plate linings

(c) Slip

1 Check 1 in (a) ; and 2 in (b)
2 Weak diaphragm spring
3 Seized clutch cable
4 Insufficient clutch cable free play

(d) Judder

1 Check 1, 3 and 4 in (a)
2 Contact area of friction linings unevenly worn
3 Bent or worn splined shaft
4 Badly worn splines in driven plate hub
5 Faulty engine or transmission mountings

(e) Tick or knock

1 Badly worn driven plate hub splines
2 Worn release bearing
3 Bent or worn splined shaft
4 Loose flywheel

CHAPTER 6

MANUAL TRANSMISSION

6 : 1 Description

The four-speed gearbox has synchromesh on all forward speeds and is operated by a centrally mounted remote control gearlever. The clutch housing is bolted to the front of the main gearbox case, the extension housing to the rear. All gears have helically-cut teeth except those in the reverse train which are straight-toothed spur gears.

The rear end of the main drive pinion runs in a ballbearing in the gearbox housing, while its front end engages the needle roller pilot bearing in the rear of the engine crankshaft. The mainshaft is supported at the front end by needle rollers in the main drive pinion and by a ballbearing at the rear of the gearbox housing. The mainshaft first-speed gear operates on a needle roller bearing and a sleeve which is pressed on to the shaft, the remaining gears operating directly on the shaft journals.

The synchromesh mechanism incorporates two sleeves and hub assemblies, one at the front end of the mainshaft between the main drive pinion and third-speed gear, the other at the rear between the first- and second-speed gears. The synchromesh hubs slide on the mainshaft splines. The sleeves have internal splines which slide on external splines on the hubs.

The countershaft gear assembly is supported at each end by needle rollers on a stationary shaft.

The reverse pinion is a sliding gear incorporating a grooved hub to take the reverse striking fork mounted on a rod in the transmission casing. An intermediate selector lever mounted in the casing has two arms, one of which is permanently engaged with the reverse striking fork shaft. The remaining two striking forks are secured to rods located in the transmission casing. The striking lever shaft is mounted transversely below the rods. A striking lever secured to each end of the shaft can engage the slot in either striking fork rod or the reverse intermediate selector lever.

The gear selector lever is connected to an intermediate lever which pivots on a bush located in the top of the transmission rear cover. The extended finger of the gearlever locates in the intermediate shaft within the intermediate lever pivot bush. Forward or rearward movement of the gearlever is transmitted through the intermediate lever to a control rod on the righthand side of the transmission. Sideways movement of the gearlever is transmitted by the extended finger and intermediate shaft to a control rod on the lefthand side of the transmission.

Instructions for servicing and overhaul of gearbox

FIG 6:1   Speedometer driven gear removal

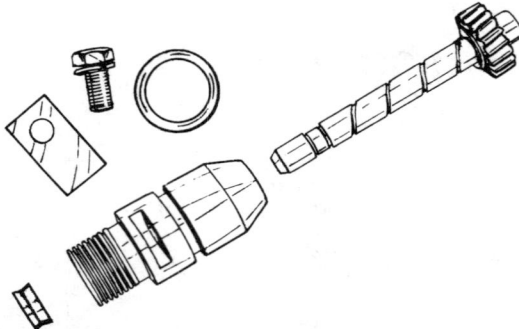

FIG 6:2   Speedometer driven gear components

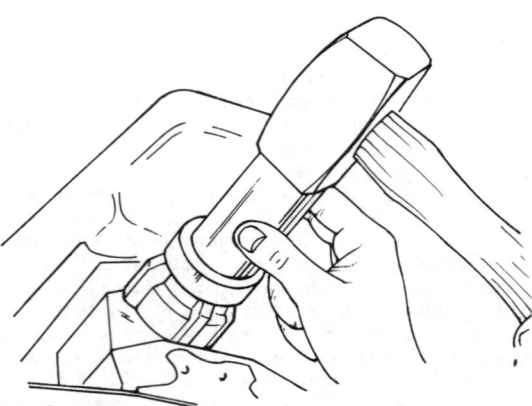

FIG 6:3   Rear cover oil seal installation

components are given in this chapter, but it should be noted that for some overhaul work certain special tools are essential and the owner would be well advised to check on the availability of these tools or suitable substitutes before tackling the items involved.

6:2 Routine maintenance

The oil level in the gearbox should be maintained at the bottom of the threaded hole for the filler plug, which is located at the lefthand side of the gearbox casing and is removed using an suitable hexagon key. Periodic draining and refilling are not necessary between gearbox overhauls. When checking the oil level, make sure that the car is standing on level ground. Clean away all dirt from around the filler plug before removing it. Top up to the correct level if necessary using an approved grade of gearbox oil, then allow all excess oil to drain away fully before refitting and tightening the plug.

6:3 Speedometer drive and reversing light switch

Speedometer driven gear:

The speedometer driven gear assembly can be removed with the gearbox in the car.

Disconnect the speedometer cable from the gearbox and remove the drive gear retainer plate. Prise the assembly from the casing, using a screwdriver as shown in **FIG 6:1**. Push the gear shaft through the seal from the threaded end of the guide and remove the rubber ring and oil seal (see **FIG 6:2**). Reassemble and refit the components in the reverse order of removal, renewing both rubber ring and seal.

Reversing light switch:

The reversing light switch is of the spring loaded plunger type and is located at the rear of the transmission case. The switch is operated by movement of the reverse gear striking fork rod.

To remove the switch, pull off the two wiring connectors and unscrew the unit from the case. When refitting, make sure that the sealing ring is in position.

6:4 Rear cover oil seal

If leakage from the gearbox rear cover oil seal occurs, the seal can be renewed without removing the gearbox, in the following manner:

Remove the propeller shaft as described in **Chapter 8**. Use a suitable pointed tool to prise out the old seal, taking care not to damage the seal housing. Clean the inside of the housing, then coat the lips of a new seal with recommended grease and drive the seal fully home using a suitable piece of tube as shown in **FIG 6:3**.

6:5 Gearchange linkage

Removal:

Remove the four screws arrowed in **FIG 6:4**, then remove the small access panel and withdraw the centre console. Ease the upper and lower rubber gaiters up the gearlever to provide access to the mountings. Detach the gearlever tension spring and, after removing the

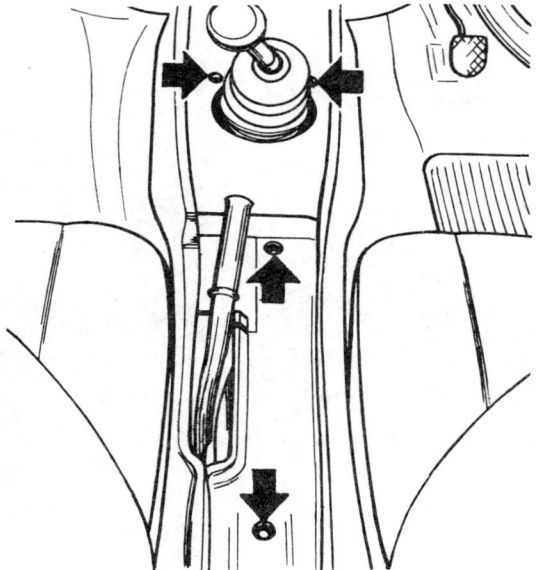

FIG 6:4 Centre console fixing screws

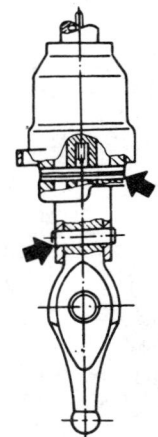

FIG 6:5 Spiral pin and spring pin locations

E-clip from pivot pin, withdraw pin from intermediate selector lever and lift off the gearlever.

If the gearlever is to be completely dismantled, drive off the gearlever knob with a soft mallet then remove the spring and slacken the two grub screws securing the lift collar cable. Note, that a new gearlever knob must be fitted during reassembly. If necessary, the tube can be withdrawn from the lever assembly after removing circlip from bottom of tube. To remove the cable, drive spiral pin and spring pin from striker tube and stop sleeve (see **FIG 6:5**). Remove striker and withdraw cable together with spring from gearlever.

To remove the intermediate selector lever or to renew the bush, the transmission must be removed from the vehicle as described in **Section 6:6** and the oil drained. This done, remove gear selector rod, selector lever and intermediate shaft, as shown by the arrows in **FIG 6:6**. If the intermediate lever pivot shaft bush is to be renewed, remove the locking ring then drive out the bush using a suitable drift as shown in **FIG 6:7**. The new bush must be installed into the lever and rear cover, locking ring end first, from the righthand side of the transmission. The cutaway section of bush must point vertically towards the gearlever. This can be checked using a set square against the rear face of the rear cover and the bush cut away as shown in **FIG 6:8**. Lubricate intermediate lever before installing lever and bush. After driving bush fully home, install locking ring.

Refitting:

When installing gear selector rod, lever ,and intermediate shaft, lubricate all joints with recommended grease. Assemble dished washer and shim at each mounting point for selector rod and selector lever. Before installing transmission as described in **Section 6:6**, adjust reverse gear stop sleeve as follows.

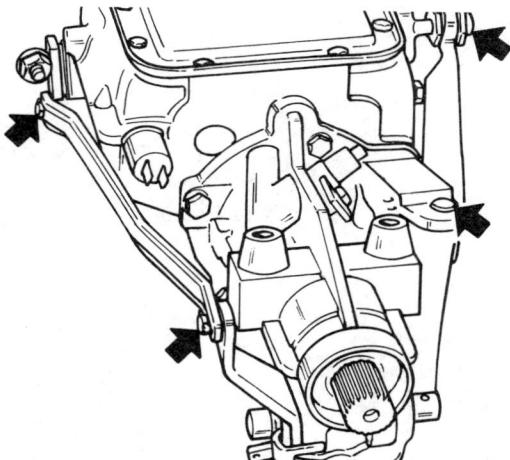

FIG 6:6 Removing gearlever linkage components

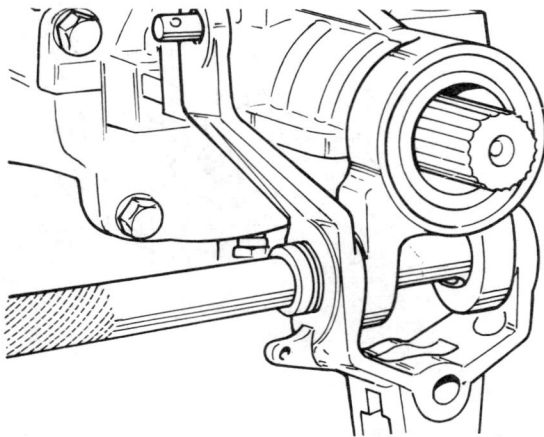

FIG 6:7 Removing intermediate lever pivot shaft bush

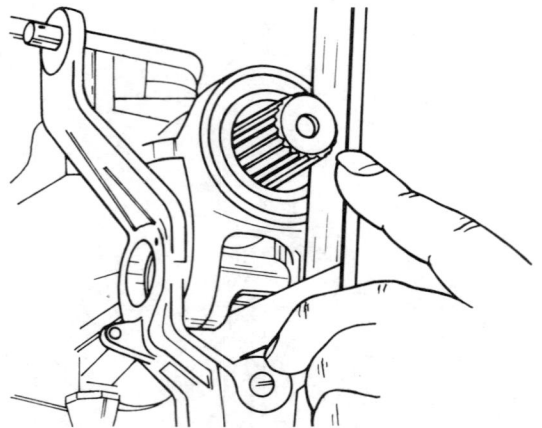

FIG 6:8   Checking bush installation

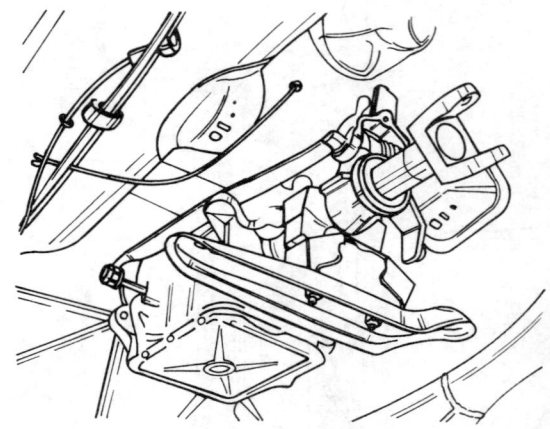

FIG 6:11   Transmission removal

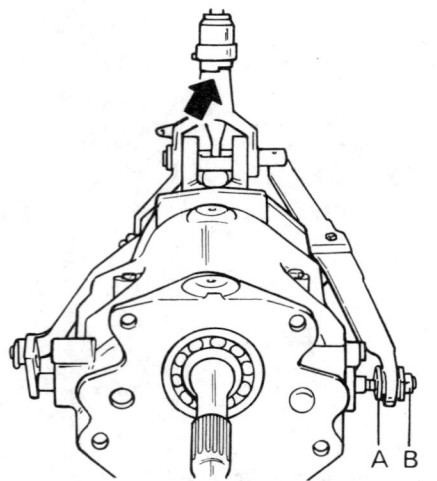

FIG 6:9   Adjusting reverse gear stop sleeve

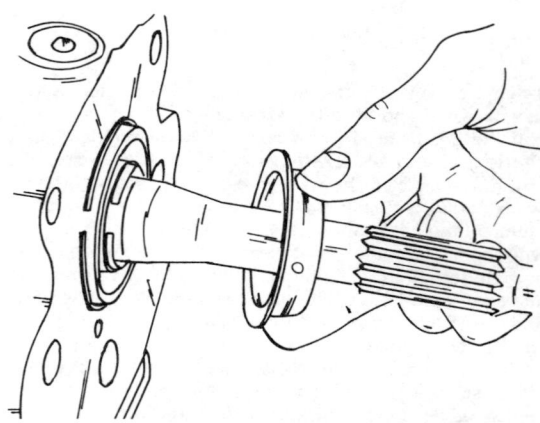

FIG 6:12   Main drive pinion oil seal and retainer

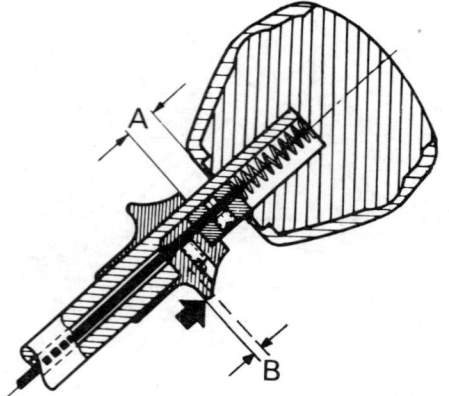

FIG 6:10   Gearlever knob installation and lift collar free travel

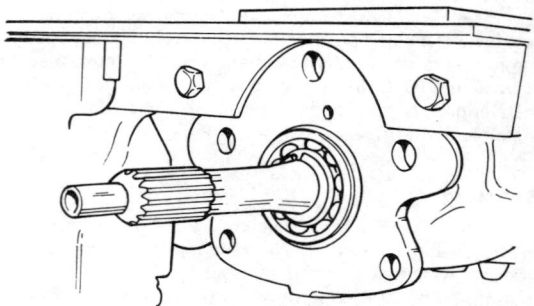

FIG 6:13   Supporting transmission on shaped steel angle

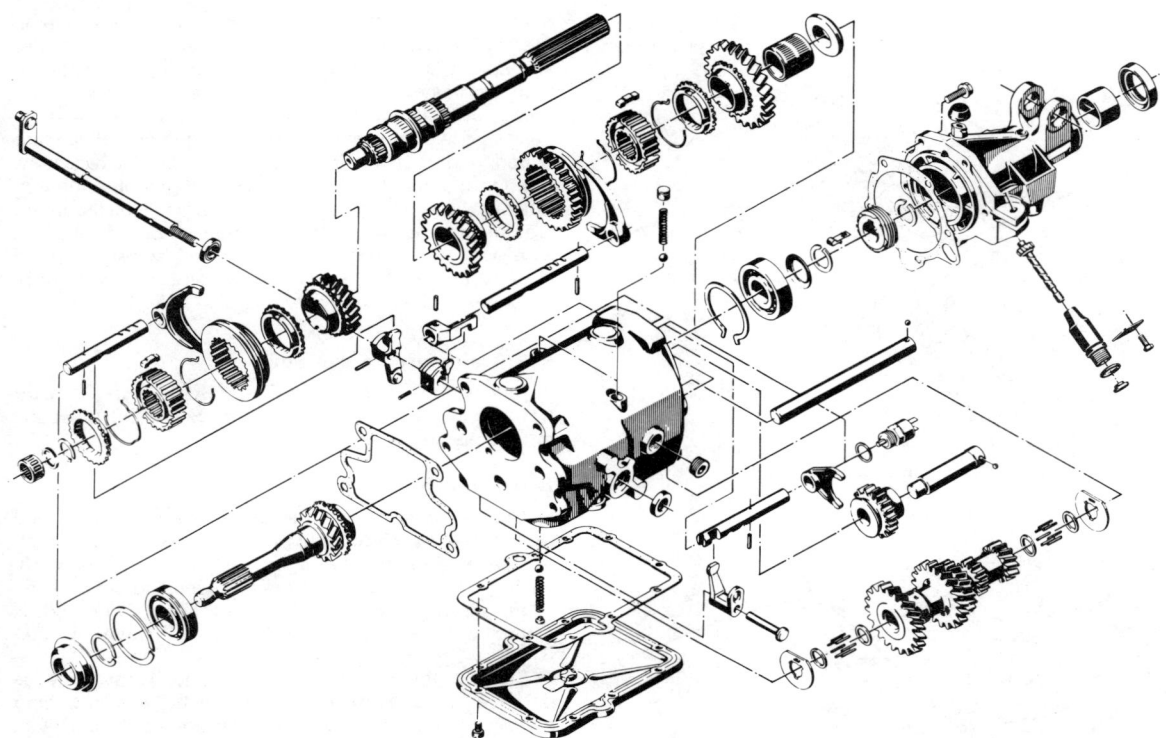

FIG 6:14   Gearbox components

Temporarily install gearlever but do not assemble tension spring. Refer to **FIG 6:9**. Engage second gear and adjust selector ring **A** so that stop sleeve (arrowed) contacts the stop on intermediate selector lever. Turn selector ring back a quarter of a turn and secure with locknut **B**. Check for correct engagement in all gear positions.

To reassemble the gearlever, lubricate gearlever stop sleeve with engine oil and insert cable and spring. Locate stop sleeve so that cutout is towards left of lever and secure cable and sleeve with spring pin. Assemble lift collar and clamping piece to cable then tighten grub screws. Heat new gearlever knob in hot water to approximately 80°C (176°F) and drive it into position using a soft mallet until dimension **A** is 8mm (0.30in) as shown in **FIG 6:10**. Insert striker in gearlever so that countersink for wave washer is towards the front and secure with spiral pin.

Before installing gearlever assembly, coat striker and bearing with recommended grease and retain the lower wave washer in the countersink on striker with grease. After installing the lever, check lift collar for free travel **B** (see **FIG 6:10**). This should be 1.0 to 2.0mm (0.040 to 0.079in). If necessary, slacken both grub screws securing cable and adjust as required. Tighten the screws on completion. Refit the lower and upper gaiters, noting that the upper gaiter should be located so that the distances between its top flange and the top of the gearlever knob is 225mm (8.80in).

If the transmission has been drained for work on the selector linkage, refill to the correct level with fresh oil (see **Section 6:2**).

6:6 Transmission removal and refitting

Remove the gearlever and rubber gaiters as described in **Section 6:5**. Raise and safely support the vehicle on floor stands to provide access for gearbox removal from beneath the car. Disconnect the propeller shaft from the transmission as described in **Chapter 8**. Disconnect the speedometer cable from the speedometer gear assembly and disconnect the wires from the reversing lamp switch.

Refer to **FIG 6:11** and detach the rear mounting crossmember from the vehicle underbody. Support the transmission by means of a suitable jack, then remove the four bolts securing the transmission to the clutch housing. Move the gearbox assembly rearwards to disengage the splined input shaft from the clutch hub, then lower the assembly and remove from beneath the car. Take care not to allow the weight of the assembly to rest on the splined shaft while it is in the clutch unit, otherwise serious damage to clutch components may result.

Refitting:

Check the rear mounting for deterioration and renew as necessary. Ensure that the oil return hole in the front of the casing adjacent to main drive pinion is clear. Pack cavity of main drive pinion oil seal and

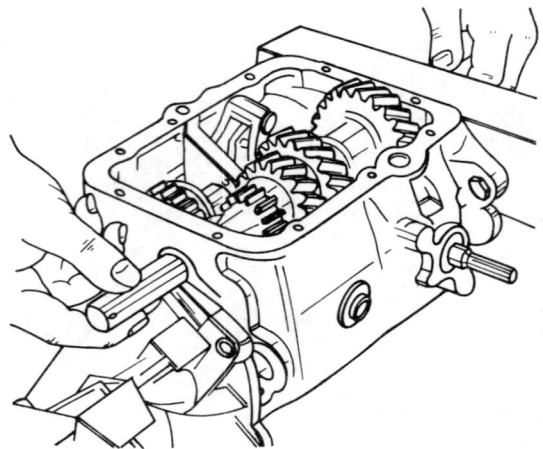

FIG 6:15   Countershaft removal

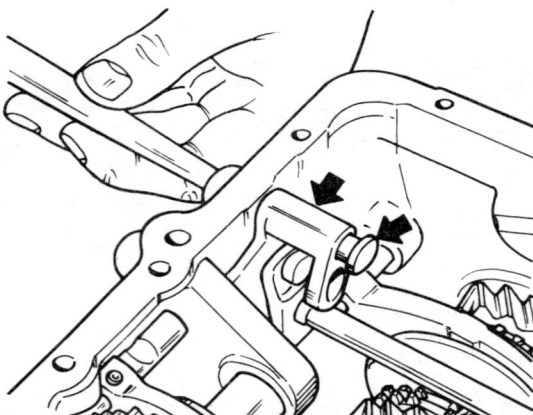

FIG 6:16   Reverse gear selector lever pivot removal

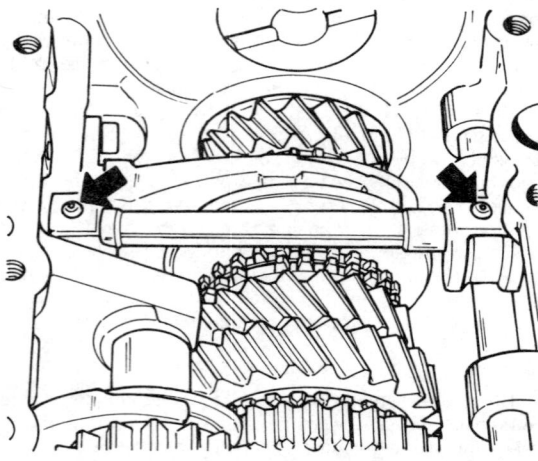

FIG 6:17   Removing striking lever shaft

retainer with recommended grease and install on pinion (see **FIG 6:12**). Lightly smear main drive pinion splines and spigot and the clutch release bearing guide sleeve with recommended grease. Use grease to stick a new gasket on clutch housing before installing transmission. Take care when inserting main drive pinion splines into clutch hub to avoid damage to the clutch assembly. Support the gearbox while fitting and tightening the four retaining bolts. Using new lockplates, install the mounting crossmember to the underbody. Refit the propeller shaft as described in **Chapter 8**, then check transmission oil level as described in **Section 6:2**. Refit the gearlever as described in **Section 6:5**.

6:7 Transmission overhaul

Remove the transmission as described in **Section 6:6**. Remove the gearbox bottom cover and drain the oil into a suitable waste container.

Dismantling:

The transmission can be completely dismantled and reassembled when mounted on a suitably shaped length of steel angle secured in a vice, as shown in **FIG 6:13**. Failing this, use suitable blocks of wood to support the gearbox case in the appropriate attitudes while work is carried out. Gearbox components are shown in **FIG 6:14**.

Remove the speedometer driven gear assembly as described in **Section 6:3**. Remove the reversing lamp switch and the bolts securing transmission rear cover. Rotate the rear cover to expose rear of countershaft, then drive shaft out from front to rear as shown in **FIG 6:15**. Remove the countershaft gear and thrust washers from casing.

Use a suitable drift to drive out the bearing pivot of reverse gear intermediate selector lever, as shown in **FIG 6:16**.

The selector mechanism striking levers are secured to shaft by spring pins, as shown arrowed in **FIG 6:17**. Drive out first the pin for third- and fourth-speed lever then for first- and second-speed lever and withdraw the shaft to the left. The striking fork rod locking balls and springs are retained in transmission casing by drive-in plugs, as shown arrowed in **FIG 6:18**. Remove the plugs by engaging a pair of pincers in the groove and tapping the pincers down with a hammer. Collect the springs and balls as the plugs are removed.

Engage first-gear and drive retaining pins, which are arrowed in **FIG 6:19**, out of striking forks and first and second selector fork sufficiently to release forks on rods. Do not drive the pins out completely otherwise they may jam against transmission casing. After rotating rear cover to gain access, selector rods can be driven out from rear to front.

Turn the rear cover so that it is clear of the work, then use a suitable remover tool to withdraw the reverse pinion shaft as shown in **FIG 6:20**. Remove the main drive pinion and the mainshaft assembly from transmission casing.

Remove the circlip from the main drive pinion, then use suitable press tools to remove main drive pinion bearing as shown in **FIG 6:21**. Use suitable circlip pliers to remove the circlip as shown in **FIG 6:22**, then

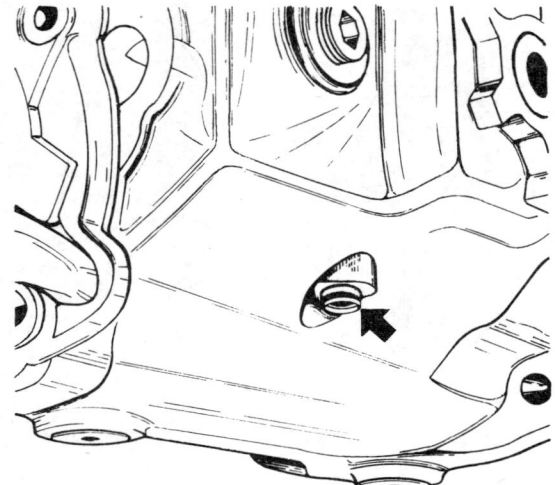

FIG 6:18   Locking ball and spring retaining plug

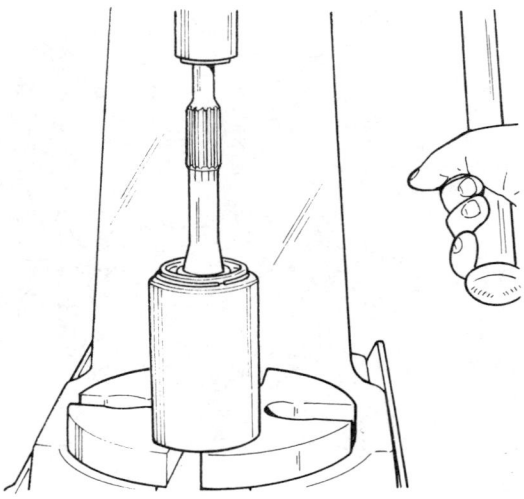

FIG 6:21   Main drive pinion bearing removal

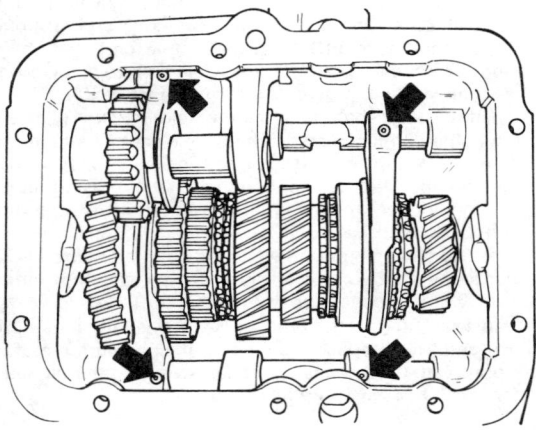

FIG 6:19   Striking fork retaining pins

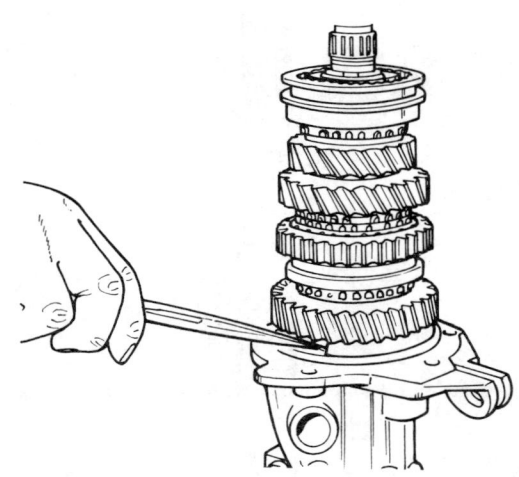

FIG 6:22   Mainshaft bearing circlip removal

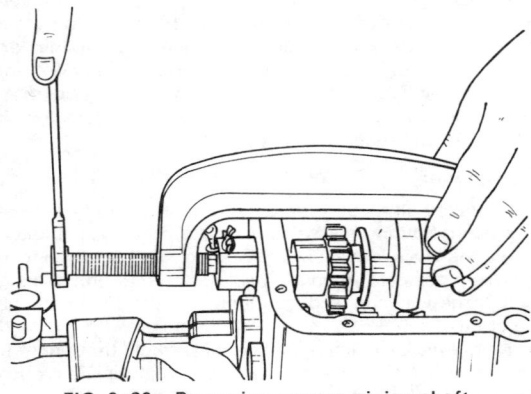

FIG 6:20   Removing reverse pinion shaft

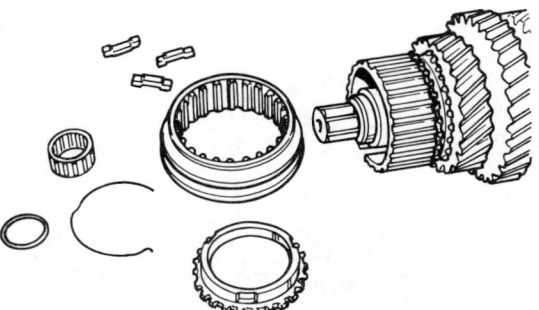

FIG 6:23   Removing needle bearing and synchromesh from mainshaft

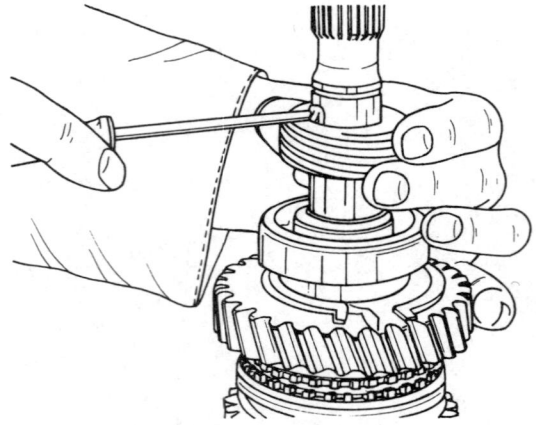

FIG 6:24   Speedometer drive gear removal

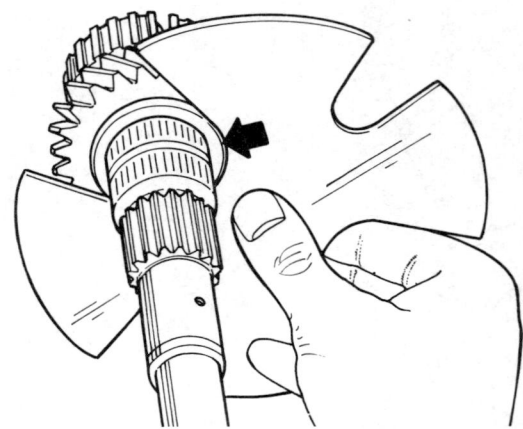

FIG 6:27   Press plate must clear mainshaft collar

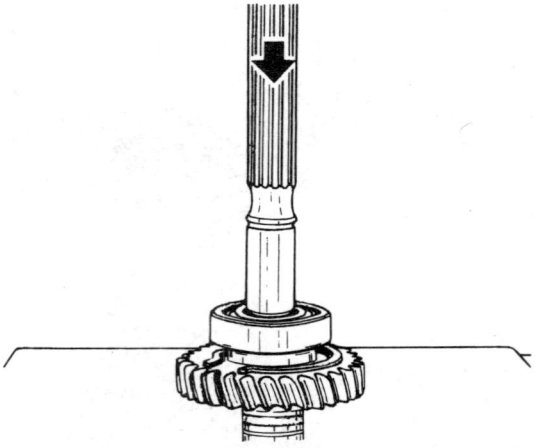

FIG 6:25   Removing mainshaft bearing and first gear

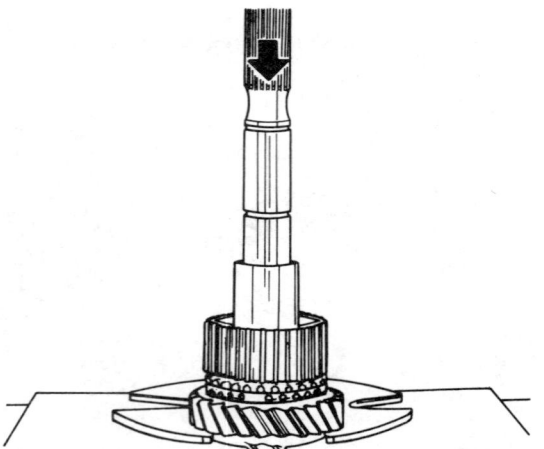

FIG 6:26   Removing second gear and synchromesh

remove the mainshaft assembly from the rear cover. Prise the oil seal from the rear cover. Remove the breather cap and clean the breather in the rear cover.

Remove needle bearing, spacer ring, synchronising ring, clutch, sliding keys and front key spring from the mainshaft (see **FIG 6:23**). Remove propeller shaft spring and circlip, then depress spring clip and remove speedometer driving gear as shown in **FIG 6:24**.

Remove mainshaft rear bearing circlip and washer. Fit suitable support plates behind first-gear as shown in **FIG 6:25**, then press off bearing, first-gear, spacer and large circlip. The needle bearing, synchronising ring, first- and second-speed clutch, keys and rear key spring can now be withdrawn.

With suitable plates under second gear, press first- and second-speed clutch hub and needle bearing inner sleeve from mainshaft, as shown in **FIG 6:26**. Remove circlip from spigot at front end of mainshaft. Press off third- and fourth-speed clutch hub, making sure that the support plate used clears the collar which is integral with the mainshaft (see arrow in **FIG 6:27**).

Inspection:

Thoroughly clean all parts and inspect carefully for wear or damage. Check all parts for nicks, scoring or other damage. Check gears for worn, chipped or broken teeth and bearings for roughness or binding. Check for wear on splines and similar mating parts. The splines on the gearbox main drive pinion should be checked for backlash by inserting in the splined clutch hub disc. Renew all worn or damaged components. Always renew all gaskets, oil seals and circlips.

Reassembly:

Lubricate all moving parts with an approved grade of gearbox oil during reassembly, unless otherwise stated.

Fit the main drive pinion bearing so that the circlip groove is towards the pinion splines. Secure the bearing with a new circlip and assemble a new circlip to the outer race.

Before reassembling mainshaft, assemble the synchromesh clutches to their hubs. The synchronising rings and springs of the two assemblies are of different diameter

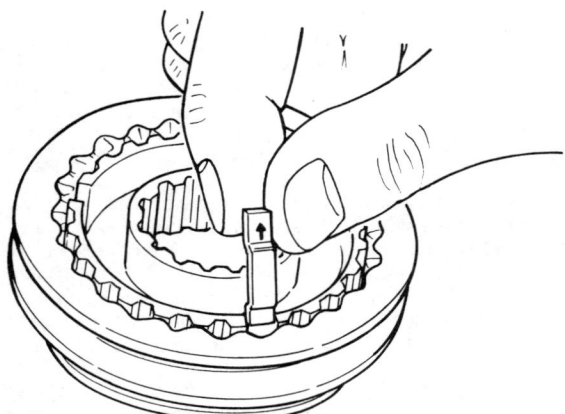

FIG 6:28 Installing sliding key to synchromesh unit

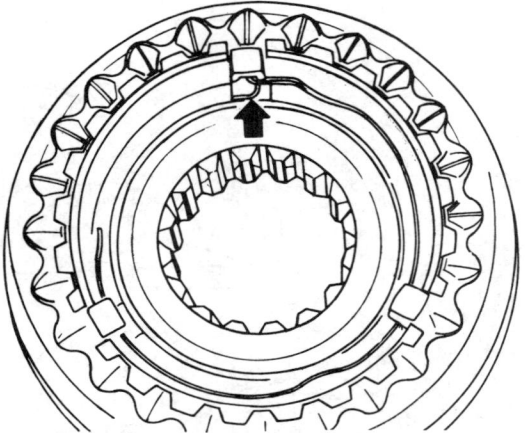

FIG 6:29 Synchromesh spring installation

and the keys also differ. The striking fork groove on the clutch for third and fourth gears and also the arrow on the sliding keys are located towards the spigoted end of the hub and the front end of the mainshaft (see **FIG 6:28**). Locate a spring each side of hub so that turned-out end of each spring engages slot in same key and the other end of the springs point in opposite directions (see **FIG 6:29**).

Place third-speed gear and synchronising ring over front end of mainshaft, then press on third- and fourth-speed clutch and hub so that selector fork groove in clutch is towards front of shaft. Make sure that sliding keys engage slots in synchronising ring. Secure hub with a new circlip.

Place second-speed gear and synchronising ring over end of mainshaft, then press first- and second-speed clutch and hub together with needle bearing inner sleeve on to mainshaft. Ensure that sliding keys engage slots in synchronising ring and that selector fork groove is towards rear of shaft.

Install needle bearing, synchronising ring, first-speed gear, rear bearing circlip for rear cover and the spacer. Chamfered side of spacer must be to rear of mainshaft. Press the bearing home. Install dished washer with concave side towards bearing and secure with a new circlip.

Assemble spring clip and speedometer driving gear to mainshaft, followed by propeller shaft spring circlip. Before installing mainshaft assembly in rear cover, coat a new oil seal with recommended grease. Fit a new rear cover gasket in position and insert mainshaft assembly into casing. Place spacing ring on mainshaft spigot followed by needle roller bearing coated in recommended grease. Install synchronising ring and main drive pinion.

Reverse pinion must be installed with striking fork groove towards front of casing. Locate selector fork as shown in **FIG 6:30**, with flanged side towards front. Make sure that locking ball in shaft is aligned with recess in casing before driving shaft home. Coat sealing lips of striking lever shaft oil seals with recommended grease then drive fully and squarely home open side first.

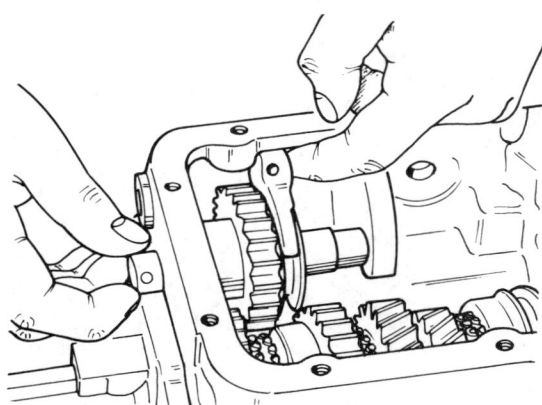

FIG 6:30 Installing release pinion and striking fork

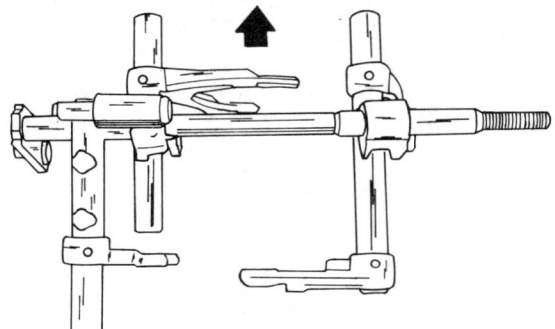

FIG 6:31 Selector mechanism installation

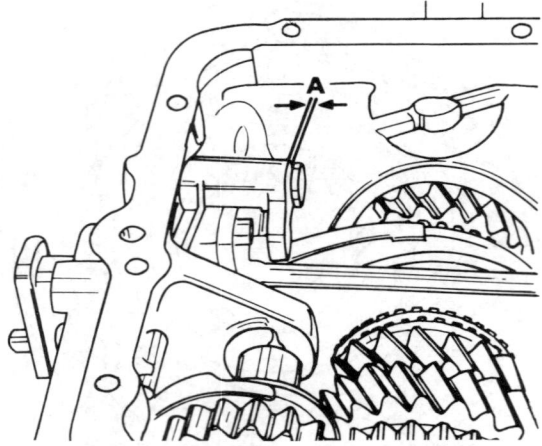

FIG 6:32 Reverse gear bearing pivot end float

FIG 6:33 Countershaft gear thrust washer installation

When installing selector mechanism, insert selector rods for forward gears from front to rear of casing and selector rod for reverse gear from rear to front after engaging forks and sliding dog on shafts, secure with new retaining pins and allow pins to project 2mm (0.079in). The relative locations of selector mechanism components is shown in **FIG 6:31**. Note, that the components are shown as viewed during overhaul when the transmission is inverted with an arrow to indicate the front of transmission.

After inserting striking lever shaft and levers, drive retaining pin into first and second gear lever, then drive pin into third and fourth lever. Allow pins to project 2mm (0.079in). Install striking fork rod locking balls and springs for forward gears and drive in plugs. Make sure that the groove in plugs is left exposed to permit removal later if necessary. Install reverse gear intermediate selector lever and drive in bearing pivot until end float **A** is 0.1 to 0.3mm (0.004 to 0.012in) as shown in **FIG 6:32**.

Before installing countershaft gear, secure thrust washers in position with recommended grease, as shown in **FIG 6:33**. Make sure that the needle rollers are properly fitted into the countershaft gear bores, retaining them with recommended grease. Place gear in position and locate rear cover so that countershaft can be inserted at rear and driven home with locking ball in place. When installing rear cover bolts, smear the threads with suitable jointing compound. Install locking ball, spring and dome-headed thrust pad for reverse gear selector rod before refitting transmission bottom cover.

Refit the gearchange linkage as described in **Section 6:5**, then install the transmission as described in **Section 6:6**.

6:8 Fault diagnosis

(a) Jumping out of gear

1 Weak or damaged locking ball spring
2 Locking ball broken or omitted on reassembly
3 Badly worn retaining groove in selector shaft
4 Worn synchromesh components
5 Striking fork loose on shaft
6 Worn striking forks

(b) Noisy gearbox

1 Insufficient or incorrect lubricant
2 Excessive end floats and clearances
3 Worn or damaged bearings
4 Worn or damaged gear teeth

(c) Oil leaks

1 Blocked breather
2 Too high lubricant level
3 Defective oil seals
4 Defective gaskets or loose attachments
5 Damaged joint faces

(d) Difficult gear changing

1 Excessively worn clutch
2 Incorrectly adjusted clutch
3 Defective spigot bearing in end of crankshaft
4 Worn synchromesh assemblies
5 Stiff gearlever mounting

CHAPTER 7

AUTOMATIC TRANSMISSION

7:1 Description

Automatic transmission is supplied as an optional extra to take the place of the usual clutch and gearbox. The automatic transmission consists of a torque converter and hydraulically controlled automatic epicyclic gearbox with three forward speeds and one reverse. In all gears the drive is through the torque converter which results in maximum flexibility, especially in top gear. The gears are selected automatically as the hydraulic control system engages clutches and/or applies a brake band in various combinations. The hydraulic control system and the torque converter assembly are supplied with pressure fluid from a pump mounted within the transmission case. A manually controlled mechanical parking pawl is incorporated so that the transmission output shaft can be locked when the vehicle is stationary.

The torque converter consists of an impeller connected through a drive plate to the engine crankshaft, a turbine which is splined to the transmission input shaft and a stator connected to the unit by a one-way clutch. The impeller, driven by the engine, transmits torque by means of the transmission fluid to the turbine which drives the automatic gearbox. The stator redirects the flow of fluid as it leaves the turbine so that it re-enters the impeller at the most effective angle.

When the engine is idling, the converter impeller is being driven slowly and the energy of the fluid leaving it is low, so little torque is imparted to the turbine. For this reason, with the engine idling and drive engaged, the vehicle will have little or no tendency to move from rest. As the throttle is opened impeller speed increases and the process of torque multiplication begins. As the turbine picks up speed and the slip between it and the impeller reduces, torque multiplication reduces progressively until, when their speeds become substantially equal, the unit acts as a fluid coupling. In this condition, the stator is no longer required to redirect the fluid flow and the roller clutch permits it to rotate with the impeller and turbine.

The maintenance and adjustment procedures which can be carried out by a reasonably competent owner are given in this chapter. More serious performance faults which require pressure take-off points to be opened and pressure measurements taken to diagnose the fault, adjustment of the governor or clutches and band, partial or complete dismantling to replace worn or failed internal components dictate that the services of a fully equipped

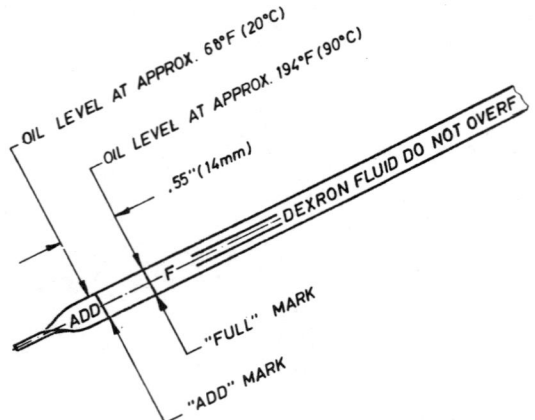

FIG 7:1   Dipstick markings and fluid levels

specialist should be enlisted. Quite apart from the specialised knowledge which is required, test equipment and a large number of special tools are essential.

7:2 Maintenance

Routine checking of transmission fluid level and periodic changing of transmission fluid and strainer should be carried out at the intervals specified in the manufacturer's service schedule. As brake band adjustment is required when the fluid is changed as part of routine maintenance, this operation should be carried out by a fully equipped service station. If, however, the transmission is to be removed, the oil may be drained by removing the plug from the oil pan. Replace with approximately 2.5 litres (4.5 pints) of new oil poured in the dipstick tube using a clean funnel. Check and correct the level as described next.

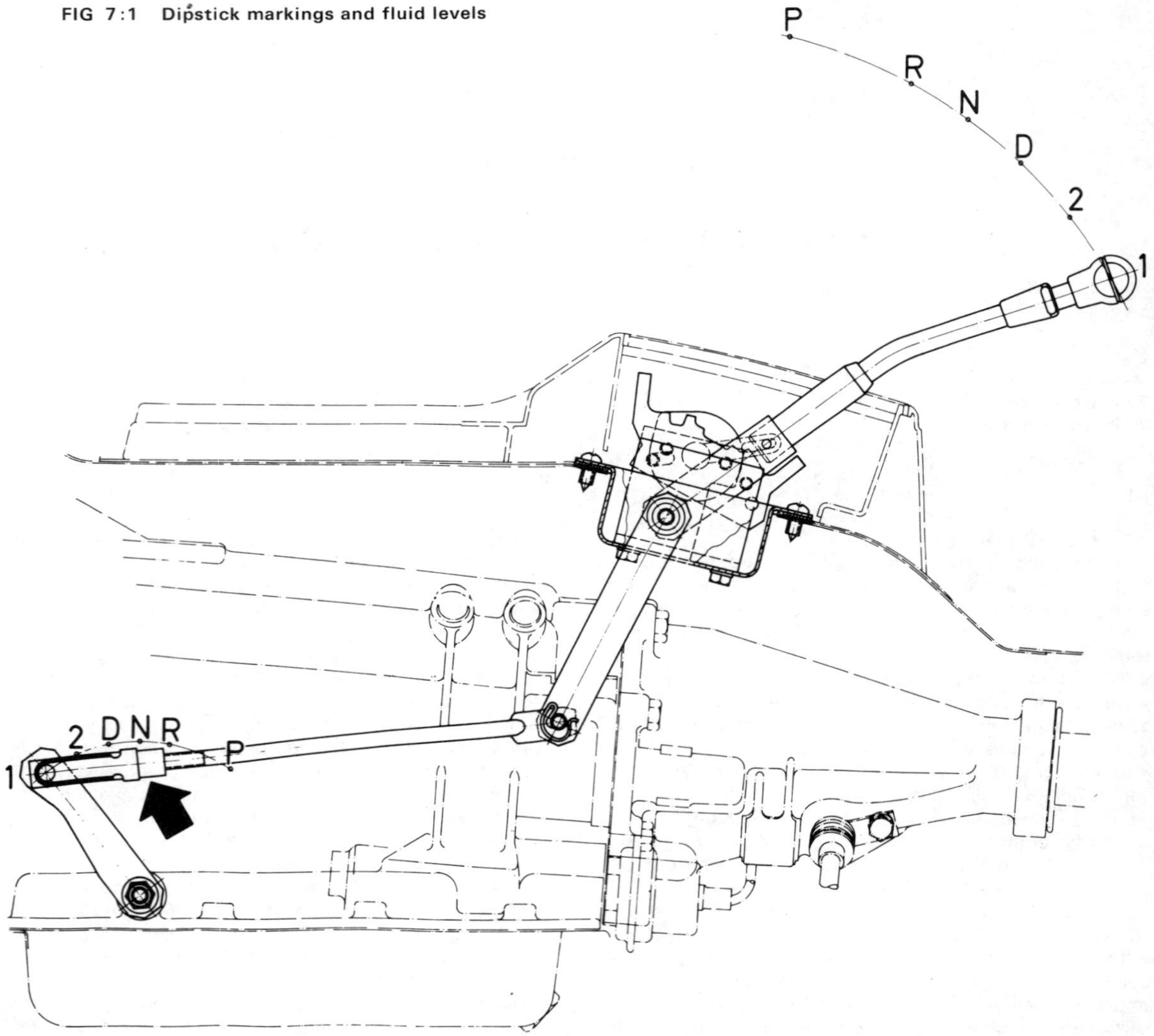

FIG 7:2   Selector linkage adjustment

Checking fluid level:

The automatic transmission is designed to operate with the fluid level at the FULL mark on the dipstick at normal operating temperature of approximately 90°C. This temperature will only be reached after approximately 12 miles of driving. With the transmission at operating temperature, clean the area around the dipstick and tube then start the engine with the selector lever in the **P** (Park) position. Do not race the engine. Move the selector lever through each position on the quadrant and return the lever to the **P** position. Leave the engine idling and immediately remove the automatic transmission dipstick, wipe it clean on a lint-free cloth and refit it fully. Remove the dipstick again and check the level of fluid against the marks (see **FIG 7 : 1**). Top up through the dipstick tube if necessary to bring the fluid level to the FULL mark on the dipstick. Add fluid slowly, checking with the dipstick after each addition. Do not overfill. Use Dexron Automatic Transmission Fluid. **Never use anything but the recommended fluid in the automatic transmission.**

If the vehicle cannot be driven a sufficient distance to bring the fluid up to normal operating temperature, the fluid level may be checked at room temperature (approximately 20°C) as just described but, when a reading is made, the fluid level should be just below the ADD mark on the dipstick as shown in **FIG 7 : 1**. Checking is carried out as described previously, but the engine should be allowed to idle with the selector in the **P** position for 10 minutes before carrying out the operation. Normal thermal expansion of the fluid will bring the level to the FULL mark on the dipstick when the transmission is at normal operating temperature.

If the transmission has been inadvertently overfilled, the excess should be siphoned off by inserting a suitable pipe down the dipstick tube and drawing fluid up into a suitable flexible plastic bottle. A pipe inserted through the dipstick tube cannot touch any internal moving parts of the transmission.

Make sure that all containers, funnels and pipes used for adding or removing automatic transmission fluid are perfectly clean and dry, as dirt or oil in the fluid can cause failure of transmission internal components.

Checking fluid condition:

Whenever the transmission fluid level is checked, examine the condition of the fluid adhering to the dipstick. Under normal conditions, the fluid should flow freely and the colour should not vary significantly from that of new fluid of similar type.

A grey appearance of the fluid can be caused by metallic particles, which indicates worn or damaged internal components. Black colouration of the fluid, perhaps accompanied by particles of friction materials and a burnt smell, indicates a failure of internal clutch discs or the brake band. Brownish fluid colouring indicates that the fluid has decomposed as a result of overheating.

If any yellow or white colouring is discernible in the fluid, it indicates that cooling water from the radiator has entered the transmission fluid cooler and formed an emulsion with the fluid.

If any of the conditions described are evident, the vehicle should be taken to a fully equipped service station so that checks and any necessary remedial work can be carried out before the fault becomes more serious.

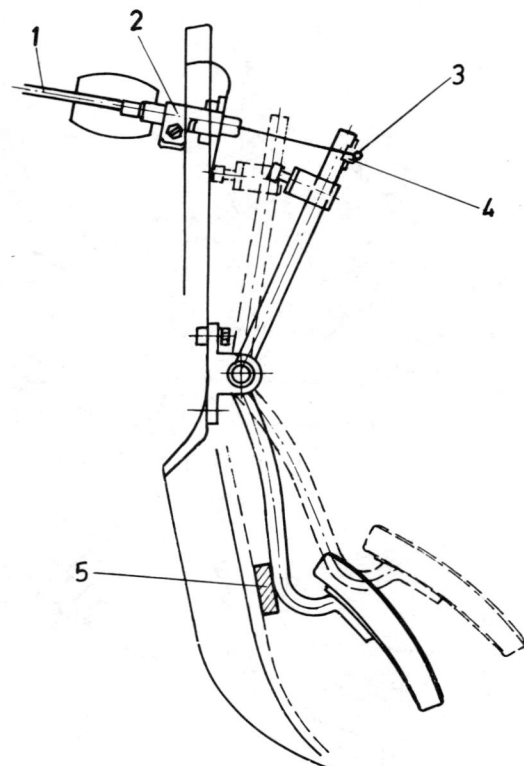

FIG 7 : 3   Kick-down cable adjustment

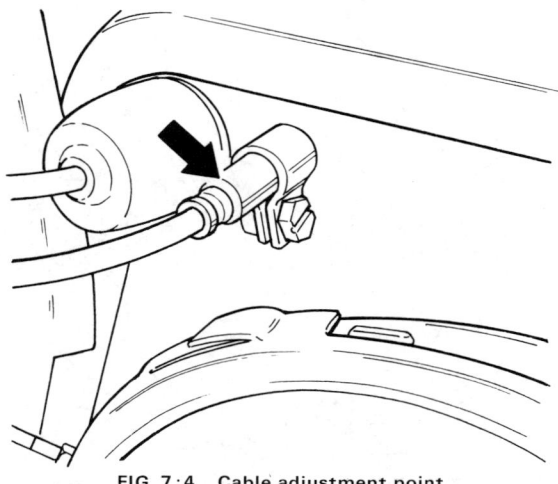

FIG 7 : 4   Cable adjustment point

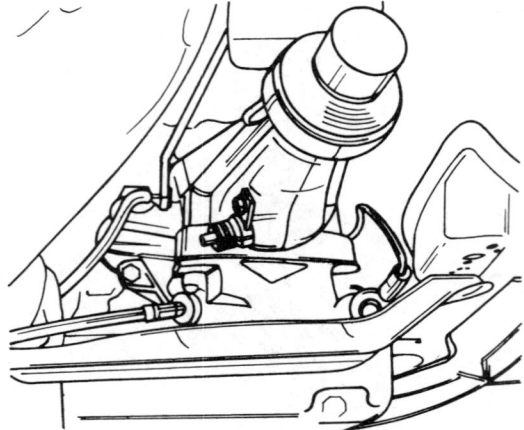

FIG 7:5 Disconnecting speedometer cable

FIG 7:6 Disconnecting and sealing fluid cooler lines

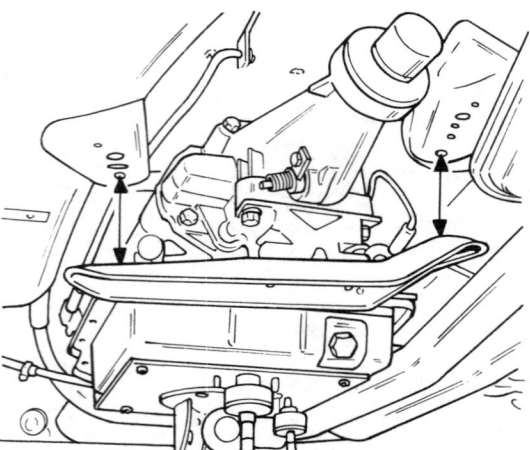

FIG 7:7 Transmission rear mounting bracket

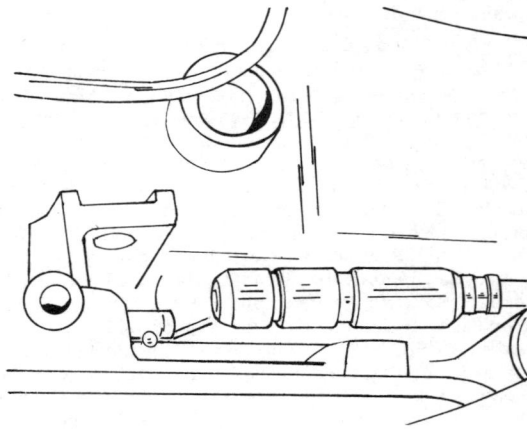

FIG 7:8 Disconnecting kick-down cable

7:3 Gear selector linkages

Selector linkage adjustment:

Linkage adjustment is not likely to be needed unless difficulty is encountered in gear selection, or if the transmission has been removed and refitted for servicing purposes. If adjustment is necessary, carry out the work in the following manner, referring to **FIG 7:2**.

Make sure that the car is standing on level ground and fully apply the handbrake. From beneath the car, disconnect the fork on the end of the selector rod from the selector lever on the transmission. Make sure that the selector levers in the car and on the transmission are both in position 1, as shown in the illustration. Adjust the length of the selector rod by turning the fork at the end of the rod (arrowed) until the fork can be reconnected to the selector lever without binding. From this position, unscrew the fork by exactly four and a half turns, then connect the fork to the selector lever. Hold the locking catch on the selector lever inside the car, then move the selector through all six gear positions, checking that a definite click can be felt as each position is selected. If necessary, make further slight adjustments to the length of the selector rod to ensure accurate engagement of all selector positions.

Kick-down cable adjustment:

This adjustment is necessary to ensure that the transmission makes downward changes for maximum acceleration when the accelerator pedal is pushed fully to the floor, into the kick-down position.

Adjustment is correct when the ball 3 (see **FIG 7:3**) at the end of the control cable rests in grommet 4 when the accelerator pedal is 9mm from the pedal stop. To check, place a suitable 9mm thick block in position 5, then depress the accelerator pedal until it contacts the block and check that the ball 3 seats firmly in grommet 4 without undue strain on the operating cable.

If adjustment is necessary, slacken the cable clamp located on the bulkhead in the engine compartment and slide the cable sleeve arrowed in **FIG 7:4** in or out until the correct cable setting is achieved. Tighten the clamp to secure the adjustment, then recheck.

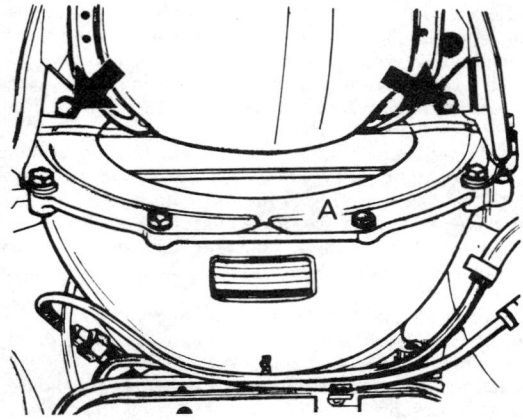

FIG 7:9   Converter cover removal

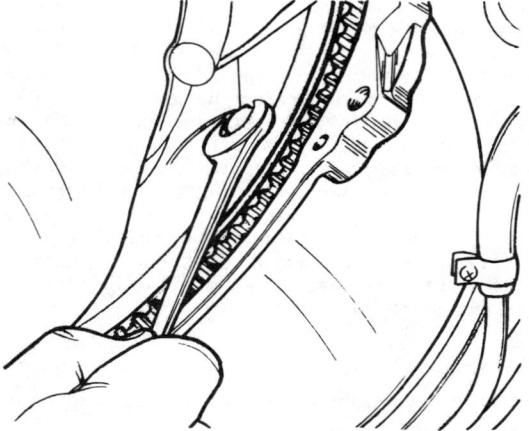

FIG 7:10   Converter securing bolts

Linkage damper adjustment:

Linkage damper adjustment is described in **Chapter 2**, **Section 2:8** or **2:9**.

7:4 Transmission removal and refitting

Disconnect the battery. If the cooling fan is provided with a cowl, remove the fixing screws securing the cowl to the radiator but leave the cowl in position. Remove the starter motor upper fixing bolt and the bolt securing the bracket at the front of the starter motor to the engine.

Remove the upper clip securing the kick-down control cable to the fluid filler pipe. Withdraw the transmission fluid dipstick and plug the filler tube to prevent the entry of dirt. Raise and safely support the car on floor stands, to provide sufficient underbody clearance for transmission removal.

Disconnect the exhaust pipe flange from the exhaust manifold. Refer to **Chapter 8** and remove the propeller shaft. Fit a suitable plug or cover to the rear end of the transmission to prevent loss of fluid.

Refer to **FIG 7:5** and disconnect the speedometer cable from the rear of transmission. Pull the modulator pipe from modulator diaphragm assembly. Slacken one of the clips at each of the fluid cooler hoses, then pull one end of each hose from the pipe and push each free end on to the adjacent pipe to seal the system against the entry of dirt, as shown in **FIG 7:6**.

Raise a suitable jack beneath the transmission to just support its weight. Remove the bolts securing the rear mounting bracket to the underbody, then slowly lower the transmission as shown in **FIG 7:7** until the jack is just free. Disconnect the selector lever. Remove the clamps securing modulator pipe and kick-down control cable to oil filler pipe. Force the modulator pipe from clip at transmission housing.

Refer to **FIG 7:8**. Clean the transmission housing in the area of the control cable connection, unscrew the bracket, withdraw kick-down cable end and unhook control cable from valve. Refer to **FIG 7:9**. Remove earth strap from stay bolt, remove converter cover fixing bolts and stay bolt, then just slacken the two screws

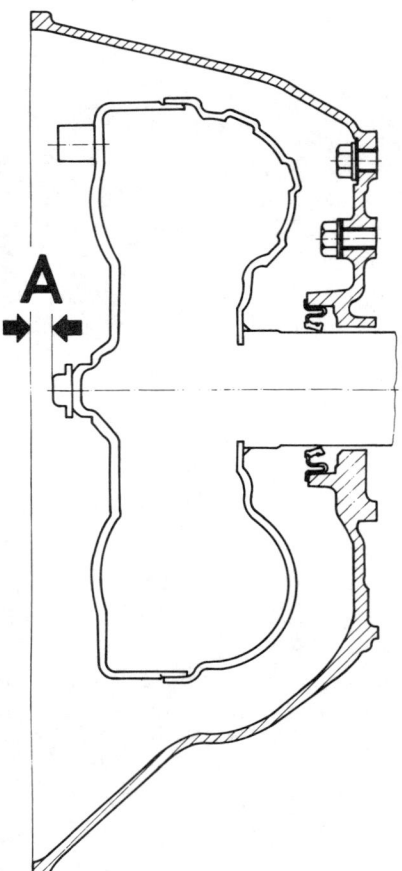

FIG 7:11   Checking converter installation

(arrowed) and remove converter cover **A**. Remove the three converter securing bolts as shown in **FIG 7:10**, turning the converter for access to each bolt in turn. Remove the cap from the converter housing.

Remove the bolts securing the transmission to the engine. Withdraw the starter from the converter housing and support in the engine compartment so that the starter wiring is not strained. With the jack supporting the weight of the transmission, move the transmission rearwards, carefully levering the converter from the drive plate, if necessary. Wedge or hold the converter assembly in the transmission housing to prevent it falling out as the transmission is removed. Lower the transmission carefully and remove from beneath the car.

Refitting:

This is a reversal of the removal procedure, noting the following points.

Before installation, check for correct location of converter assembly in transmission. If converter hub is meshing fully with drive gear wheel in transmission, distance **A** between flange of converter housing and end face of centring pivot will be approximately 5 to 7mm (0.20 to 0.28in) (see **FIG 7:11**).

Coat the front spigot of the converter and bearing point in centring piece with an approved grade of grease. Note that the converter is marked with a blue line and the drive plate at the rear of the crankshaft is marked by a white line. When securing converter to drive plate, make sure that the blue and white lines are as close as possible to one another.

On completion, check that the air filter intake hose has not been pulled from the port at the air deflector during the removal procedure, refitting the hose if necessary. Check the selector linkage and kick-down cable adjustment as described in **Section 7:3** and check transmission fluid level as described in **Section 7:2**.

CHAPTER 8

THE PROPELLER SHAFT, REAR AXLE AND REAR SUSPENSION

8:1 Description

Power is transmitted from the transmission output shaft to the differential unit pinion shaft by a one-piece open tubular propeller shaft, this shaft incorporating two universal joints of the trunnion and needle roller type. The yoke of the front universal joint carries an internally splined sleeve which can slide on the splined transmission output shaft to compensate for movement of the rear axle. The rear universal joint is bolted to a flange attached to the pinion shaft at the rear axle.

The rear axle is of the semi-floating type with a hypoid final drive enclosed in a one-piece axle housing with detachable rear cover. The differential and hypoid gear, and the hypoid pinion, are carried on tapered roller bearings. The pinion extension shaft is splined to the hypoid pinion and is supported at the front end by a ballbearing in the pinion extension housing. On some models, a limited-slip differential unit is available as an optional extra.

The rear suspension incorporates coil springs, lower arms, telescopic dampers and a Panhard rod as shown in **FIG 8:1**. The axle is located longitudinally by the suspension arms and pinion extension housing, lateral movement being prevented by the Panhard rod. Rubber bump stops are attached to the vehicle underbody, suspension rebound being controlled by double-acting dampers. An anti-roll bar is attached at each end by links bolted to the underbody and is secured to the rear axle housing by U-shaped clamps.

The items of maintenance and overhaul which can be carried out by a reasonably competent owner/mechanic are given in this chapter, but it is not advised that any further operations be attempted. Special tools and equipment are essential to overhaul the drive shafts and differential components and set the necessary preloads so, for these reasons, the components mentioned should be dismantled and serviced only by a service station having the necessary equipment and trained fitters.

8:2 Routine maintenance

The level of oil in the rear axle unit should be checked at the intervals specified in the manufacturer's service schedule. Note, that special hypoid gear oil is required. The combined oil level and filler plug is on the axle housing rear cover as can be seen in **FIG 8:2**. Clean all dirt from around the plug before removing it. The oil level should be at the bottom of the filler plug hole, checked with the car unladen and on level ground. Top up with

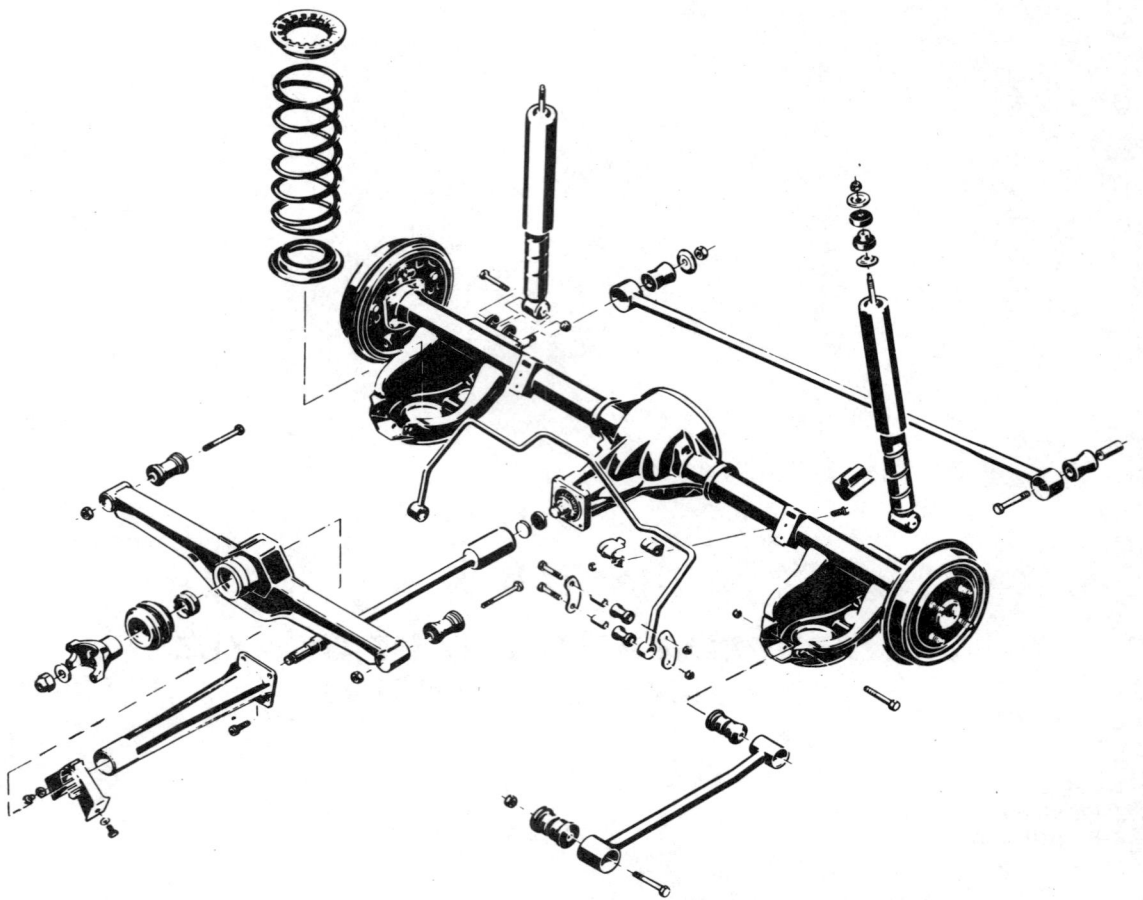

FIG 8:1   Layout of the rear axle and suspension

the correct grade of oil, then allow all excess oil to drain away before refitting the filler plug. Periodic draining and refilling of the rear axle is not required.

8:3 Propeller shaft

Propeller shaft joint bearings are pre-packed with lubricant on assembly, then staked into place as shown in **FIG 8:3**. No servicing of the bearings is possible, so if a bearing unit is worn or damaged, the unit in question must be renewed complete.

Removal:

Have ready a spare sliding sleeve or suitable plug or cover to fit to the transmission rear cover to prevent oil loss when the propeller shaft is removed.

Mark the relationship between the rear universal joint flange and the rear axle pinion shaft flange with quick drying paint. Remove the locking nuts and bolts securing the flanges.

After withdrawing the sliding sleeve from the transmission, protect the outer surface of the sleeve by binding with tape to prevent damage. Burrs or scratches on this surface may cause premature wear on the transmission rear cover bush and oil seal.

Refitting:

Smear the lip of the transmission rear cover seal with recommended lubricant and ensure that the surface of the sliding sleeve is free from burrs or scores. Fit the spring into the bore of the sliding sleeve before inserting it into the transmission, as shown in **FIG 8:4**.

Align the paint marks on rear universal joint flange and rear axle pinion shaft flange and fit the retaining bolts, noting that the heads of the bolts are towards the propeller shaft. Fit new lock tabs and tighten the nuts, then bend over the tabs to secure. On models fitted with manual transmission, check gearbox oil level as described in **Chapter 6**, after a short run to circulate the oil. On models fitted with automatic transmission, check transmission fluid level as described in **Chapter 7**.

8:4 Rear axle

Removal of the rear axle is only likely to be called for if a replacement unit is to be fitted. As already stated,

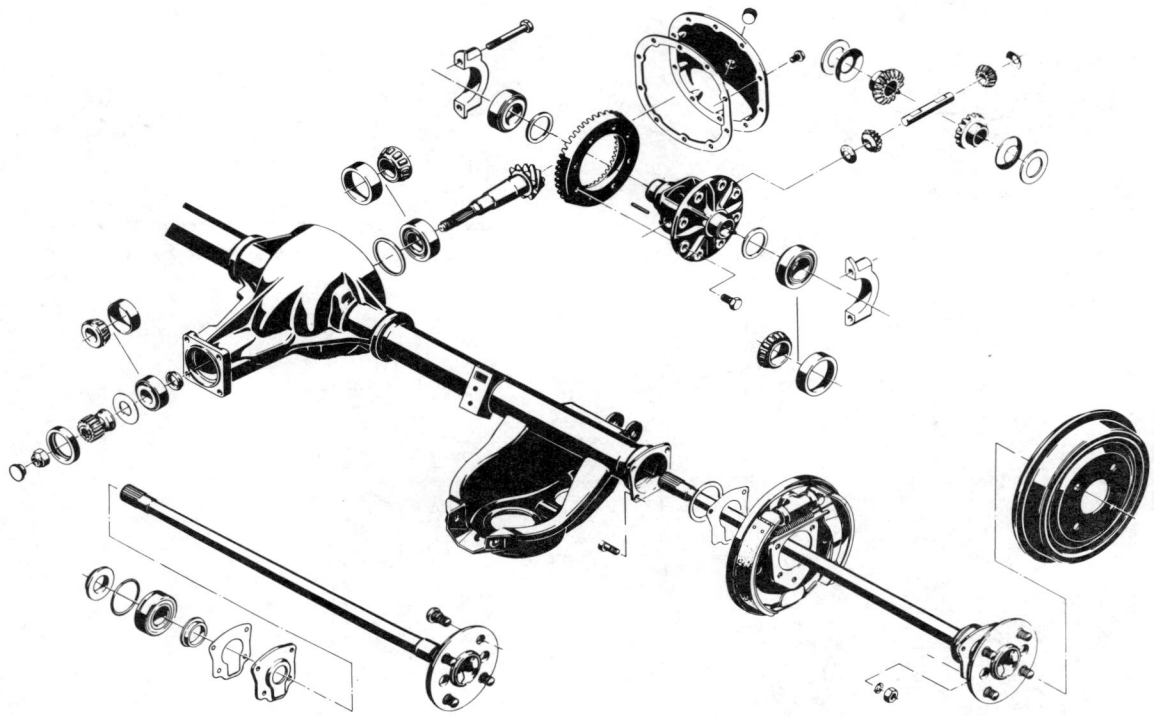

FIG 8:2 Typical rear axle components

dismantling of the axle and differential should be carried out by a fully equipped service station. **FIG 8:1** shows layout of the rear axle and suspension, **FIG 8:2** typical rear axle components.

The spring-loaded seal which prevents oil leaking from around the pinion shaft can be renewed without the need for axle removal, as described later.

Axle removal:

Raise the rear of the car and safely support on floor stands placed beneath the suspension arm front under-body brackets. Use a suitable jack to take the weight of the axle unit. Remove the rear road wheels.

Disconnect the handbrake adjuster mechanism to separate the front and rear handbrake cables. Refer to **Chapter 11** for detailed instructions concerning braking system components. Remove the brake drums and unhook cable from brake shoe operating levers after removing E-clips securing cable guides to flange plates. Disconnect the hydraulic brake pipes from the wheel cylinders at each brake backplate and from the rear axle housing. Plug the open ends of the brake pipes to prevent loss of fluid and entry of dirt, then tie the brake pipes up out of the way of further operations.

Disconnect the suspension arms, dampers, Panhard rod and anti-roll bar at the axle end.

Lower the jack supporting the rear axle assembly until sufficient clearance is obtained for coil spring removal. Disconnect the pinion extension housing from the axle using an M8 tri-square bit and withdraw the axle from beneath the car.

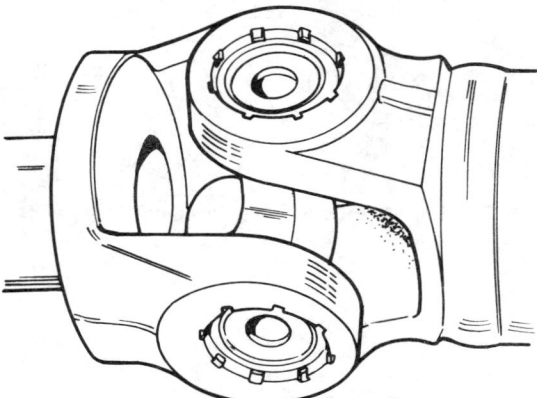

FIG 8:3 Universal joint bearings are staked in position and cannot be renewed separately

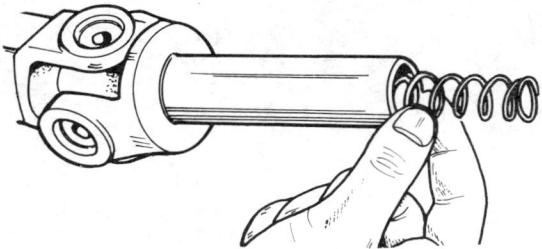

FIG 8:4 Installing the spring in the sliding sleeve bore

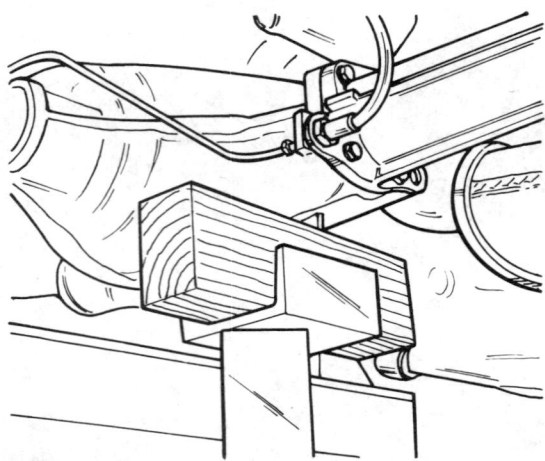

FIG 8:5 Supporting the pinion extension housing

FIG 8:6 Removing pinion extension housing seal

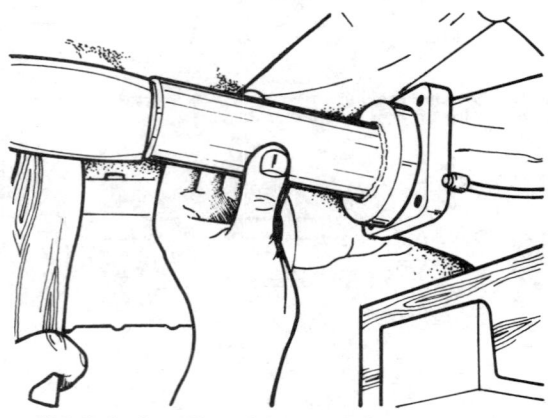

FIG 8:7 Installing pinion extension housing seal

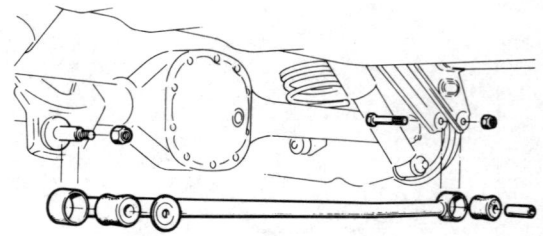

FIG 8:8 Panhard rod removal

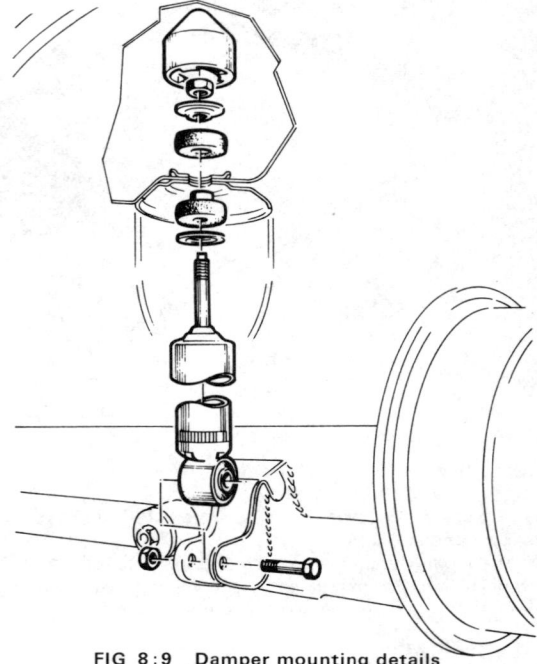

FIG 8:9 Damper mounting details

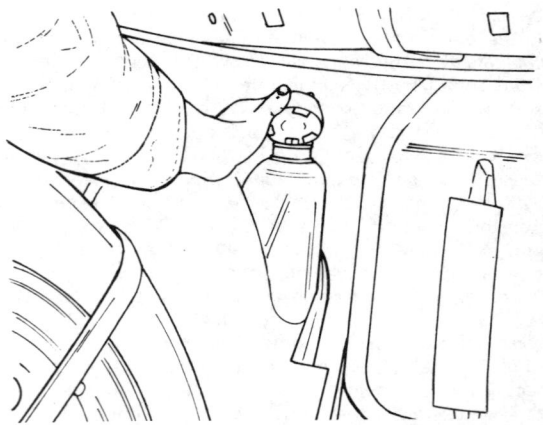

FIG 8:10 Damper upper mounting nut

Refitting:

Refitting the rear axle is a reversal of the removal procedure, noting the following points:

Connect the pinion extension housing to axle housing and tighten bolts to the correct torque before installing the coil springs. Make sure that the springs and suspension components are correctly installed as described in **Section 8:5**. Note that the weight of the car must be resting on the road wheels before the suspension arm fixings are fully tightened.

On completion, bleed the braking system, reconnect the handbrake cable and check brake adjustment (see **Chapter 11**). Check the level of oil in the rear axle as described in **Section 8:2**.

Pinion shaft seal renewal:

Before any work is carried out on the axle which involves removal of the pinion extension housing crossmember bolts, the rear axle must be supported with a jack or stand immediately behind the housing to relieve downward pressure from the coil springs (see **FIG 8:5**).

Disconnect the rear end of the propeller shaft as described previously, then tie the shaft up so that the sliding sleeve is not disconnected from the transmission. Disconnect the brake fluid pipe from the pinion housing flange and plug the open ends of the pipe to prevent loss of fluid or the entry of dirt. With the housing properly supported, remove the bolts securing the pinion extension housing to the axle, using an M8 tri-square bit. Disconnect the pinion housing crossmember and remove the housing.

Carefully prise the seal from the housing, using a suitable pointed tool as shown in **FIG 8:6**. Install the new seal, open end first, using a suitable driver tool so that the seal face is flush with the end of the axle housing (see **FIG 8:7**).

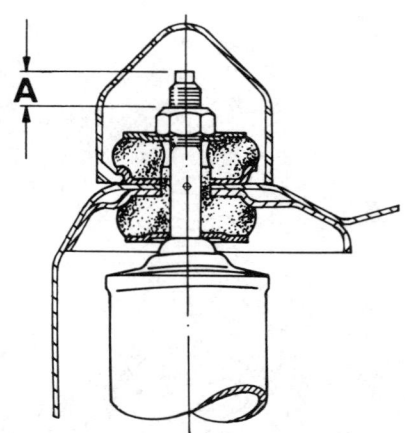

FIG 8:11 Damper upper nut must be tightened so that dimension A is 11mm (0.44in)

Refit the components removed for seal renewal and, on completion, bleed the braking system as described in **Chapter 11**. Check the oil level in the axle as described in **Section 8:2**.

8:5 Rear suspension

The layout of the rear suspension components is shown in **FIG 8:1**.

Panhard rod:

The Panhard rod is fitted between an anchorage on the underbody and a bracket on the axle tube. Both ends of the rod are provided with rubber bushes and the end secured to the underbody has an additional internal sleeve.

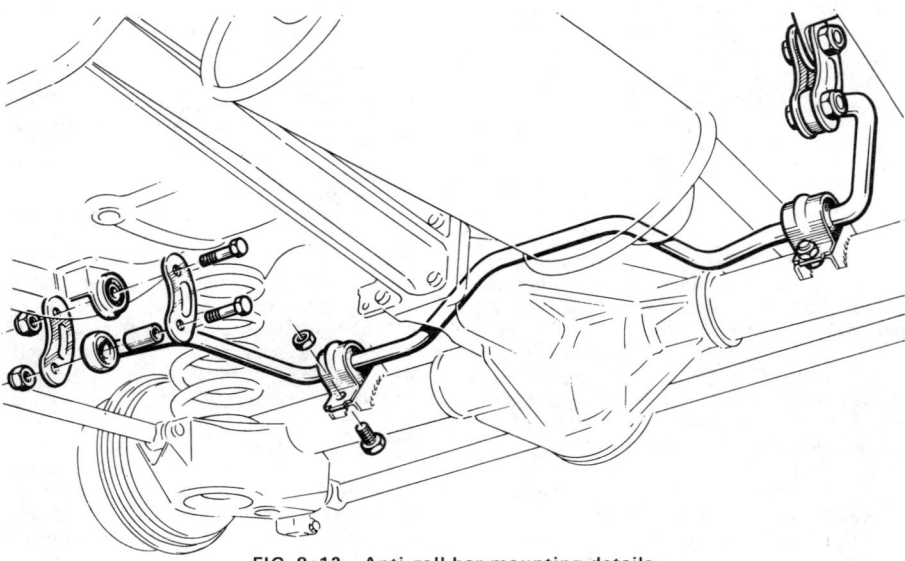

FIG 8:12 Anti-roll bar mounting details

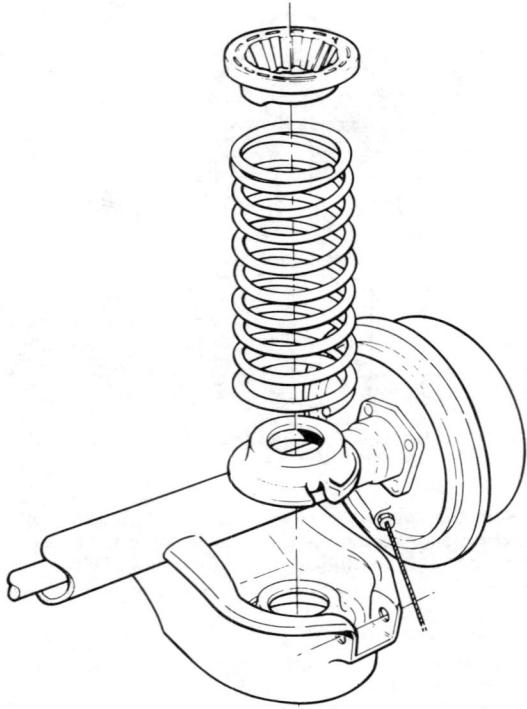

FIG 8:13   Coil spring mounting details

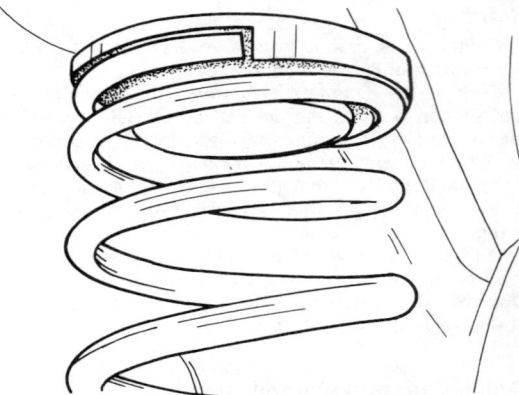

FIG 8:15   Correct location of upper spring seat

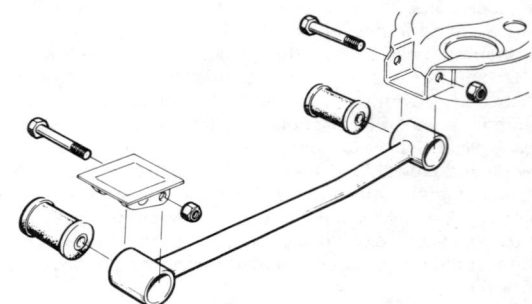

FIG 8:16   Suspension arm mountings

FIG 8:14   Coil spring removal

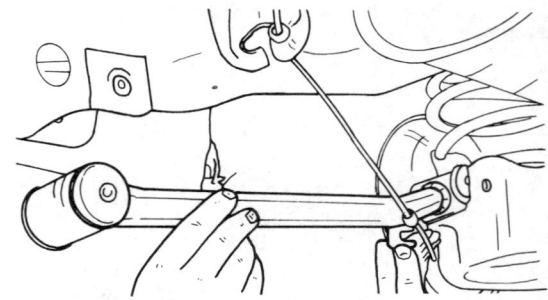

FIG 8:17   Suspension arm removal

To remove the Panhard rod, remove the nuts and bolt shown in **FIG 8:8**. Inspect the rubber bushes and renew them if worn or perished. New bushes should be dipped into a soap solution before fitting.

Dampers:

The dampers have a rubber-bushed stud fixing to the underbody and a rubber-bushed eye attachment to the rear spring mounting bracket on the axle tubes. Mounting details are shown in **FIG 8:9**.

Before removing a damper, support the car beneath the rear axle to prevent the damper from extending fully. The upper mounting nuts are accessible from inside the luggage compartment after removing the partition board

and prising off the plastic caps (see **FIG 8:10**). Hold the squared end of the damper rod with one spanner while slackening the upper mounting nut with a second spanner.

When refitting a damper, ensure that the upper mounting bushes and cups are located correctly, as shown in **FIG 8:11**. Tighten the upper mounting nut until dimension **A** is 11mm (0.44in).

Anti-roll bar:

The anti-roll bar is attached at each end by links bolted to the underbody and is secured to the axle tube by U-shaped clamps. The clamps incorporate rubber insulators and at each end of the links rubber bushes with internal sleeves are fitted (see **FIG 8:12**). Removal and refitting of the anti-roll bar are straightforward operations. Renew the rubber bushes if they are worn or perished.

Coil springs:

The rear coil springs are supported on rubber seats located in the axle tube brackets and on the underbody. Mounting details are shown in **FIG 8:13**.

To remove a coil spring, support the rear of the body on floor stands and support the axle with a suitable jack. Disconnect the anti-roll bar from both axle mountings (see **FIG 8:12**). Disconnect both dampers at their lower mounting points and slacken the suspension arm mounting bolts. As a precaution against stretching the brake hose, remove the hose securing clip at the pinion extension housing before lowering the axle. Lower the axle until the side being worked on can be pulled down sufficiently to allow coil spring removal as shown in **FIG 8:14**.

Before installing a coil spring, make sure that the spring seat is correctly located in the axle tube bracket and fits the spring with the straightened coil end towards the axle. Fit the upper spring seat to the spring so that the step in the seat contacts the end of the spring coil, as shown in **FIG 8:15**. Before tightening the suspension arm bolts, the car weight must be resting on the road wheels.

Suspension arms:

The rubber bushed suspension arms are clamped between brackets on the underbody and axle housing (see **FIG 8:16**). The bushes incorporate internal sleeves. Suspension arms can be removed regardless of axle position relative to the car body, after removing the handbrake cable guide from the clip beneath the arm (see **FIG 8:17**).

As special tools and press equipment are required to remove and refit suspension arm bushes, this work should be carried out by a fully equipped service station.

Refit the suspension arm with the handbrake cable clip towards the rear and facing downwards. Before finally tightening the suspension arm bolts, the weight of the vehicle must be resting on the road wheels.

8:6 Fault diagnosis

(a) Noisy axle

1 Incorrect or insufficient lubricant
2 Worn bearings
3 Worn gears
4 Damaged or broken gear teeth
5 Incorrect adjustments in differential
6 General wear

(b) Excessive backlash

1 Worn gears or bearings
2 Worn propeller shaft splines
3 Worn universal joints
4 Loose wheel attachments

(c) Oil leaks

1 Defective oil seals
2 Defective gaskets or distorted casing
3 Overfilled rear axle

(d) Vibration

1 Propeller shaft out of balance
2 Worn universal joints

(e) Rattles

1 Worn universal joints
2 Worn suspension rubber bushes
3 Worn spring seat

(f) Knock

1 Check (a)
2 Badly worn splines on propeller or axle shaft
3 Worn universal joints

NOTES

CHAPTER 9

FRONT SUSPENSION AND HUBS

9:1 Description

The independent front suspension is of the short and long arm type with coil springs and is shown in **FIG 9:1**. The wishbone type suspension arms are rubber bushed at their inner ends and pivot on fulcrum bolts attached to the crossmember which is bolted to the underbody. At the outer ends of upper and lower arms ball joints carry the steering knuckles. The coil springs are fitted between the crossmember and the lower arms. The telescopic dampers are fitted between the body and upper arms. Each lower arm incorporates an outrigger which is secured to the crossmember brace. The anti-roll bar is mounted on the underbody and linked to the lower arms. Rubber bump stops are mounted on the crossmember to limit suspension movement under compression, rebound being controlled by the dampers.

The suspension ball joints are packed with lubricant on assembly and sealed for life, so apart from a periodic check on the general condition of all suspension components, no routine maintenance is required.

9:2 Front hubs

The front hubs are mounted on taper roller bearings and the wheel bolts are splined and pressed into the hub flange. A spring loaded lip type seal is incorporated in the hub at the inner end and the hub is retained by a keyed washer, slotted nut and splitpin. **FIG 9:2** shows a section through the front hub assembly.

Jack up the front of the car so that the road wheels are clear of the ground. Spin the wheels and check that they rotate freely without bearing noise, taking care not to confuse noise from the brake with that from a defective bearing. Grasp the tyre at the top and bottom of the wheel and attempt to rock the top of the wheel in and out while noting the play. Repeat the test with the tyre gripped at each side of the wheel. If excessive play is evident, the wheel bearings should be adjusted first and, if roughness is still apparent, the bearings should be dismantled for inspection.

Adjustment:

Jack up the front of the car and remove the road wheel. Remove the grease cap from the centre of the hub. Remove the splitpin and tighten the nut to a torque of 27Nm (20lb ft) while turning the wheel. The nut must then be slackened to give a hub end float of 0.02 to 0.10mm (0.001 to 0.004in). End float is best measured using a dial gauge assembly. When the bearings are

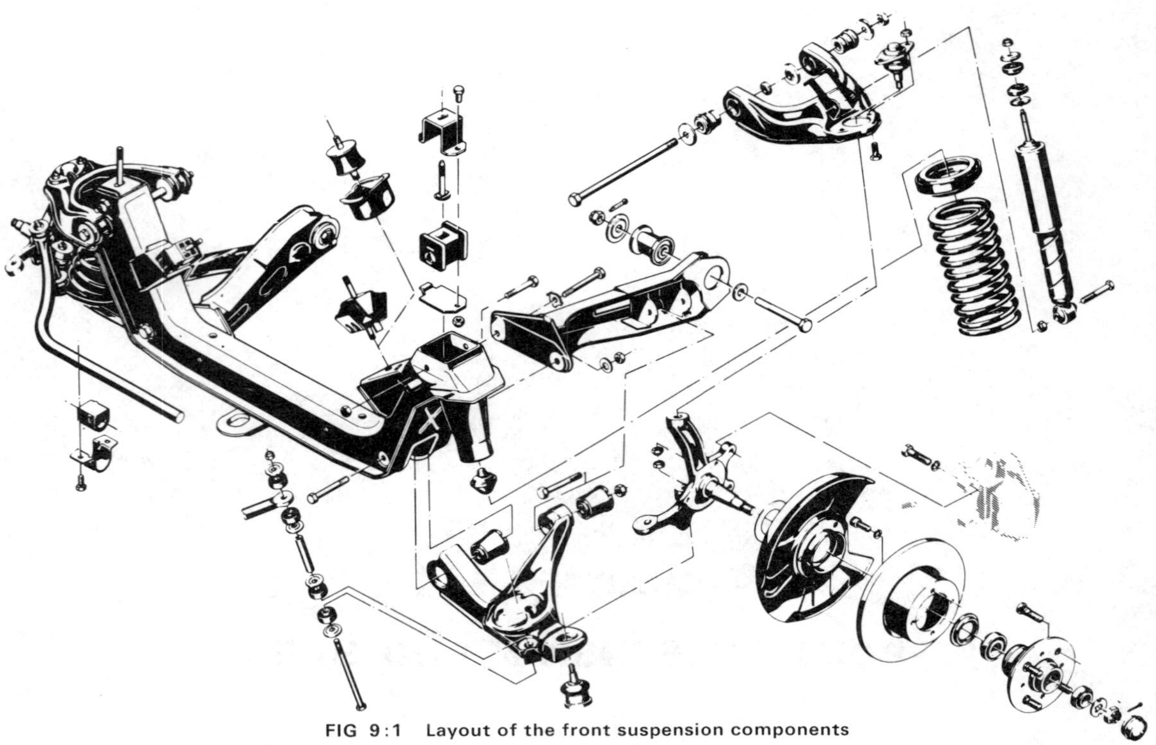

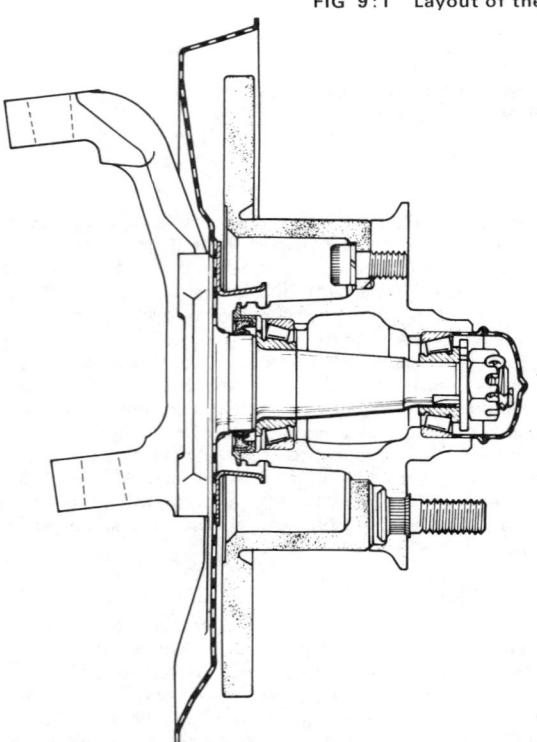

FIG 9:1   Layout of the front suspension components

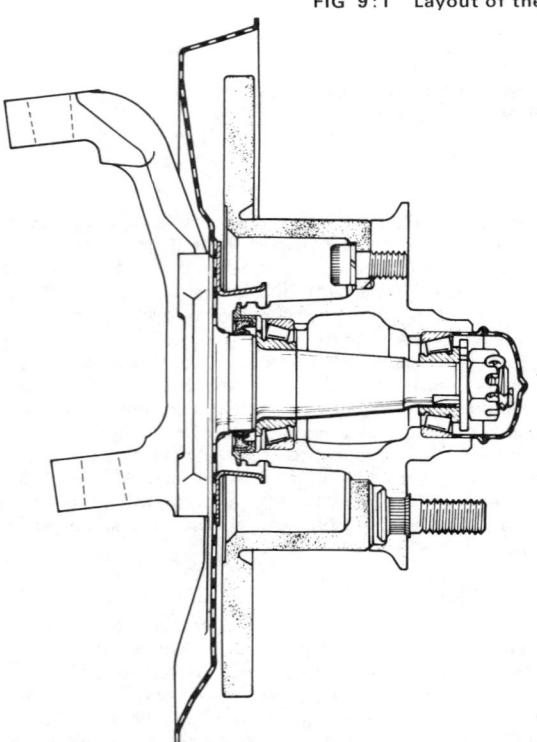

FIG 9:2   Section through the front hub assembly

correctly adjusted, slacken the nut a fraction more if necessary to align the splitpin hole, then insert and lock a new splitpin.

Removal:

Slacken the road wheel fixings and raise the front of the car on to stands. Remove the road wheels. Remove the brake caliper as described in **Chapter 11** and wire it to the suspension to avoid straining the hose.

Remove the grease cap from the hub. Remove the splitpin and hub nut. Remove the hub assembly from the steering swivel, using a suitable puller if necessary. Collect the inner race of the outer bearing as it comes free. Remove the oil seal from the hub and remove the inner race of the inner bearing.

Servicing:

Wipe the old grease from the hub and bearings, then thoroughly degrease the parts in petrol, paraffin or a similar solvent. Wash the bearing races separately by rotating them in a bowl of clean solvent. The brake disc must be thoroughly washed with solvent to remove all traces of grease or dirt.

Examine the operating face of the stub axle on which the oil seal operates for scoring or nicks. Light damage can be smoothed with fine grade emerycloth. Check the stub axle for hairline cracks or other damage, which would dictate renewal.

Check the outer races of the bearings for fretting, scoring or wear. If damage is found, both outer races must be driven out with a suitable copper drift, working evenly around the races to prevent jamming, then both bearings renewed.

Lubricate the inner races with light oil. Press each inner race firmly back into its outer and rotate the bearing to check for any roughness in operation. Dirt can be a cause of roughness, so wash the bearing again thoroughly before repeating the test. If an air-line is used to dry the bearings, do not allow them to spin in the air blast as this chips the faces. If a bearing is defective, both bearings must be completely renewed, including the outer races in the hub.

Reassembly:

If the outer races of the hubs have been removed they should be driven back evenly and fully using a suitable drift.

The wheel bearing must be lubricated with an approved grade of grease. Evenly pack the inside of the hub with fresh grease and liberally pack the inner race of the inner bearing, working grease well into the rollers. Install the inner race of the inner bearing into the hub and press a new oil seal into the hub to retain the race in position.

Slide the hub assembly back on to the stub axle, taking care not to damage the seal. Pack the inner race of the outer bearing with grease and fit it back into place, followed by the washer and nut. Adjust the wheel bearings as described previously and fit a new splitpin. Install the grease cap. Refit the brake caliper as described in **Chapter 11**, being sure to pump the brake pedal hard several times on completion to take up the adjustment in the brakes. Refit the road wheel.

9:3 Dampers and anti-roll bar

Dampers:

The front dampers have a stud fixing to the wheel house panel and an eye mounting to the front suspension upper arm, both fixings being provided with rubber bushes. The upper mounting nuts are accessible from inside the engine compartment. Never attempt to remove the damper from upper or lower mountings when the front wheels are off the ground, unless the car is supported

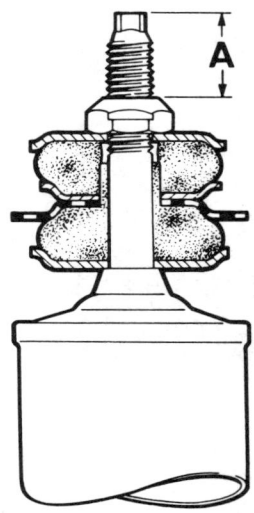

FIG 9:3 Install damper so that dimension A is 20mm (0.8in)

under the suspension lower arms or a spring compressor fitted, as the dampers control suspension rebound and therefore extension of road springs.

When installing a damper, ensure that the upper mounting bushes and washers are located correctly as shown in **FIG 9:3**. Hold the squared end of the damper rod with one spanner while tightening the upper mounting nut with a second spanner until dimension **A** is 20mm (0.8in).

Anti-roll bar:

The anti-roll bar is connected by means of links to brackets welded to the lower arms. Metal straps and insulator rubbers secure the bar to the front underbody (see **FIG 9:4**). The underpan must be removed, if fitted, for access to the anti-roll bar.

Anti-roll bar removal is straightforward, but refit the insulator rubbers with the split towards the front of the

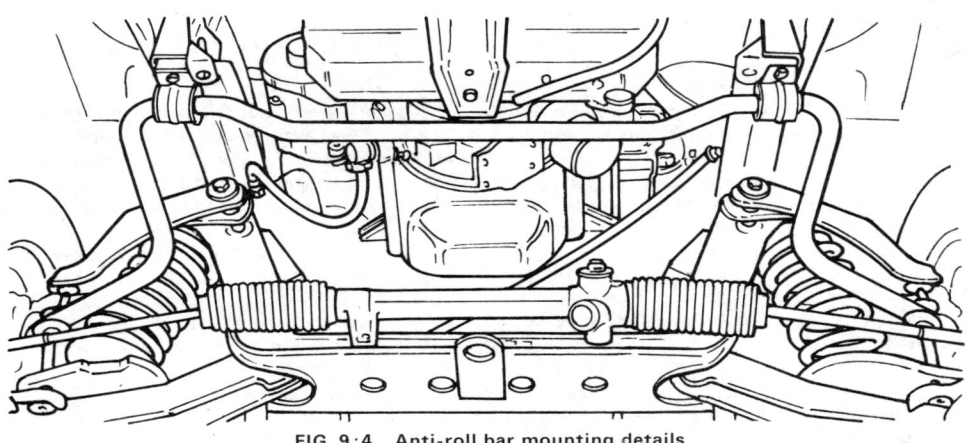

FIG 9:4 Anti-roll bar mounting details

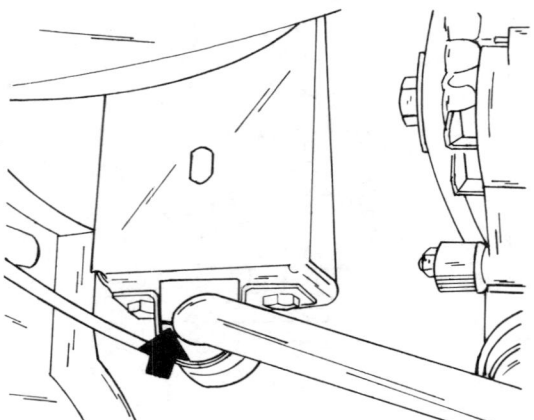

FIG 9:5 Anti-roll bar insulator position

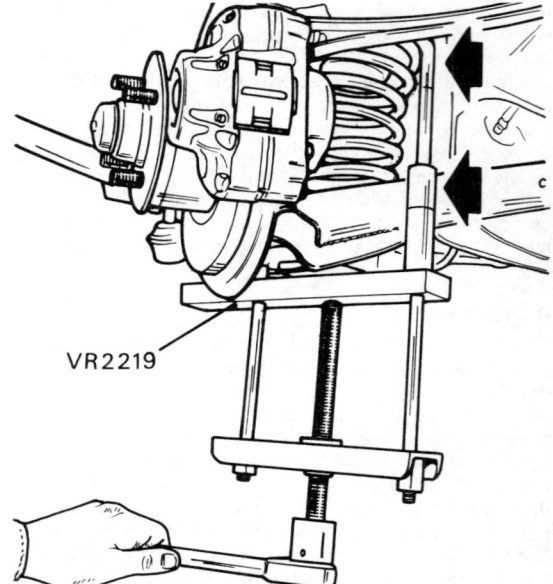

VR2219

FIG 9:7 Spring compressor installation

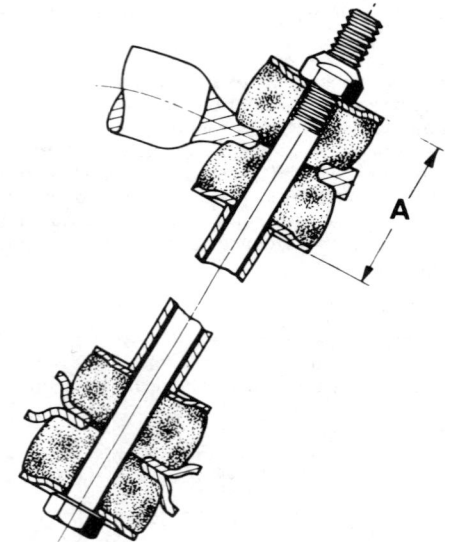

FIG 9:6 Install anti-roll bar so that dimension A is 38mm (1.50in)

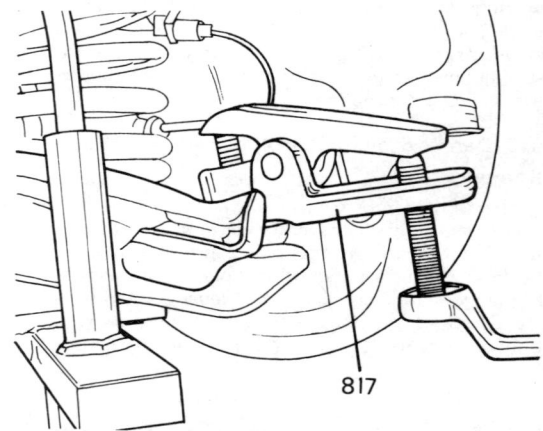

817

FIG 9:8 Removing lower arm ball joint

vehicle (see **FIG 9:5**). Insulator rubbers should be smeared with an approved grade of rubber grease before installation.

Install the anti-roll bar ends to the lower suspension arms with the cup washers and bushes as shown in **FIG 9:6**. Tighten the nut until dimension **A** is 38mm (1.50in).

9:4 Coil springs

The front coil springs are equal in length and may be interchanged side to side.

Removal:

In order to remove a coil spring it is necessary to use a spring compressor such as tool VR2219 (see **FIG 9:7**).

Slacken the suspension lower arm and outrigger fulcrum bolts and remove the anti-roll bar connections from both lower arms. Refer to **Chapter 10** and disconnect the tie rod ball joint from the steering arm on the side of the car from which the coil spring is to be removed.

Fit the spring compressor as shown in **FIG 9:7**, ensuring that the hooks are positively located over approximately seven coils. The end of guide plate and hook painted red should always be to the right as viewed from the side of the vehicle.

Remove the nut from the lower arm ball joint. Use remover 817 or other similar tool to remove the ball joint from steering knuckle, as shown in **FIG 9:8**. Wedge or tie the upper arm and steering knuckle away from the lower arm and spring to avoid straining the brake hose.

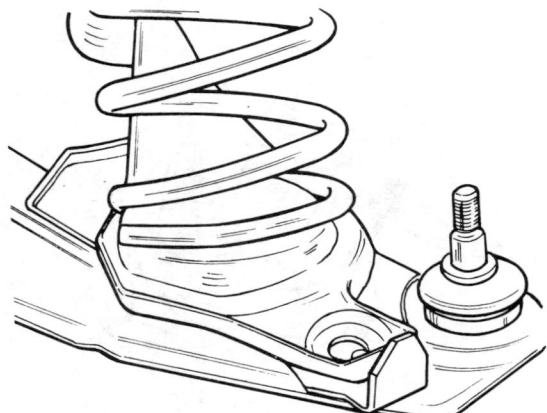

FIG 9:9 Correct position of spring in lower arm recess

Remove the fulcrum and outrigger bolts and withdraw the lower arm complete with spring from the vehicle. Slacken the spring compressor to remove the spring.

Refitting:

Refitting is a reversal of the removal procedure. Make sure that the end of the spring with the straight portion seats correctly in the lower arm recess as shown in **FIG 9:9**. Use the compressor tool in the manner previously described when refitting the spring. Fit the insulator to the top end of the spring and install spring and lower arm to the vehicle. Make sure that the mating tapers are clean and free from grease before attaching the ball joint to the steering knuckle. Tighten the suspension arm fulcrum and outrigger bolts to the specified torque when the weight of the vehicle is resting on the road wheels.

9:5 Suspension ball joints

The upper suspension arm ball joints, which are bolted to the arms, have seatings which are preloaded to eliminate vertical clearance. Lower suspension arm ball joints are of the pendant type and may have up to 0.2mm (0.008in) vertical clearance when new. The lower joint socket is splined externally and is pressed into corresponding splines in the suspension arm aperture during manufacture.

Checking ball joints:

Raise the front of the car and support on floor stands placed beneath the lower front suspension arms. Rock the road wheel while holding the upper and lower ball joints in turn. If any slackness of the ball in its seating can be felt, the joint should be renewed. **FIG 9:10** shows ball joint mounting details. The ball joint must also be renewed if the rubber boot is chafed or split, as the boot is not available separately. Rapid wear of the ball joint can occur if the rubber boot is damaged, due to the ingress of dirt and grit.

Ball joint renewal:

In order to remove either of the ball joints, the coil spring must be compressed as described previously. No

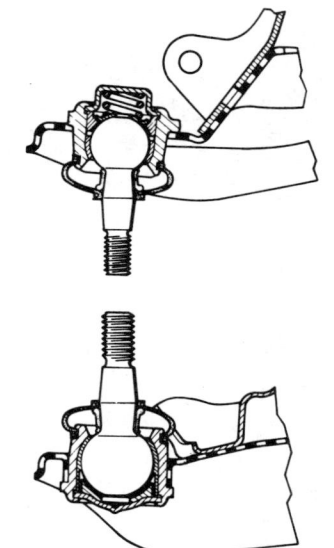

FIG 9:10 Ball joint installation details

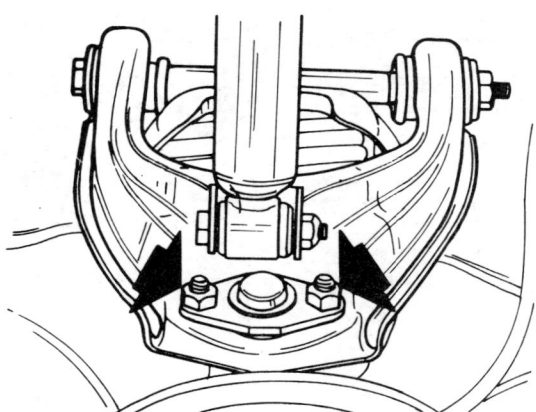

FIG 9:11 Upper ball joint mounting nuts

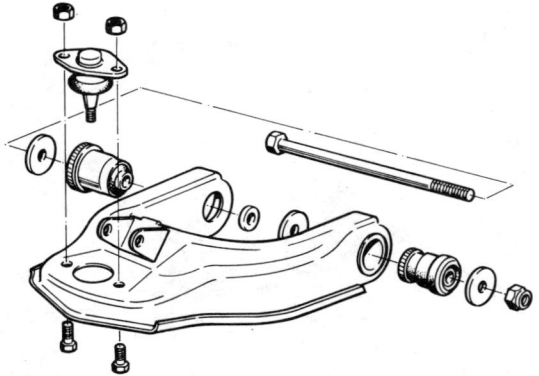

FIG 9:12 Upper suspension arm components

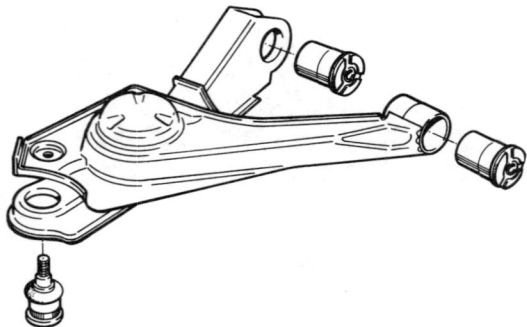

FIG 9:13   Lower suspension arm components

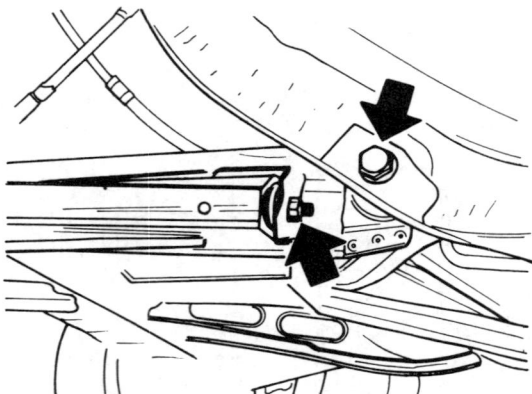

FIG 9:14   Outrigger fulcrum and brace rear mounting bolts

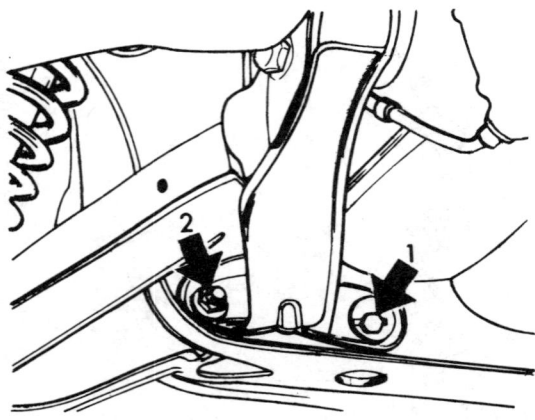

FIG 9:15   Steering gear attachment and lower arm fulcrum bolts

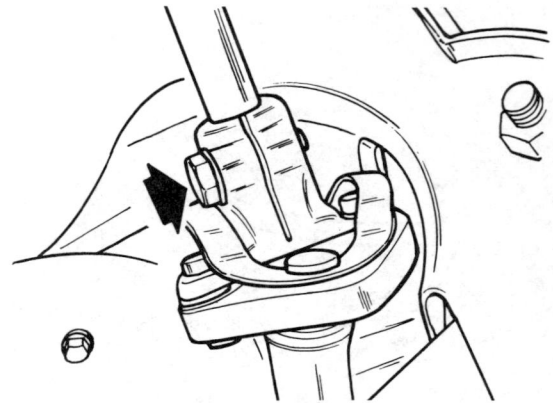

FIG 9:16   Steering coupling pinch bolt

attempt should be made to renew a ball joint without using a spring compressor.

To remove the upper ball joint, it is not necessary to remove the upper suspension arm from the car. Disconnect the steering knuckle with remover 817 or similar tool as described previously, then release the nuts retaining the joint to the arm (see **FIG 9:11**). Make a note of the position of the ball joint before removal. When reassembling, make sure that the new joint is installed in the same position as the old joint to prevent alteration of the camber angle.

The lower ball joint can be removed without the need for suspension arm removal but, as special tools and press equipment are needed to remove the ball joint from the arm, the work should be carried out by a fully equipped service station. If desired, the lower arm and ball joint assembly can be removed as described previously, then the assembly taken to a service station for ball joint renewal. Note that the lower suspension arm fulcrum and outrigger attachments must be finally tightened when the weight of the car is on the road wheels.

9:6 Suspension arms

The components of the suspension arms are shown in **FIGS 9:12** and **9:13**. Removal of the lower arm is

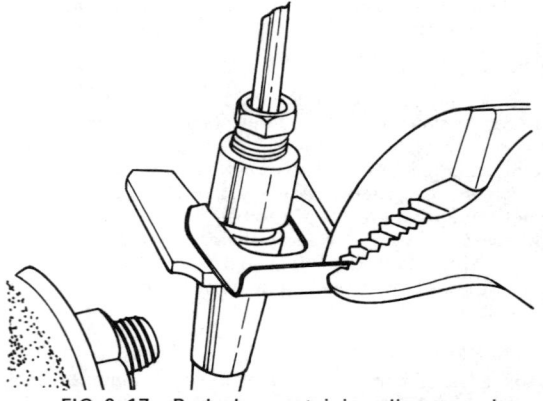

FIG 9:17   Brake hose retaining clip removal

described in **Section 9:4**. To remove the upper arm, partially compress the road spring as described previously, disconnect the ball joint and withdraw the damper lower mounting bolt. Support the front hub to avoid straining the brake hose, then remove the fulcrum bolt.

Both bushes for the lower suspension arms and outriggers incorporate inner and outer sleeves. On the upper suspension arms, the front bush incorporates an inner and outer sleeve whilst the rear bush has no outer sleeve. As removal and installation of suspension arm bushes require the use of special tools and press equipment, the work should be carried out by a fully equipped service station.

9:7 Front axle

The front axle crossmember assembly is bolted directly to the underbody, the lower suspension arm outriggers being attached independently to the crossmember braces. These braces are bolted directly to the crossmember and are secured to the side members through rubber bushes (see **FIG 9:1**).

Crossmember brace removal:

Remove both the suspension lower arm outrigger fulcrum bolt and the crossmember brace rear mounting bolt, these being arrowed in **FIG 9:14**. Refer to **FIG 9:15**. Bend back tab washer and remove steering gear attaching bolt 1, then finally remove lower arm fulcrum bolt nut 2 and withdraw crossmember brace.

As removal and installation of the crossmember brace bush requires many special tools and a press, the work should be carried out by a fully equipped service station.

Refit the crossmember brace in the reverse order of removal, noting that the lower arm and outrigger fulcrum bolts must be finally tightened to the specified torque when the weight of the car is on the road wheels.

Front axle removal:

Remove the pinch bolt shown in **FIG 9:16**. Disconnect the steering coupling from the steering shaft. If the coupling will not slide away from the shaft, turn the steering wheel each way to facilitate removal. Do not

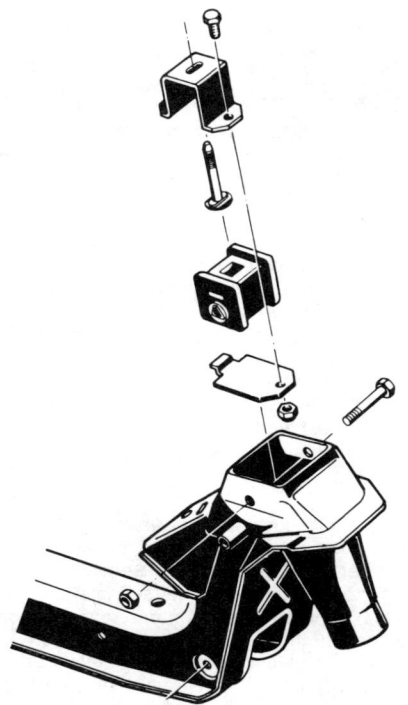

FIG 9:18 Front axle upper mounting details

strike the coupling with a hammer as this may damage the plastic injections in the shaft and make it unfit for further service.

With the weight of the car on the road wheels, remove the damper lower mounting bolts, remove the crossmember braces, and disconnect the anti-roll bar underbody mountings, all as described previously.

Disconnect the brake pipes and remove the hose retaining clips as shown in **FIG 9:17**.

Fit suitable lifting equipment to take the weight of the front of the engine and use a suitable jack to support the weight of the front axle assembly. Remove the nuts

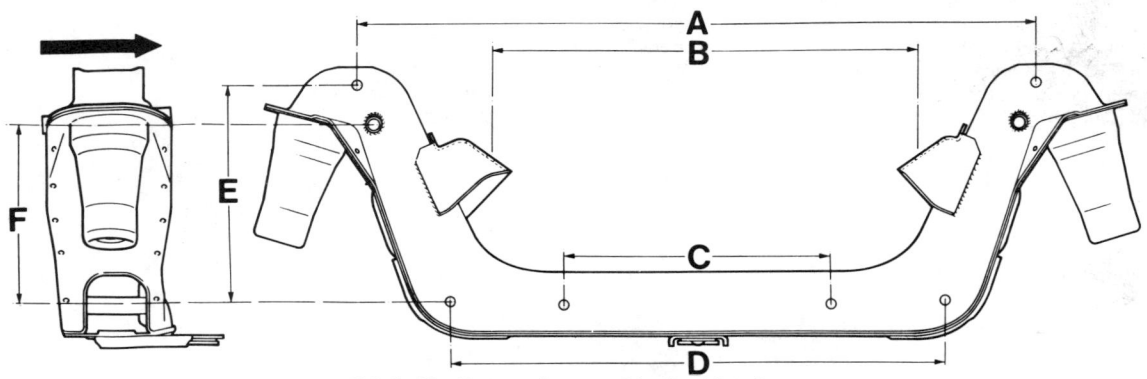

FIG 9:19 Front axle assembly checking data

Key to Fig 9:19　　A = 748mm (29.45in)　　B = 711mm (27.99in)　　C = 294mm (11.57in)　　D = 544mm (21.42in)　　E = 245mm (9.65in)　　F = 200mm (7.87in)　　Arrow above side elevation indicates front of vehicle

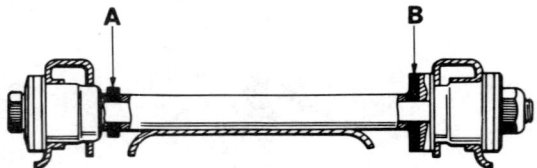

FIG 9:20 Locations of spacers used for castor angle adjustment

securing the engine mountings to the brackets, which are accessible from inside the engine compartment (see **Chapter 1**). Refer to **FIG 9:18** and remove the through bolts from the crossmember and separate the mounting clamp. Lower the jack supporting the axle and remove the assembly from beneath the car.

The front axle crossmember can be checked for distortion or accidental damage by comparing with the dimensions given in **FIG 9:19**.

Refitting:

Refit the front axle assembly in the reverse order of removal, tightening all fixings to the specified torque figures. Refer to **Chapter 10, Section 10:4** when connecting the coupling to the steering shaft. Note, that the lower arm and outrigger fulcrum bolts must be finally tightened when the weight of the car is on the road wheels. On completion, bleed the braking system as described in **Chapter 11**. It is also recommended that suspension geometry be checked as described in the next section.

9:8 Suspension geometry

Due to the need for special optical measuring equipment for accurate results, the checking and adjusting of front wheel caster and camber angles should be carried out by a fully equipped service station.

The camber angle is adjusted by rotating the upper ball joint mounting flange through 180°. As the mounting flange is offset from the joint centre, the camber angle will be altered by approximately 0° 50'. Adjustment is carried out by supporting the lower suspension arm, slackening the upper ball joint nut and releasing the taper from the knuckle using remover 817 or similar tool. With the knuckle supported to avoid brake hose strain, the ball joint retaining nuts which are arrowed in in **FIG 9:11** must be removed. The ball joint flange is then rotated through 180° and the components reassembled.

The caster angle is adjusted by changing spacers **A** and **B** between the upper suspension arm and axle mounting (see **FIG 9:20**). Spacer **A** has a smaller external diameter and is installed towards the front of the vehicle. Production spacers are 6mm (0.24in) thick. To alter the caster angle, spacers must be replaced with one 3mm (0.12in) spacer and one 9mm (0.35in) spacer in the following manner. To increase the caster angle, spacer **A** must be replaced with one of 3mm thickness and spacer **B** with one of 9mm thickness. To decrease the caster angle, spacer **A** must be replaced with one of 9mm thickness and spacer **B** with one of 3mm thickness. In either case, the total thickness of spacers installed must be 12mm (0.47in).

The method for setting the correct toe-in of the front wheels is described in **Chapter 10**.

9:9 Fault diagnosis

(a) Wheel wobble (see also **Chapter 10**)

1 Worn hub bearings
2 Weak front springs
3 Uneven tyre wear
4 Worn suspension bushes

(b) Car pulls to one side

1 Unequal tyre pressures
2 Incorrect suspension geometry
3 Defective suspension bushes or damaged parts
4 Weak spring on one side
5 Fault in steering system

(c) Bottoming of suspension

1 Bump rubbers damaged or missing
2 Broken or weak front coil spring
3 Defective damper

(d) Excessive body roll

1 Check 2 and 3 in (c)

(e) Rattles

1 Check 2 and 4 in (a); 2 and 3 in (c)
2 Defective damper mounting bushes
3 Defective suspension arm bushes

(f) Suspension hard

1 Tyre pressures too high
2 Suspension arm ball joints stiff
3 Dampers faulty

CHAPTER 10

THE STEERING GEAR

10:1 Description

The rack and pinion type steering gear is secured to the front axle crossmember. A tie rod is connected to each end of the rack by a ball joint enclosed in a concertina type rubber boot. The outer end of each tie rod is threaded into a ball joint attached to the steering arms. Steering lock is controlled by the lock stops, which are integral with the steering knuckle, contacting pads on the suspension lower arms. A flexible coupling is connected to the splined ends of the steering gear pinion shaft and steering shaft. The energy absorbing steering column is supported by brackets to the upper and lower dash panels. The column incorporates a combined steering lock and ignition switch.

The steering wheel is a push fit on the splined steering shaft and secured by a nut.

There are no grease nipples on the steering gear or connections. Maintenance is confined to renewal of the rubber boots on the rack and pinion gear should these become defective. The tie rod outer ball joints are lubricated and sealed during assembly, the checking and renewal of these components being described in the next section.

10:2 Tie rod ball joints

The tie rod outer ball joints are of the spring loaded type with nylon seatings and it is therefore possible to move the socket in line with the stud against compression of the spring when a load is applied. **FIG 10:1** shows a section through a ball joint assembly. Check the joint by grasping the tie rod adjacent to the joint and attempting to move the joint up and down. If any free movement can be felt in the ball joint without applying pressure, this indicates wear or a broken spring and the joint must be renewed.

Ball joint renewal:

To prevent ball joint housing damage while slackening the locknut, hold the housing by means of a spanner fitted on the flats provided (see **FIG 10:2**).

Use remover 817 or similar tool to detach the ball joint from the steering arm (see **FIG 10:3**). Unscrew the ball joint assembly from the tie rod, carefully counting the number of turns taken to do so.

Screw the new ball joint on to the tie rod by the same number of turns as counted during removal. Ensure that the mating tapers are clean and free from grease, then

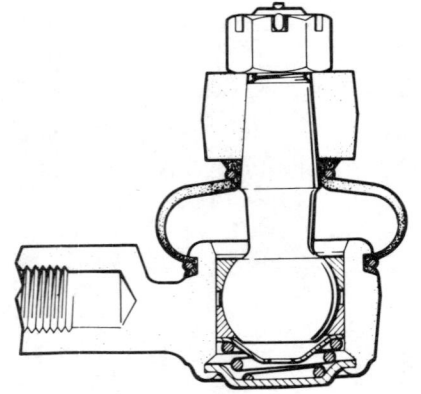

FIG 10:1   Section through a ball joint assembly

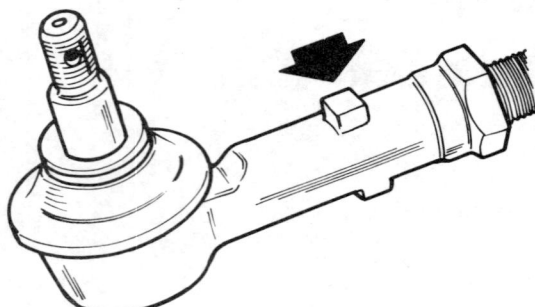

FIG 10:2   Flats machined on ball joint housing

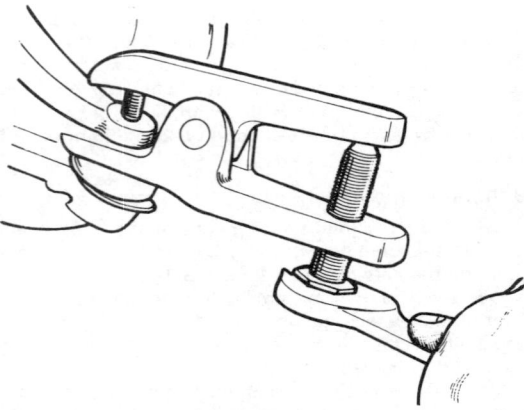

FIG 10:3   Removing the ball joint from the steering arm

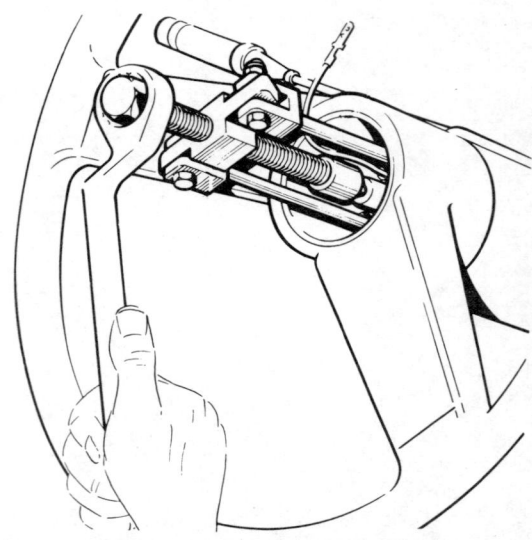

FIG 10:4   Steering wheel removal

fit the ball stud to the steering arm and tighten the nut securely. Tighten the nut a fraction more if necessary to align the splitpin holes, then fit and lock a new splitpin. Hold the ball joint by means of a spanner on the flats provided and tighten the locknut. On completion, check and if necessary adjust the front wheel alignment as described in **Section 10:7**.

10:3 Steering wheel removal

On the two-spoked steering wheel, pull the horn button assembly from steering wheel boss and disconnect single wire after depressing locking tongue. On the four-spoked steering wheel, carefully prise the horn button assembly from the steering wheel boss and disconnect the two wiring connectors after depressing the locking tongues.

Make sure that the road wheels are pointing straight-ahead, then remove the steering wheel securing nut. Use a suitable puller assembly, such as that shown in **FIG 10:4**, to pull the steering wheel from the shaft splines. The claws of the puller must point outwards. Do not strike the steering wheel or steering shaft during removal or refitting, as this may damage the plastic injections and render the shaft unfit for further service.

To refit the steering wheel, make sure that the road wheels are pointing straightahead and align the steering wheel with the spokes horizontal. Make sure that the spring is located over the shaft. Tighten the nut to the specified torque and secure with the tabwasher. Re-connect the wiring and install the horn push button assembly.

10:4 Steering shaft and column

The energy absorbing steering column and steering shaft are designed to collapse in the event of a heavy impact on the front of the car or on the steering wheel. The column has a lattice section which compresses when sufficient force is applied to either end. The steering shaft is of telescopic construction, the two sections being held together by plastic injections which shear under impact. Two pads with plastic injections are incorporated in the column attachment bracket which will shear when a heavy impact is imposed on the steering wheel.

It is essential that great care be taken when working on the steering column assembly to avoid applying any shock loading to the steering shaft column, column outer jacket or mounting brackets as this may cause irreparable damage.

Inspection for damage:

The steering column and mounting bracket can be checked for damage without the need for removal from the car, but if steering shaft damage is suspected, the shaft must be removed for inspection as described later.

Damage to the column and mounting bracket is indicated if gaps are observed between pads 1 and mounting bracket 2 shown in **FIG 10:5**. If gaps are found, the plastic injections which secure the pads to the bracket have sheared allowing the bracket to move forward and the steering column to collapse. Damage to the steering column itself is indicated by bulging or bending of the lattice section (see **FIG 10:6**). Note that this section is slightly corrugated during manufacture and collapsing will only have occurred if the overall length of section **A** is less than 263.4mm (10.37in).

To check the steering shaft for damage its overall length must be measured. If this is more than 802.5mm (31.59in) or less than 800.5mm (31.52in), it indicates that the plastic injections have sheared and the shaft must be renewed (see **FIG 10:7**).

Steering column components:

The steering intermediate shaft and universal joint, steering column canopies, steering lock, steering shaft assembly and the upper and lower steering column bearings can all be serviced without the need for steering column removal.

Intermediate shaft and universal joint:

To remove the intermediate shaft, first make sure that the steering is in the straightahead position, then remove the two pinch bolts arrowed in **FIG 10:8**. Slide the shaft down into the pinion flange until the upper universal joint is free from the steering shaft splines, then pull the universal shaft upwards to disconnect from the pinion flange.

The intermediate shaft universal joint is serviced as an assembly only and no attempt should be made to dismantle the unit. If the universal joint is removed, make sure that the spring is located over the steering shaft before reassembly. When refitting the intermediate shaft, note that the shaft must be installed with the larger cut-out towards the steering gear pinion flange. The universal joint pinch bolt should first be tightened to the specified torque then the intermediate and steering shafts pushed up against spring pressure before tightening the pinion flange pinch bolt to the specified torque.

Column canopies:
Removal:

Remove the two fixing screws and detach the lower column canopy. To facilitate withdrawal of the upper

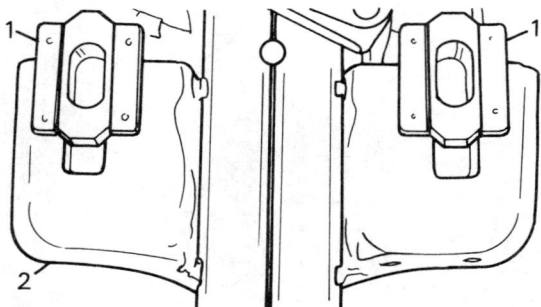

FIG 10:5 Checking the column mounting for gaps between pads 1 and bracket 2

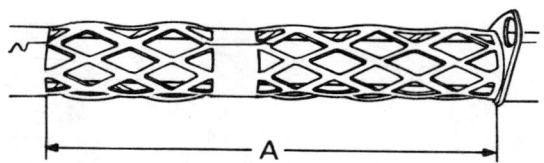

FIG 10:6 Checking length of lattice section of steering column

FIG 10:7 Locations of the steering shaft plastic injections

FIG 10:8 Intermediate shaft pinch bolts

FIG 10:9   Lower instrument panel securing screws

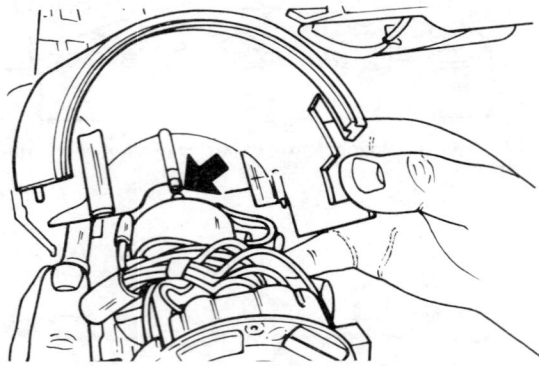

FIG 10:10   Upper canopy spigot

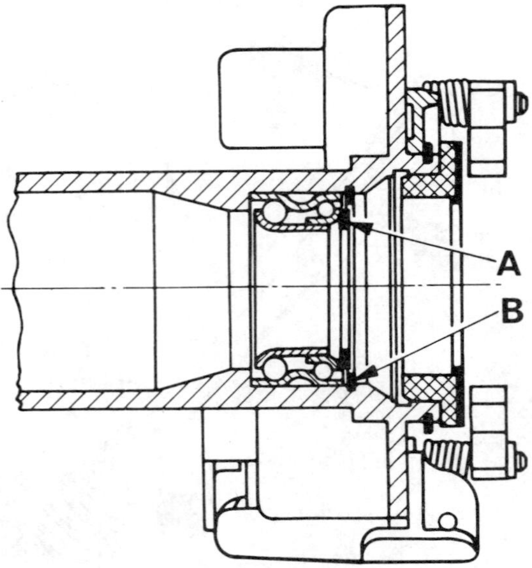

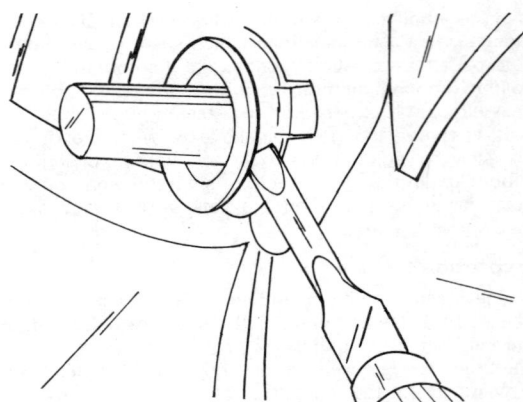

FIG 10:12   Removing column lower bearing

canopy, first remove the righthand instrument lower panel which is secured by the two screws shown arrowed in **FIG 10:9**. The canopy can then be withdrawn, after removing the column upper mounting nuts and lowering the column slightly.

Refitting:

Refit in the reverse order of removal, making sure that the spigot arrowed in **FIG 10:10** locates in the hole in the steering column.

Steering column bearings:

Upper bearing renewal:

Remove the steering wheel, spring and upper and lower column canopies as described previously. Remove the switch housing, which is secured to the steering column by three bolts. Carefully lever the horn button contact ring from the switch housing at the top of the steering column, ensuring that the lead is not damaged.

Refer to **FIG 10:11**. Remove thrust ring **A** and retaining clip **B**, then pull the bearing from the switch housing using a suitable puller tool.

Carefully press the new bearing into position, making sure that it is correctly installed as shown in **FIG 10:11**. Make sure that the horn button contact ring is fully installed in the housing and that the lead is pulled back into the wiring harness. Refit the remaining components in the reverse order of removal.

Lower bearing renewal:

Remove the intermediate shaft and universal joint assembly as described previously. Refer to **FIG 10:12** and carefully prise the bearing from the nylon retainer, ensuring that both inner and outer tracks are removed together. The nylon retainer may then be removed from the steering column.

Lubricate the 27 balls in the new bearing with a recommended grade of grease and assemble inner and outer tracks to the nylon retainer, making sure that the lip of the inner track which is arrowed in **FIG 10:13** is located through the retainer. Push the bearing and retainer fully into the steering column, making sure that the spigot on the retainer locates the slot in the column.

FIG 10:11   Column upper bearing installation

Refit the intermediate shaft and universal joint assembly as described previously.

Steering shaft removal:

Remove the intermediate shaft upper pinch bolt arrowed in **FIG 10:8**. Remove the steering wheel, column canopies, switch housing and upper bearing assembly as described previously. Withdraw the steering shaft from the column assembly. Check the steering shaft for damage as described previously. Refitting is a reversal of the removal procedure.

Steering column removal:

The steering shaft and column components can be completely dismantled while the column is mounted in the vehicle, as described previously. However, if it is necessary to remove the column, the lower mounting shear-head bolt, which is arrowed in **FIG 10:14**, should be centre-punched then drilled with a 3mm ($\frac{1}{8}$in) diameter high-speed drill and removed using a suitable extractor tool.

Before installing the steering column, ensure that the rubber gaiter is in a serviceable condition and correctly located over the aperture in lower dash panel. If the shaft and column are being installed as an assembly, ensure the spring is positioned over the shaft and that the cut-out in shaft is towards pinch bolt side of universal joint.

With the column mounting and steering coupling nuts and bolts loosely assembled, initially tighten a new steering column mounting shearhead bolt to a torque of 11Nm (8lb ft). Tighten the column upper mounting nuts and coupling pinch bolt to specified torque, check that the steering gear operates smoothly, then finally tighten the shearhead bolt until the head breaks off.

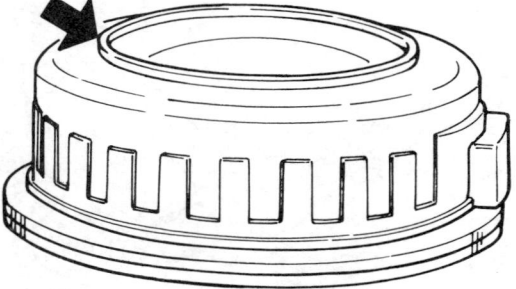

FIG 10:13   Column lower bearing assembly

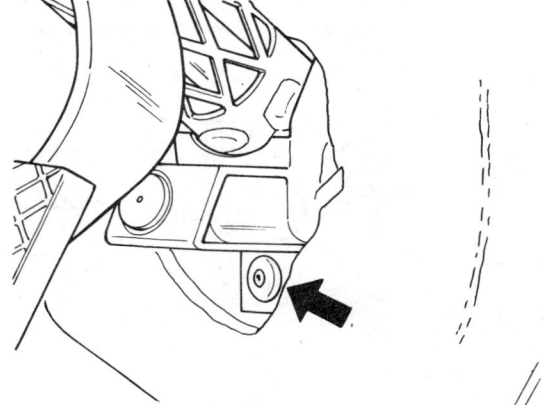

FIG 10:14   Column lower mounting shearhead bolt

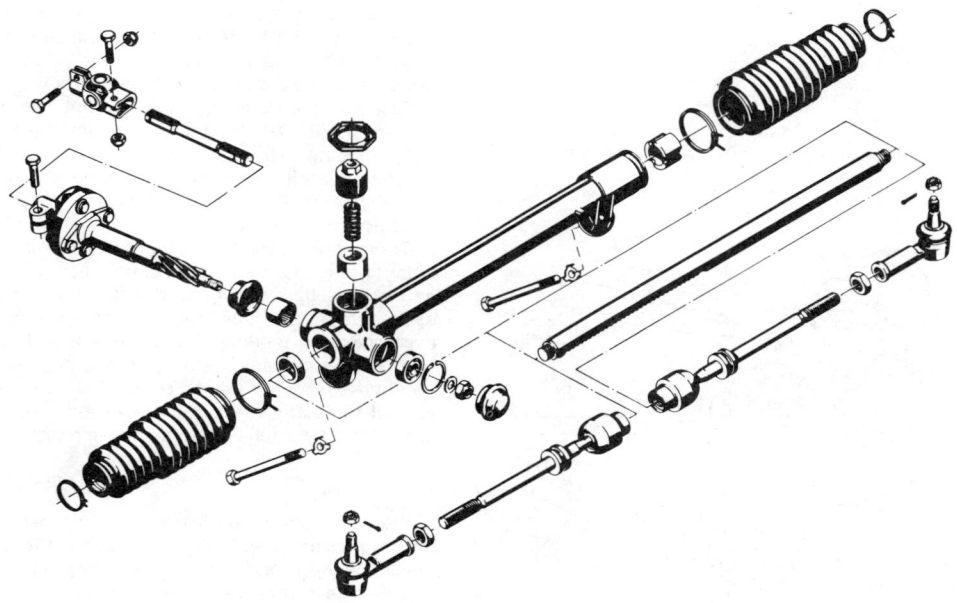

FIG 10:15   Steering gear components

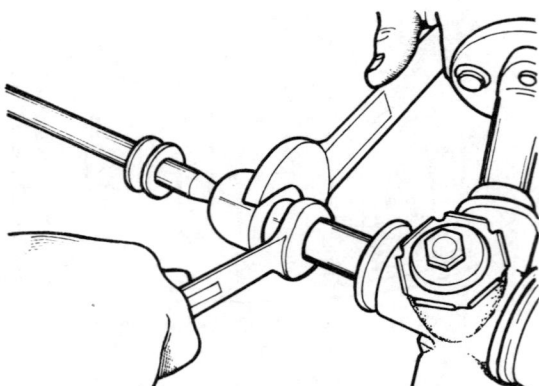

FIG 10:16   Tie rod and inner ball joint removal

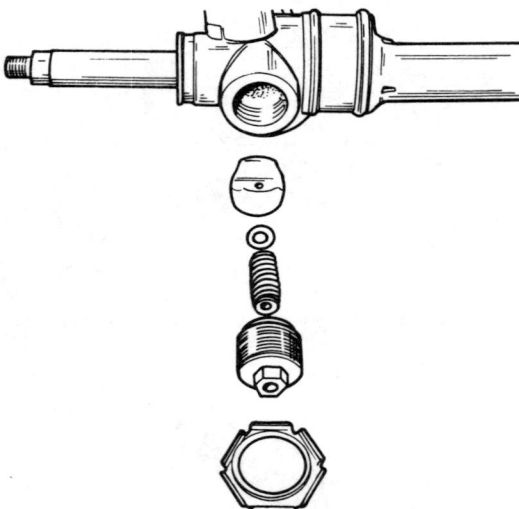

FIG 10:17   Rack and pinion adjustment mechanism

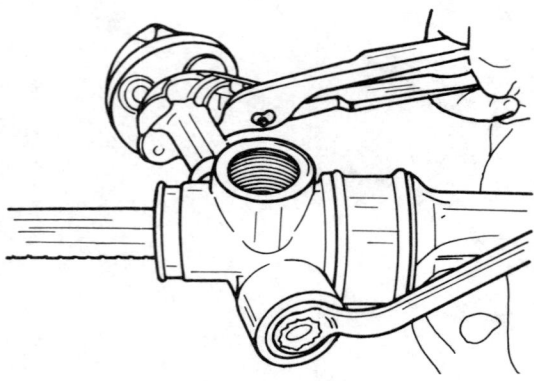

FIG 10:18   Removing pinion shaft nut

10:5 Steering gear

The steering rack is supported at both ends of the steering gear housing by pre-finished bushes. The pinion is supported in the housing by means of a needle roller bearing at the upper end and a ballbearing on the lower end of the shaft. A spring loaded adjustable thrust bearing controls the loading of the rack with the pinion. Lock stops integral with the steering knuckle contact pads on the suspension lower arms to control steering lock. **FIG 10:15** shows the steering gear components.

Removal:

Remove the underpan, if fitted. Make sure that the steering is in the straightahead position. Detach the tie rod ball joints from the steering arms as described in **Section 10:2**. Remove the intermediate shaft lower pinch bolt, shown by the lower arrow in **FIG 10:8**. Lift the intermediate shaft to disengage from the steering gear pinion shaft. If the coupling will not slide away freely, ease the assembly by turning the steering wheel each way. Do not strike the coupling with a hammer as this may damage the plastic injections in the steering shaft. Remove the bolts securing the steering gear to the front axle crossmember, then carefully remove the assembly from the vehicle.

Dismantling:

Remove the tie rod outer ball joint assemblies as described in **Section 10:2**. Release the retaining clips and remove the rubber gaiters from the tie rods. Hold the rack with one spanner and use a second spanner to remove the tie rod and inner ball joint assembly, as shown in **FIG 10:16**.

Slacken the locknut and remove the adjusting screw, spring, washer and thrust bearing from the rack housing, as shown in **FIG 10:17**. Withdraw the dust cover and hold the pinion shaft while removing the pinion retaining nut as shown in **FIG 10:18**. Remove the pinion shaft and rack, withdrawing the rack from the pinion end of the housing to avoid damaging the housing bushes.

Remove the retaining circlip from the housing as shown in **FIG 10:19**, then drive out the lower pinion shaft bearing. The upper pinion shaft needle bearing can be pulled from the housing using a suitable internal race extractor. Alternatively, drive out the bearing using a suitable mandrel and spacer.

Thoroughly clean all components and inspect for wear or damage. Renew any components found to be in an unserviceable condition. Check the bearing bushes at each end of the rack housing for wear or scoring. If excessive rack working clearance is found to be due to worn bushes, or if any bush is scored or otherwise damaged, the bushes should be renewed. Due to the need for special tools and press equipment, this work should be carried out by a fully equipped service station.

Reassembly:

Press the pinion shaft upper needle bearing into the housing using a suitable tube. Install the pinion shaft lower bearing and secure with the circlip. Fill the steering gear housing bore between the bushes with approximately 50g (2oz) of an approved grade of grease.

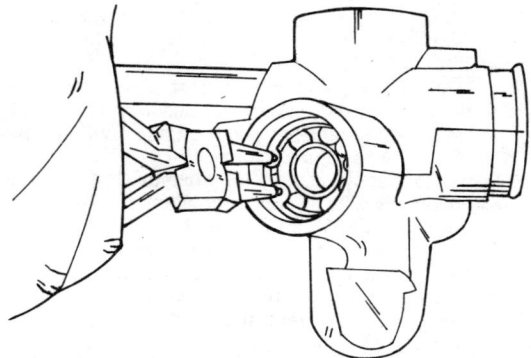

FIG 10:19   Lower pinion shaft bearing and circlip

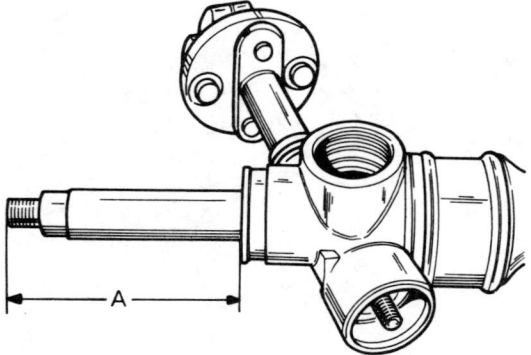

FIG 10:20   Install the rack so that protrusion A is equal on both sides

Install the rack into the housing from the pinion end and position the rack so that it protrudes an equal distance from each end of the housing, as shown at **A** in **FIG 10:20**.

Lubricate the pinion shaft and housing with approved grade of grease and fit the shaft so that the slot in the coupling is aligned with rack thrust bearing adjustment screw. Fit the washer to the pinion shaft, then tighten the retaining nut to the specified torque and install the dust cover. Install the rack thrust bearing, spring and adjusting screw to the steering gear housing. Make sure that the rack is still in the midway position and tighten the adjuster screw until a resistance is felt, then back off the screw 30° (A) to 60° (B) (see **FIG 10:21**). Make sure that the steering gear operates without binding through the full movement of the rack, then tighten the locknut to the specified torque.

Install the tie rod and inner ball joint assemblies to the rack ends and tighten to the specified torque. Use staking lever VR2213 or other suitable means to lock the assemblies in position, as shown in **FIG 10:22**. Fit the rubber gaiters and secure with the clips. Fit the outer tie rod ball joint assemblies to the tie rods, making sure that they are screwed on by equal amounts, as described in **Section 10:2**.

Refitting:

Centralise the steering gear and align the flat on the steering shaft with the pinion coupling flange. Do not tighten the coupling pinch bolt at this stage. Tighten the steering gear mounting bolts and nuts to the specified torque and secure with the lock tabs. Install the coupling pinch bolt, then push the intermediate and steering shafts up against spring pressure before tightening the pinch bolt to specified torque. Connect the tie rod ball joints to the steering arms as described in **Section 10:2**. On completion, adjust the tie rods to obtain the correct front wheel alignment as described in **Section 10:7**.

10:6 Steering column lock

The steering lock cylinder can be removed after detaching the column lower canopy as described previously. Turn the key to position 1 then depress the retainer by inserting a length of wire in the hole as shown in **FIG 10:23**. The ignition and starter switch and wiring harness can be withdrawn after removing the two attaching screws. To avoid damage to the steering column

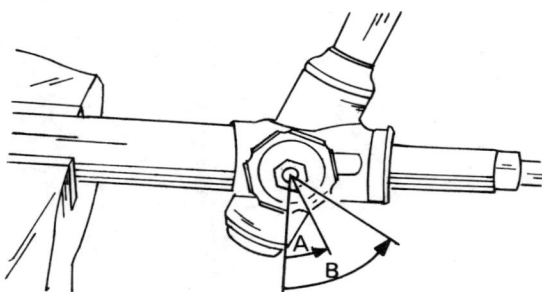

FIG 10:21   Setting rack adjustment screw in correct position

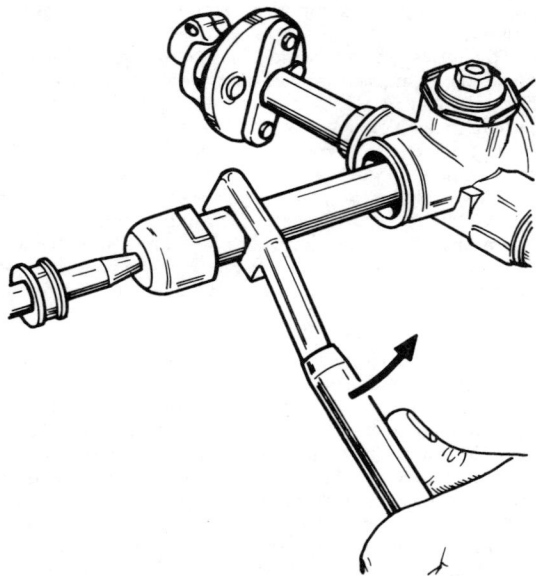

FIG 10:22   Staking the tie rod ball joint attachments

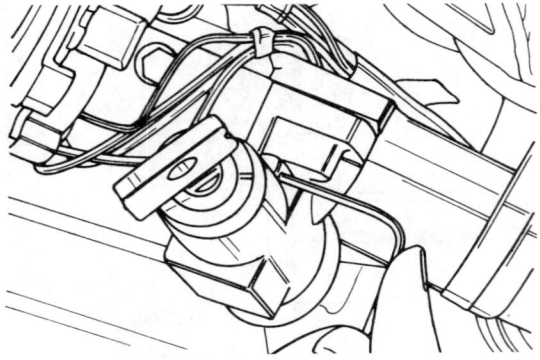

FIG 10:23   Lock barrel removal

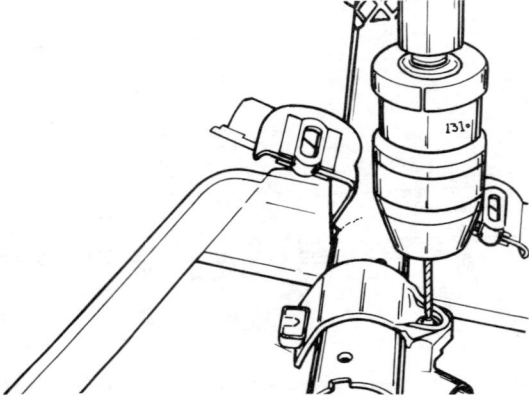

FIG 10:24   Lock assembly shearhead bolt location

lock, ignition and starter switch or lock barrel, only withdraw either the switch or lock barrel independently, leaving the other component retained in the steering column lock.

To remove the steering lock assembly, first remove the steering column assembly as described in **Section 10:4**. The lock can be released from the column after centre-punching and drilling the shearhead bolt with a 3mm ($\frac{1}{8}$in) diameter high-speed drill as shown in **FIG 10:24**, then removing the bolt with a suitable extractor tool. When installing the lock, tighten the shearhead bolt sufficiently to hold the lock in position then check the operation of the lock before finally tightening the bolt until the head shears off. Install the steering column assembly as described in **Section 10:4**.

10:7   Front wheel alignment

Front wheel alignment is correct when the wheels toe-in by 30' to 50', which is equivalent to 2.8 to 4.8mm (0.11 to 0.19in) at the wheel rims. Although this measurement is best made and the adjustment set by a service station having special optical equipment, an acceptable degree of accuracy can be obtained by using the following method, provided that a suitable track-setting gauge is available.

Place the car on level ground with the wheels in the straightahead position. Make sure that the tyres are correctly inflated.

Check the toe-in setting with the gauge equipment. If toe-in is not within the limit stated, adjustment will be required.

To adjust front wheel alignment, first release the inner circlips from the tie rod gaiters and position the circlips over the ends of the rack, so that the gaiters will not be twisted when the tie rods are turned.

Slacken each outer ball joint locknut, holding the ball joint assembly with a spanner on the flats provided to avoid damage (see **FIG 10:2**). Both tie rods have right-hand threads. Adjust the toe-in by turning the rods by equal amounts, so that the same amount of thread is visible at each end. Tighten the locknuts and recheck the toe-in. On completion, refit the circlips securing the rubber gaiters.

Toe-out on turns is a measurement which is not adjustable, this being controlled by the shape of the steering arms. Its purpose is to enable the wheels to be turned so that the inside front wheel on a turn can follow a path with a smaller radius than the outside wheel. Special equipment is needed to accurately check these settings. If the measurements do not come within the specified limits given in **Technical Data** it indicates that the steering arms are distorted and that the faulty components must be renewed.

10:8   Fault diagnosis

(a)   Wheel wobble

1 Unbalanced wheels and tyres
2 Slack steering connections
3 Incorrect steering geometry
4 Excessive play in steering gear
5 Steering gear loose on crossmember
6 Worn hub bearings

(b)   Wander

1 Check 2, 3, 4 and 5 in (a)
2 Front and rear wheels not in line
3 Uneven tyre pressures
4 Uneven tyre wear
5 Defective dampers
6 Weak coil spring

(c)   Heavy steering

1 Incorrect steering geometry
2 Very low tyre pressures
3 Lack of lubricant in steering gear
4 Tie rod or suspension ball joints tight
5 Wheel alignment incorrect
6 Steering column out of line or strained
7 Steering shaft bent or damaged
8 Steering shaft bearings tight

(d)   Lost motion

1 Play in intermediate shaft joint
2 Loose steering wheel
3 Steering gear loose on crossmember
4 Play in steering gear rack and pinion
5 Worn tie rod ball joints
6 Worn suspension ball joints

(e)   Irregular front tyre wear

1 Front wheel alignment incorrect
2 Front wheel geometry incorrect
3 Tyre pressures incorrect

CHAPTER 11

THE BRAKING SYSTEM

11 : 1 Description

The braking system follows conventional practice, with hydraulically operated disc brakes on the front wheels, drum brakes on the rear wheels and a cable operated handbrake linkage which operates on the rear brakes only. A vacuum servo unit to assist the pressure applied at the brake pedal is a standard fitment. A brake pressure regulating valve fitted in the hydraulic circuit reduces hydraulic pressure supplied to the rear brakes according to the load on the pedal, to minimise the possibility of the rear wheels locking under heavy braking.

The hydraulic system is of the dual circuit type, in which separate circuits are used for the front and rear brakes. The master cylinder is so designed that a failure in one half of the system will still allow the other half to operate, though with increased pedal stroke, so that the car can be safely stopped. As well as increased pedal stroke the overall efficiency of the braking system will be reduced as only two brakes will be operated. Such a fault should receive immediate attention.

The master cylinder is operated from the brake pedal via the servo unit by a short pushrod and coupling. Fluid pressure from the master cylinder is conveyed to the brake unit by means of the brake pipes and hoses.

11 : 2 Routine maintenance

According to master cylinder type, either a single reservoir with an internal division to separate supplies for the two circuits or a twin reservoir unit may be fitted.

Regularly check the level of fluid in the master cylinder reservoirs and replenish if necessary. Wipe dirt from around the cap before removing it and check that the vent holes in the cap are unobstructed. The fluid level should be maintained at the MAX mark on the reservoir. If such a mark is not provided, top up to a level approximately 12mm ($\frac{1}{2}$in) below the top of the reservoir. On twin reservoir units, make sure that both reservoirs are equally filled.

If frequent topping up is required, the system should be checked for leaks, but it should be noted that with disc brake systems the fluid level will drop gradually over a period of time due to the movement of caliper pistons compensating for friction pad wear. The recommended brake fluid is Castrol/Girling Universal Brake Clutch Fluid. **Never use anything but the recommended fluid.**

Before installing the top cover on twin reservoir units, make sure that the diaphragms are returned to their original shape as shown in **FIG 11 : 1.**

At the intervals recommended in the manufacturer's

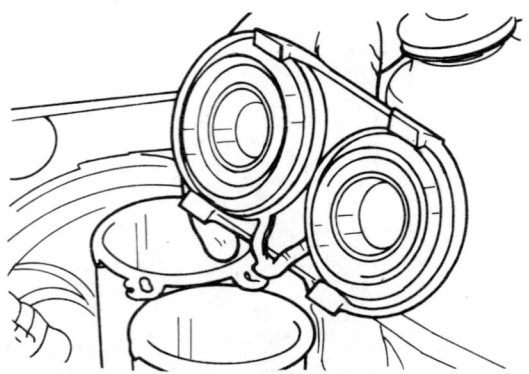

FIG 11:1   Cover diaphragms on Delco-Moraine master cylinder reservoirs

service schedule, the brake fluid in the system should be completely changed. This can be carried out by opening the bleed screws and pumping out the old brake fluid by operating the brake pedal. The system should then be filled with fresh brake fluid of the correct type and the brakes bled as described in **Section 11:9**. Alternatively, the work can be carried out very quickly by pressure-bleeding at a service station. Remember that brake fluid is poisonous, and that it will damage paintwork.

Checking brake pads and linings:

Regularly check the thickness of friction lining material on the front brake pads. To check front brake pad thickness, raise the front of the car and remove the road wheels. Look into the front of the caliper recess and examine the friction pads. If any friction lining has worn to a thickness of 1.5mm (0.06in) or if any lining is cracked or oily, all four friction pads must be renewed. **Do not renew pads singly or on one side of the car only as uneven braking will result.**

To check the lining thickness on rear brakes, the brake drum must be removed as described in **Section 11:4**. If any lining has worn down almost to the rivet heads, or if any lining is damaged or oily, all four rear brake linings should be renewed. It is not recommended that owners attempt to reline brake shoes themselves. It is important that the linings be properly bedded to the shoes and ground for concentricity with the brake drum. For this reason, it is best to obtain sets of replacement shoes on an exchange basis or have the shoes relined at a service station.

Brake adjustment:

Whenever brake pedal travel becomes excessive, the drum brakes should be adjusted to move the brake shoes closer to the drums. Always check that the linings are not worn to the limit before carrying out the adjustment procedures described in **Section 11:4**.

Adjustment of the rear brake shoes will normally maintain the handbrake adjustment correctly, but if the handbrake cable has been stretched in service, or if the mechanism has been reassembled after overhaul, the handbrake should be adjusted as described in **Section 11:8**.

Disc brakes are self-adjusting, due to the action of the operating pistons in the calipers. These pistons are returned to the rest position after each brake operation by the piston seals, the seals being slightly stretched during brake operation. As the friction pads wear, the piston will travel further than before and move through the stretched seal a little, the seal returning the piston to a new position nearer to the pad when the brakes are released.

11:3   Disc brakes

The brake discs are in unit with the front wheel hubs, the removal and maintenance of the hub assemblies being described in **Chapter 9**, **Section 9:2**. The discs are secured to the hub by four recess-headed bolts and can be detached after front hub removal. The disc brake calipers are twin piston units of either ATE or Girling manufacture, both types being similar in design and construction.

Disc brake pad renewal:

Apply the handbrake, raise the front of the car and safely support on floor stands. Remove the road wheels. Siphon sufficient brake fluid from the reservoirs to bring the level down to the halfway mark. If this is not done, fluid will overflow when the new pads are fitted and the pistons pressed back into position.

FIG 11:2 shows disc brake caliper components. On Girling units, remove spring clips 10 and drive out the retaining pins 11 towards the outside of the car. On ATE units, remove retaining pins 9 by driving them out towards the inside of the car. In either case, collect the pad retaining spring as the pins are removed.

Remove the brake pads and shims, using thin-nosed pliers if necessary. Mark the pads for refitting in their original positions if they are not to be renewed.

Check that the new pads are of the correct type and that they are free from grease, oil and dirt. Clean dirt and rust from the caliper before installing the pads. To enable the new pads to be fitted, push the caliper pistons down into their bores to allow for the extra thickness of the pads. Note that this operation will cause the brake fluid level in the master cylinder reservoir to rise, this being the reason for siphoning off some of the fluid. Use a flat wooden lever to push in the first piston, then install the pad and shim on that side. Press in the piston on the opposite side, then install the second pad and shim. If the shims are of the type shown in **FIG 11:2**, make sure that they are installed the correct way up, with the D-shaped cut-out pointing downwards. Refit the retaining pins and spring, making sure that the spring is correctly located. On Girling units, install the spring clips to lock the retaining pins. On ATE units, drive the retaining pins in until they lock in place in the caliper body. If a pin is found to be loose, it should be discarded and a new one installed in its place.

On completion, operate the brake pedal several times to bring the pads close to the disc. If this is not done, the brakes may not function the first time that they are used. Check that the pads are free to move slightly in the calipers, this indicating that the pad retaining pins are not fouling the pads. Refit the road wheels and lower the car. Top up the master cylinder reservoir to the correct level

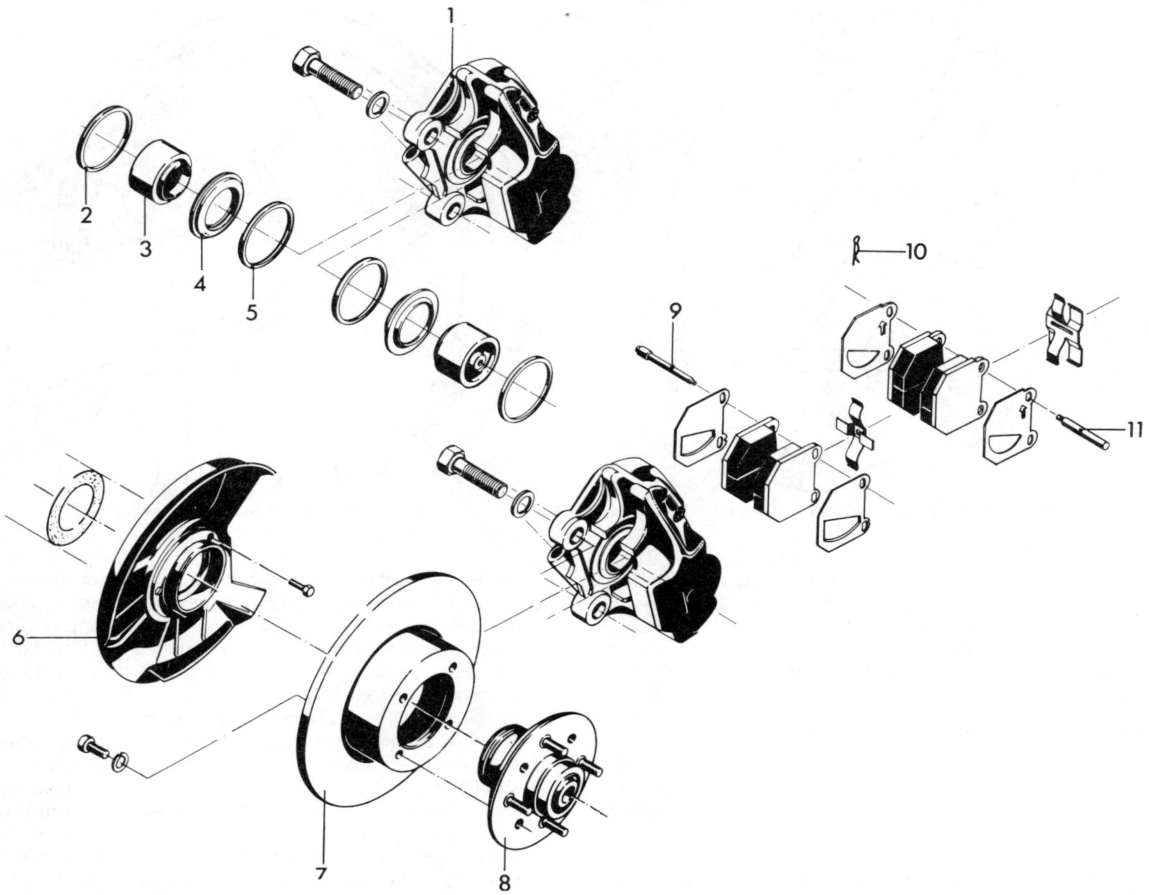

FIG 11:2 Disc brake caliper components

Key to Fig 11:2   1 Caliper body   2 Seal   3 Piston   4 Dust boot   5 Spring clip   6 Disc shield   7 Brake disc
8 Wheel hub   9 Retaining pin, ATE unit   10 Spring clip   11 Retaining pin, Girling unit

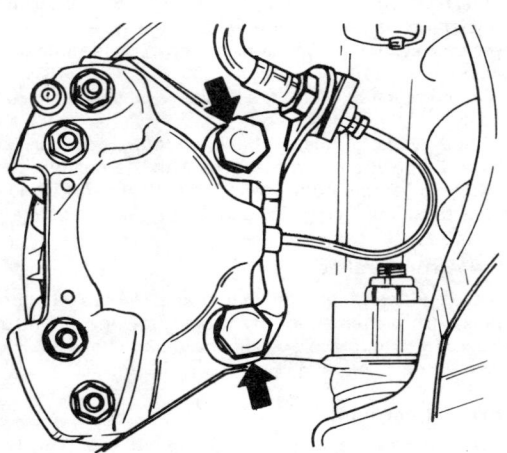

FIG 11:3 Caliper mounting bolts

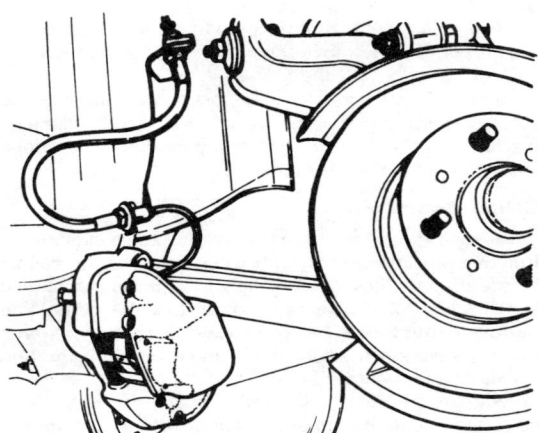

FIG 11:4 Supporting caliper to prevent damage to hose

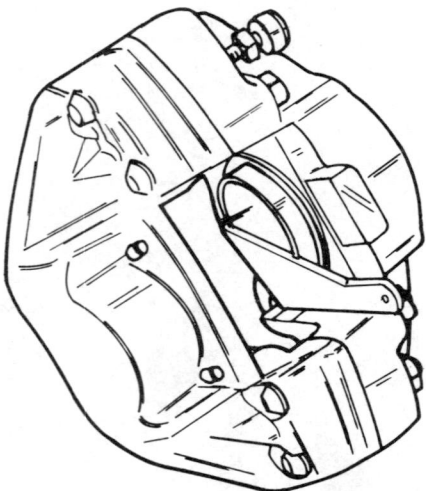

FIG 11:5　Checking piston offset

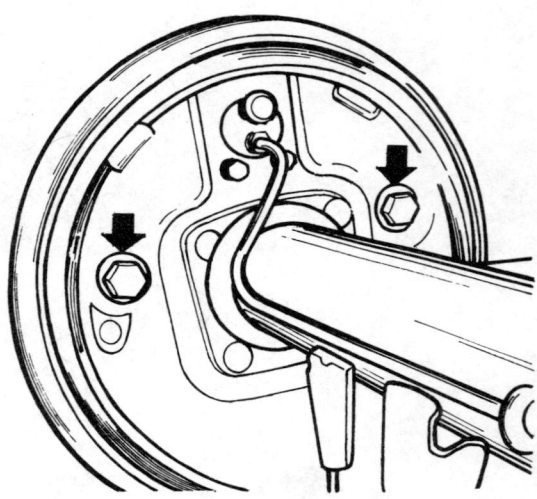

FIG 11:6　Drum brake adjusters

with new brake fluid, then road test the car to check the brakes. New brake pads should be run in gently to ensure that they bed correctly to the discs and to ensure maximum service life. To do this, avoid any unnecessary heavy braking for a distance of approximately 200km (125 miles).

Removing and refitting a caliper:

Apply the handbrake, raise the front of the car and safely support on floor stands before removing the road wheel. Remove the brake pads from the caliper as described previously.

If the caliper is to be removed for access to other components, unscrew the retaining bolts arrowed in **FIG 11:3** to release the caliper from the steering knuckle, but leave the bolts in position in the caliper body to retain the hose mounting bracket. Wire the assembly to the upper hose bracket as shown in **FIG 11:4** to prevent the hose from being strained. If the caliper is to be overhauled, disconnect the brake pipe from the caliper body and plug the end of the pipe to prevent fluid loss or the entry of dirt. Remove the two fixing bolts arrowed in **FIG 11:3** and lift off the caliper.

Refitting is a reversal of the removal procedure, taking care not to strain the brake pipe or hose. If the brake pipe was disconnected, bleed the braking system as described in **Section 11:9** on completion.

Caliper overhaul:

Remove the caliper assembly as described previously. Remove dirt and grease from the outside of the caliper before dismantling. If two calipers are to be dismantled at the same time, take care not to mix the parts. **The calipers must not be separated into two halves during servicing.** All work is carried out with the two halves bolted together.

Remove the spring clip and rubber dust cover from one piston, then fit a suitable clamp to retain the opposite piston in the caliper. Fit a suitable block of wood between the clamp and piston to prevent damage to the piston as it

is removed. Eject the piston by applying a compressed air line to the fluid pipe connection. Keep the fingers clear as the piston may be ejected at high speed. Remove the wood block and pull the piston from the caliper bore with the fingers. Carefully remove the rubber piston seal from the groove in the caliper bore, taking care to avoid damage to the bore surfaces (see 2 in **FIG 11:2**).

Discard the rubber dust cover and seal and wash the piston and the cylinder bore with commercial alcohol, methylated spirits or clean approved brake fluid. **Use no other cleaner or solvent on brake components.** Inspect the piston for scoring, pitting or corrosion, which would dictate renewal. If the cylinder bore is not in perfect condition, a new caliper should be fitted.

Dip the new seal in clean brake fluid and install in the caliper groove, using the fingers only to avoid damage to the sealing lips. Dip the piston in brake fluid and fit crown first into the bore, taking care not to dislodge the seal. Press the piston down to the bottom of its bore, then fit the new dust cover and secure with the spring clip. Transfer the clamp to secure the piston just serviced, then repeat the servicing operations on the opposite side of the caliper.

On completion, refit the caliper as described previously.

Some types of piston have an offset cut-out and should be positioned in the bore with the cut-out at an angle of 20° to the bottom edge of the caliper. **FIG 11:5** shows this angle being checked with a suitable gauge.

11:4 Drum brakes

When working on the rear brakes, chock the front wheels to prevent the car from moving, then fully release the handbrake so that the brake shoes are clear of the drum.

Brake adjustment:

Raise the rear of the car and support safely on floor stands. Locate the two brake adjusters on the backplate

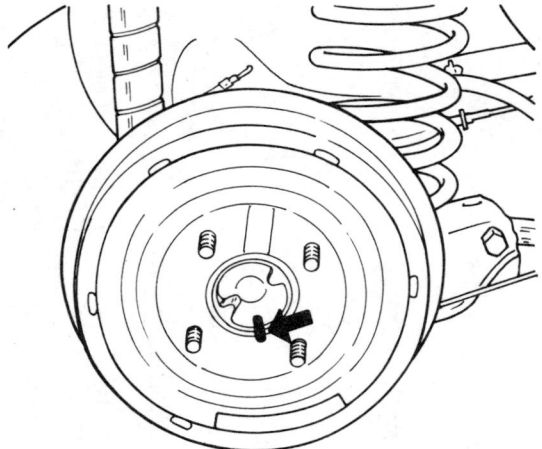

FIG 11:7   Marking brake drum position relative to axle

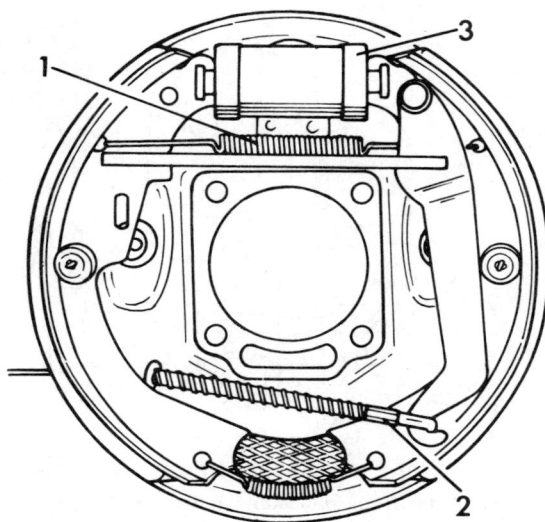

FIG 11:8   Brake shoe installation

as shown in **FIG 11:6**. Turn one adjuster at a time while spinning the road wheel. When the road wheel is locked against rotation, slacken the adjuster a little until the wheel is just free to turn without binding. Repeat the operation at the second adjuster on the same brake unit. Operate the footbrake and handbrake several times to centralise the shoes, then recheck the adjustment. Repeat the entire operation at the pair of adjusters on the opposite rear wheel.

Removing brake shoes:

Remove the hub cap and slacken the wheel nuts. Raise the rear of the car and support safely on floor stands, then remove the road wheels. Ensure that the handbrake is fully released. Mark the position of the brake drum relative to the axle shaft as shown in **FIG 11:7**, then slacken the brake adjusters fully as described previously and pull off the drum. If drum removal proves difficult, tap the unit gently with a soft-faced hammer. Do not use an ordinary hammer as this may crack the drum.

To remove the brake shoes, refer to **FIG 11:8**. First unhook the handbrake cable at point 2 then release the front shoe from the lower pedestal. Disconnect upper return spring 1 then detach the brake shoes and remove the lower return spring. Note that the rear shoe is serviced complete with handbrake operating lever.

Clean all dirt and grease from the inside of the brake assembly. Clean the inside surfaces of the brake drum, using a suitable solvent to remove all traces of grease.

Refitting:

Smear the shoe contact pads on the wheel cylinder, the pedestal, and the points on the flange plate which are arrowed in **FIG 11:9** sparingly with approved grease. Install the brake shoes in the reverse order of removal.

Lightly smear the axle shaft spigot with grease and install the brake drum. Refit the road wheel and tighten the securing nuts, then adjust the brake shoes as described previously. Check handbrake operation as described in **Section 11:8**.

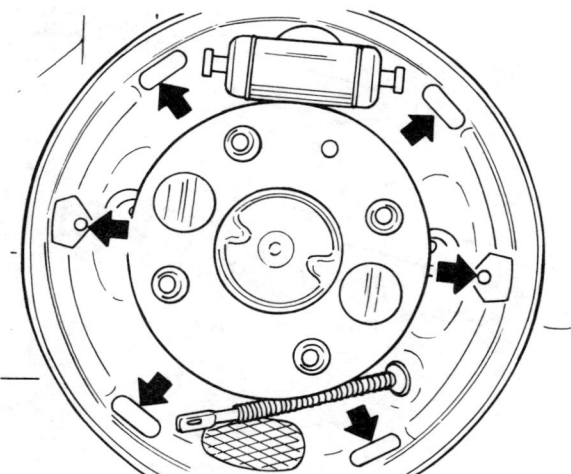

FIG 11:9   Grease points on brake flange plate

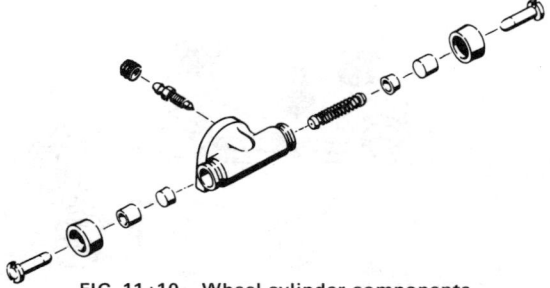

FIG 11:10   Wheel cylinder components

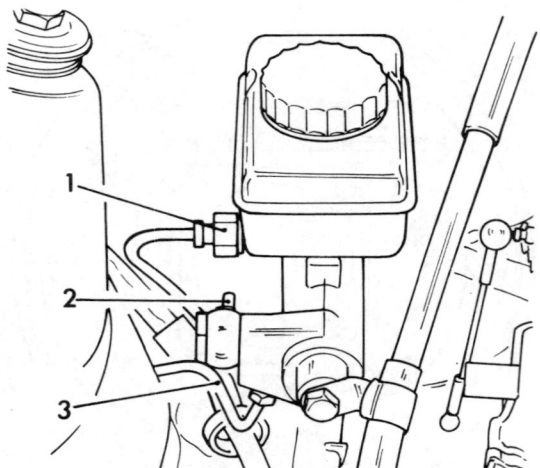

FIG 11:11　Typical master cylinder installation

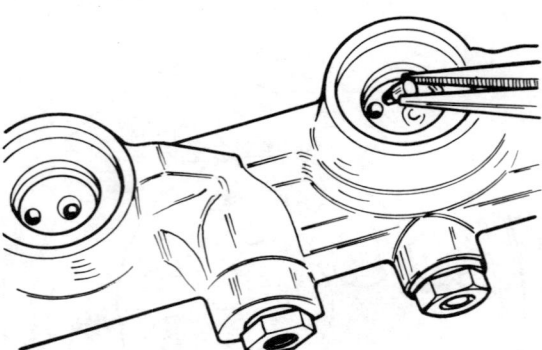

FIG 11:12　Stop pin removal, Delco-Moraine

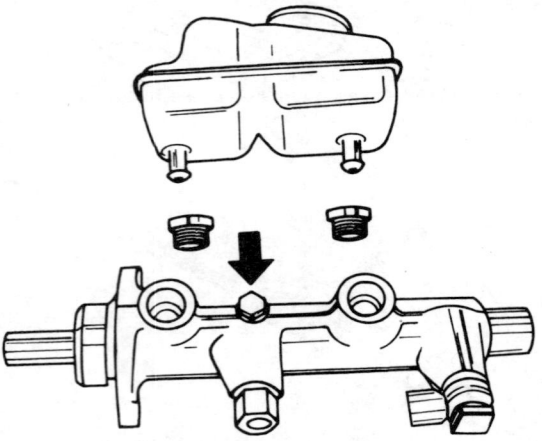

FIG 11:13　Stop screw removal, ATE

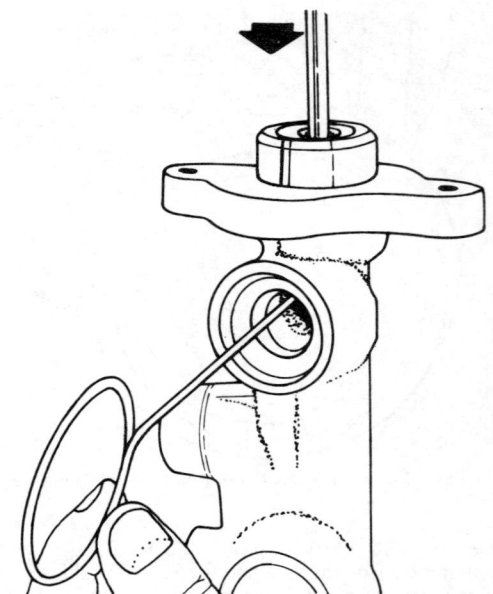

FIG 11:14　Retaining the primary piston against spring pressure

Servicing a wheel cylinder:

Raise the rear of the car and remove the road wheel and brake drum as described previously. Rotate the brake adjusters shown in **FIG 11:6** until the brake shoes are clear of the wheel cylinder pistons. Disconnect the brake fluid pipe from the wheel cylinder and plug the pipe to prevent fluid loss. Remove the mounting bolts and detach the wheel cylinder.

Remove the rubber dust boots then remove the pistons, seals and spring as shown in **FIG 11:10**. Discard the rubber dust boots and seals, then wash all remaining parts thoroughly in clean brake fluid of the correct type and inspect them for wear or damage. Any part which is unserviceable must be renewed.

Dip the pistons and new seals in brake fluid and reassemble them together with the spring, using the fingers only for this operation to avoid damage to the seals. Fill the rubber dust boots with a recommended grade of rubber grease and press them into place. **Do not use ordinary grease for this purpose.** Refit the wheel cylinder and secure with the two bolts, then reconnect the brake fluid pipe.

Smear the brake shoe contact faces sparingly with recommended grease and rotate the adjusters to fully return the shoe webs into the wheel cylinder pushrod slots. Refit the brake drum and road wheel as described previously. Bleed the braking system as described in **Section 11:9** before adjusting the brake shoes as described previously.

Rear brake shoe adjusters:

The rear brake shoe eccentric type adjusters are mounted on the flange plate. The adjusters incorporate a wave washer to provide preload. If a tight adjuster cannot be freed by turning back and forth with a spanner, or if an adjuster is excessively loose in the flange plate, a new flange plate must be fitted. No attempt should be made to lubricate adjusters or to remove from the flange plate. As renewal of the flange plate requires removal of the axle shaft and requires the selective fitting of shims during reassembly the work should be carried out by a fully equipped service station.

11:5 The master cylinder

The tandem master cylinder incorporates two pistons operating in a common bore. The primary piston operates the rear brakes through a check valve in the outlet port 1 (see **FIG 11:11**). The secondary piston operates the front brakes through two separate pipes, one to the lefthand side (2) and one to the righthand side (3).

Master cylinder removal:

Detach the fluid pipes from the master cylinder, plugging the ends of the pipes to prevent the entry of dirt. Plug the outlets in the master cylinder body to prevent loss of fluid. Note that brake fluid is toxic and can damage paintwork, so hold a piece of rag beneath the assembly to catch any spillage. Disconnect the cable clip from the end of the cylinder body, if fitted. Disconnect the switch cable from the master cylinder, if fitted. Remove the nuts securing the master cylinder to the vacuum servo unit, then lift the cylinder assembly from the car. Remove the top cover and empty the reservoir contents into a waste container.

Dismantling:

On Delco-Moraine units, remove the retaining clips from the bottom of each reservoir, then remove the reservoirs and seals from the master cylinder body. Withdraw the stop pin from the locating hole as shown in **FIG 11:12**. Take care not to lose this pin.

On ATE units, carefully pull the reservoir from the master cylinder body and withdraw the rubber sleeves. Remove the stop screw which is shown arrowed in **FIG 11:13**.

Depress the primary piston slightly and insert a length of wire into the primary piston bypass hole to hold the piston away from the retaining circlip, as shown in **FIG 11:14**. With the piston held down, remove the circlip as shown in **FIG 11:15** then remove the piece of wire and withdraw the primary piston. Discard the circlip. The secondary piston and spring may now be removed by tapping the cylinder body on a wooden block.

If necessary, remove the primary outlet port connector and check valve assembly. Note that if the check valve is faulty the assembly must be renewed complete. To dismantle the primary piston, the special factory tool or alternative suitable tool must be used as shown in **FIG 11:16**. Screw the two parts of the tool together then remove the locking ring from the rod as shown in **FIG 11:17**, or remove the screw from the rod, whichever is the case. If a locking ring is used, it must be discarded and a new one used during reassembly. Unscrew the tool and remove the piston and spring.

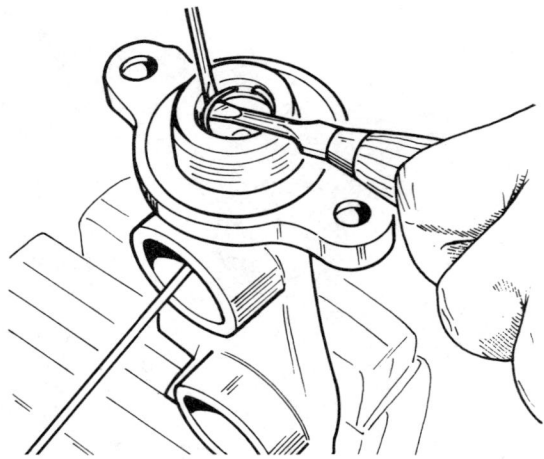

FIG 11:15   Primary piston retaining circlip

Servicing:

Wash all parts in commercial alcohol, methylated spirits or approved brake fluid. **Use no other cleaner or solvent on brake hydraulic system components.** Inspect the pistons and cylinder bore for score marks and inspect all parts for wear, damage or corrosion. Renew any faulty parts. Always use new rubber seals, locking rings and circlips.

Reassembly:

Observe absolute cleanliness to prevent the entry of dirt or any trace of oil or grease. Use the fingers only to fit the rubber piston seals to prevent damage. Take great care not to turn back the lips of the piston seals when installing them in the cylinder bore.

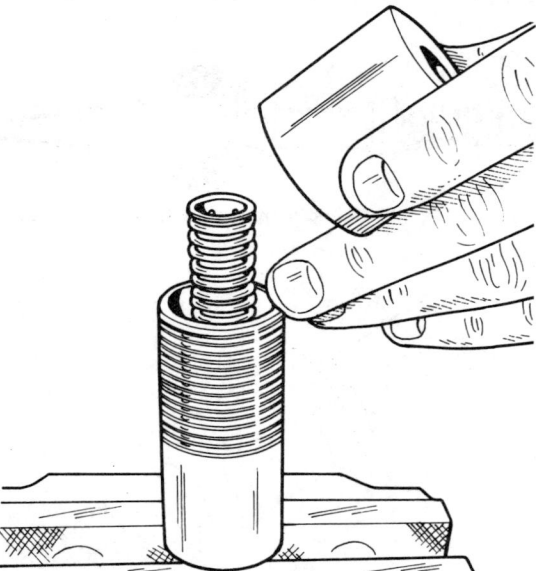

FIG 11:16 A special tool for compressing primary piston spring

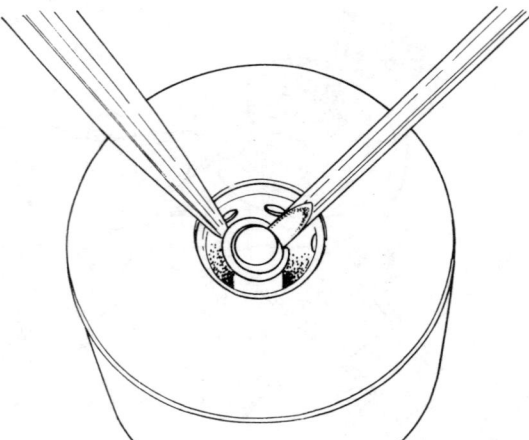

FIG 11:17 Removing primary piston locking ring

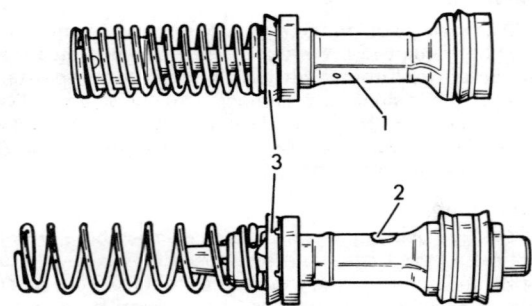

FIG 11:18 Primary piston 1, secondary piston 2 and seals 3

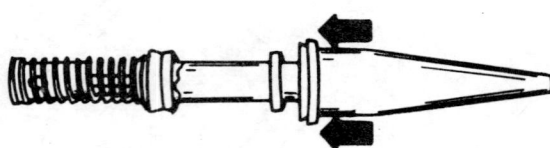

FIG 11:19 Installing piston seal with a special tool

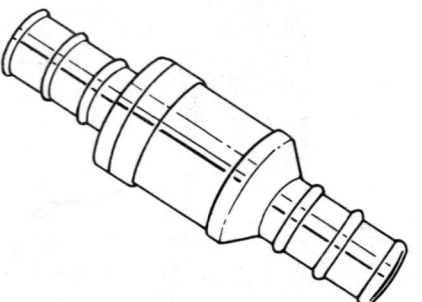

FIG 11:20 Vacuum servo check valve

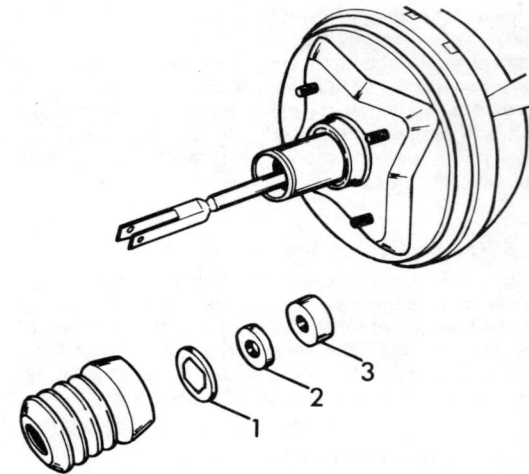

FIG 11:21 Vacuum servo filter assembly

The seals should be fitted to the primary piston 1 and secondary piston 2 as shown in **FIG 11:18**, making sure that the seal protector shims are fitted behind the front seals 3 of each piston. It is recommended that a cone-shaped special tool, such as that shown in **FIG 11:19**, is used when installing the seals in order to prevent seal deformation or damage. If the primary piston was dismantled, use the compressor tool to compress the primary piston return spring then fit a new locking ring or refit the locking screw, whichever is the case. Fit the pistons into the cylinder body then depress the primary piston and retain with a piece of wire as shown in **FIG 11:14**. Fit a new retaining circlip into the groove then remove the wire.

Install the spring and check valve, if removed. Install the secondary piston stop pin or stop screw. Smear the reservoir seals with brake fluid and press them firmly into the master cylinder body. Press the reservoir assembly firmly into the seals. On Delco-Moraine units, fit the reservoir retaining clips and make sure that they are correctly located and ensure that the diaphragms are returned to their original shape before fitting the reservoir cover.

Refitting:

This is a reversal of the removal procedure. On ATE units, always fit a new sealing ring between master cylinder and vacuum servo unit. On completion, fill the fluid reservoir to the correct level, then bleed the brakes as described in **Section 11:9**. Apply heavy pressure to the brake pedal and hold for at least 10sec, before examining the master cylinder for any signs of fluid leakage. Road test to check the operation of the brakes.

11:6 Vacuum servo unit

The vacuum servo unit operates to assist the pressure applied at the brake pedal and so reduce braking effort. The vacuum cylinder in the servo is connected to the engine inlet manifold by a hose. The vacuum servo unit is a sealed assembly and, if it is faulty or inoperative, a new unit must be fitted.

Testing:

To test the servo unit, switch off the engine and pump the brake pedal several times to clear all vacuum from the unit. Hold a steady light pressure on the brake pedal and start the engine. If the servo is working properly, the brake pedal will move further down without further foot pressure, due to the build up of vacuum in the system.

With the brakes off, run the engine to medium speed and turn off the ignition, immediately closing the throttle. This builds up a vacuum in the system. Wait one to two minutes, then try the brake action with the engine still switched off. If not vacuum assisted for two or three operations, the servo check valve is faulty. Poor overall performance of the vacuum servo unit can be caused by a clogged air filter.

Check valve renewal:

Remove and discard the old check valve, which is fitted in the hose between the servo unit and the inlet manifold. Make sure that the hose is clear, then fit a new check valve (see **FIG 11 : 20**) with the arrow on the valve body pointing towards the inlet manifold and the white section of the valve towards the servo.

Air filter renewal:

Working from the inside of the passenger compartment, remove the E-clip and pull out the clevis pin to disconnect the vacuum servo pushrod from the brake pedal. Refer to **FIG 11 : 21**. Pull the rubber boot from the pushrod, then remove retainer 1, silencer 2 and filter 3. When installing the new filter, ensure that the rubber boot is located correctly over the end cover.

When refitting the clevis to the brake pedal, check that brake pedal free play is 6 to 9mm (0.24 to 0.35in) measured at the pedal pad. If not, slacken the clevis locknut on the pushrod, then turn the clevis until the play is correct and firmly retighten the nut. Lubricate the clevis and pin with recommended grease, then lock with the E-clip.

11 : 7 Pressure regulating valve

The fluid pressure regulating valve is shown in **FIG 11 : 22**. The rear brake line fluid pressure from the master cylinder enters the valve at port **A** and passes to the rear brakes via port **B**. As pressure on the footbrake pedal increases, front and rear brake line pressures increase at the same rate until valve cut-in pressure is reached. From this point, front brake line pressure continues to increase at the same rate but the valve modifies the rear brake line pressure so that the rate of increasing pressure is reduced, thereby reducing the possibility of locking the rear brakes. Should a failure occur in the rear brake pressure system, full pressure will still be maintained in the front brakes. However, the valve is constructed in a manner which permits the reducing characteristic of the valve to be bypassed should a failure in front brake pressure occur, thereby delivering full pressure to the rear brakes. No attempts should be made to dismantle the valve if it is faulty, as it is serviced as a complete unit only. Removal and refitting of the valve is a straightforward procedure, bleeding the brakes on completion as described in **Section 11 : 9**.

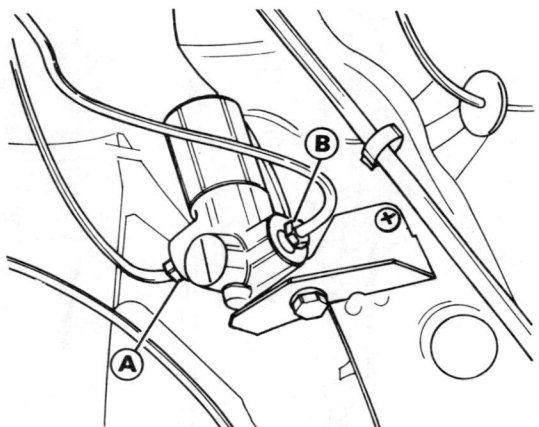

FIG 11 : 22   Brake fluid pressure regulating valve

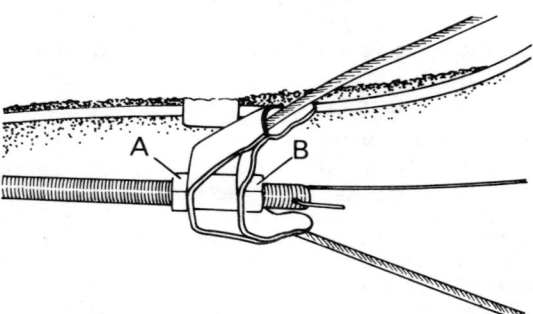

FIG 11 : 23   Handbrake cable adjustment mechanism

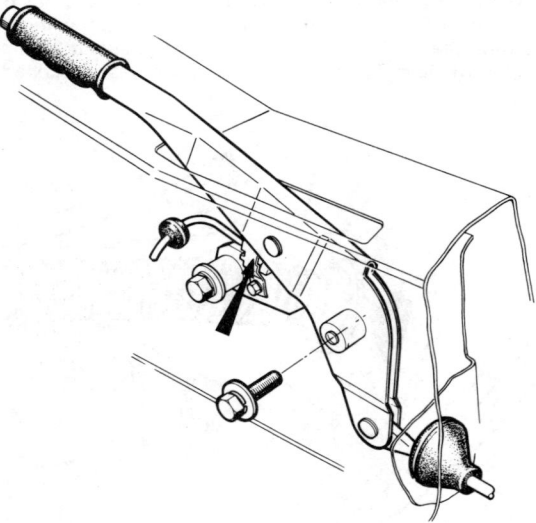

FIG 11 : 24   Handbrake lever mounting details. The warning light switch is arrowed

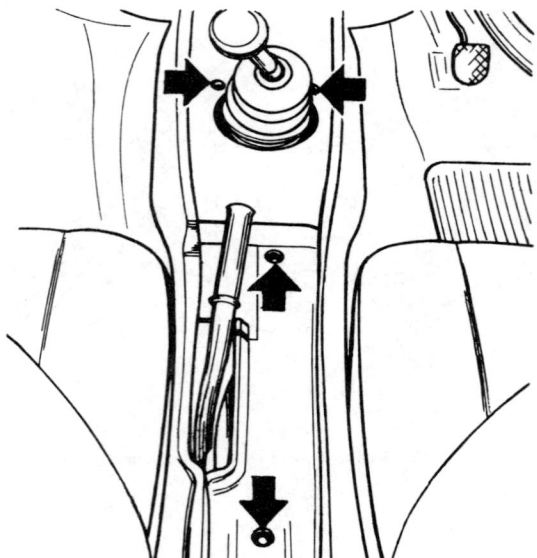

FIG 11:25 Console mounting screw positions

11:8 The handbrake

Handbrake adjustment:

Adjustment of the rear brake shoes will normally maintain handbrake adjustment correctly, but if the handbrake cable has stretched in service, or if the mechanism has been reassembled after overhaul, the handbrake should be adjusted in the following manner. Note that the rear brake shoe adjustment must always be checked first as described in **Section 11:4**.

A force of 25lb applied midway along the handbrake lever hand grip should raise the lever by four notches on the ratchet. If adjustment proves to be required, refer to **FIG 11:23** and slacken the locknut **A**. Rotate the nut **B** to eliminate any slackness in the cable but without causing the rear brakes to bind. After adjustment, check the movement of the handbrake lever as described

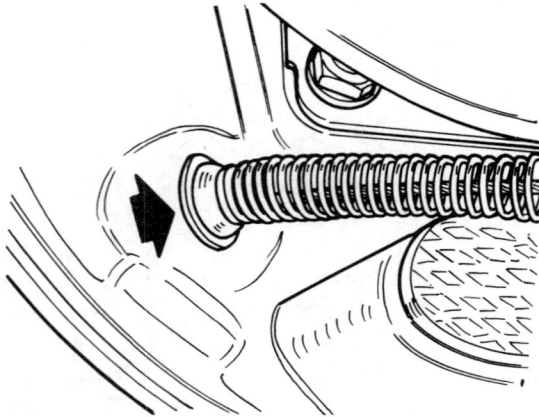

FIG 11:26 Handbrake cable guide at rear brake flange plate

previously and raise the rear of the car to check that the rear wheels rotate freely when the handbrake lever is released. On completion, tighten the locknut **A** to secure the adjustment.

Handbrake mechanism and cables:

The handbrake lever is bolted to a plate welded to the underside of the transmission tunnel (see **FIG 11:24**). The handbrake warning light switch (arrowed) is attached to the mounting bracket and actuated by the lever pawl. Access to the lever mounting bolts and warning light switch cable connector and grommet can be gained after removing the centre console, which is attached by four screws arrowed in **FIG 11:25**. The small filler plate should be lifted out prior to withdrawing the centre console. The lefthand front seat must be removed to enable the carpet to be raised for access to the lever mounting bolts. If the lever is to be removed, after removing the mounting bolts partially withdraw the lever and detach handbrake warning light switch. The lever may then be removed. After refitting, check handbrake cable adjustment as described previously.

The handbrake lever is connected to the rear cable equaliser by means of a relay rod. The one-piece rear handbrake cable passes through the equaliser, means for cable adjustment being provided as described previously. Nylon cable guides are located in brackets welded to the underbody and rear suspension lower arms. Eye-type connectors at each end of the cable hook into the brake shoe operating levers. A cable guide, which also acts as a stop for the cable return spring, is secured to each rear brake flange plate by an E-clip (see **FIG 11:26**). To gain access to the E-clip, the forward brake shoe must be removed as described in **Section 11:4**.

11:9 Bleeding the system

This is not routine maintenance and is only necessary if air has entered the hydraulic system due to parts being dismantled, or because the level in the master cylinder supply reservoir has been allowed to drop too low. The need for bleeding is indicated by a spongy feeling at the brake pedal accompanied by poor braking performance. Each brake must be bled in turn, starting with the one furthest from the master cylinder and finishing with the one nearest to the master cylinder.

Vacuum must be exhausted from the servo by depressing the brake pedal several times before starting the work and the engine must not be run whilst bleeding is carried out. Do not attempt to bleed the brakes with any drum or caliper removed.

Remove the reservoir cap and top up the reservoirs to the correct level with approved brake fluid. Clean dirt from around the first bleed screw and remove the rubber dust cap. Fit a length of rubber or plastic tube to the screw and lead the free end of the tube into a clean glass jar containing a small amount of approved brake fluid. The end of the tube must remain immersed in the fluid during the bleeding operation.

Unscrew the bleed screw about half a turn and have an assistant depress the brake pedal fully. With the pedal held down tighten the bleed screw. Allow the pedal to return fully and wait a few seconds for the master cylinder to refill with fluid before repeating the operation.

Continue operating the pedal in this manner until no air bubbles can be seen in the fluid flowing into the jar, then hold the pedal against the floor on a down stroke while the bleed valve is tightened. **Do not overtighten.**

At frequent intervals during the operation, check the level of fluid in the reservoir, topping up as needed. If the level drops too low air will enter the system and the operation will have to be restarted.

Remove the bleed tube, refit the dust cap and repeat the operation on each other brake unit in turn.

On completion, top up the fluid to the correct level. Discard all used fluid. Always store brake fluid in clean sealed containers to avoid air or moisture contamination.

11 :10 Fault diagnosis

(a) Spongy pedal

1 Leak in the system
2 Worn master cylinder
3 Leaking wheel or caliper cylinders
4 Air in the fluid system
5 Gaps between brake shoes and underside of linings

(b) Excessive pedal movement

1 Check 1 and 4 in (a)
2 Excessive lining or pad wear
3 Very low fluid level in supply reservoir
4 Rear brakes need adjustment

(c) Brakes grab or pull to one side

1 Distorted discs or drums
2 Wet or oily pads or linings
3 Loose flange plate or caliper
4 Disc or hub loose

5 Worn suspension or steering connections
6 Mixed linings of different grades
7 Uneven tyre pressures
8 Broken brake shoe return springs
9 Seized handbrake cable
10 Seized wheel cylinder or caliper piston

(d) Brakes partly or fully locked on

1 Swollen pads or linings
2 Damaged brake pipes preventing fluid return
3 Master cylinder compensating hole blocked
4 Master cylinder piston seized
5 Brake or pedal return spring broken
6 Dirt in the hydraulic system
7 Seized wheel cylinder or caliper piston
8 Rear brakes incorrectly adjusted
9 Seized handbrake mechanism or cable

(e) Brake failure

1 Empty fluid reservoir
2 Broken hydraulic pipe or hose
3 Ruptured master cylinder seal
4 Ruptured wheel cylinder or caliper seal

(f) Reservoir empties too quickly

1 Leaks in pipelines
2 Deteriorated cylinder seals

(g) Pedal yields under continuous pressure

1 Faulty master cylinder seals
2 Faulty wheel cylinder or caliper seals
3 Leak in brake pipe or hose

NOTES

CHAPTER 12

THE ELECTRICAL SYSTEM

12:1 Description

All models covered by this manual have 12-volt electrical systems in which the negative terminal of the battery is earthed to the car bodywork.

There are wiring diagrams in **Technical Data** at the end of this manual which will enable those with electrical experience to trace and correct faults.

Instructions for servicing the items of electrical equipment are given in this chapter, but it must be pointed out that it is not sensible to try to repair units which are seriously defective, electrically or mechanically. Such faulty equipment should be replaced by new or reconditioned units.

12:2 The battery

To maintain the performance of the battery, it is essential to carry out the following operations, particularly in winter when heavy current demands must be met.

Keep the top and surrounding parts of the battery clean and dry, as dampness can cause current leakage. Clean off corrosion from the metal parts of the battery mounting with diluted ammonia and coat them with anti-sulphuric paint. Clean the terminal posts and smear them with petroleum jelly, tightening the terminal clamps securely.

Check the battery earth lead connection to the car body for looseness or corrosion. High electrical resistance due to corrosion at the battery terminals can be responsible for a lack of sufficient current to operate the starter motor.

Regularly remove the screw caps from the battery and check the electrolyte level in each cell, topping up with distilled water if necessary to just cover the separator plates.

If a battery fault is suspected, test the condition of the cells with a hydrometer. **Never add neat acid to the battery. If it is necessary to prepare new electrolyte due to loss or spillage, add sulphuric acid to distilled water. It is highly dangerous to add water to acid.** It is safest to have the battery refilled with electrolyte if it is necessary by a service station.

The indications from the hydrometer readings of the specific gravity are as follows:

For climates below 27°C or 80°F	Specific gravity
Cell fully charged	1.270 to 1.290
Cell half discharged	1.190 to 1.210
Cell discharged	1.110 to 1.130
For climates above 27°C or 80°F	
Cell fully charged	1.210 to 1.230
Cell half discharged	1.130 to 1.150
Cell discharged	1.050 to 1.070

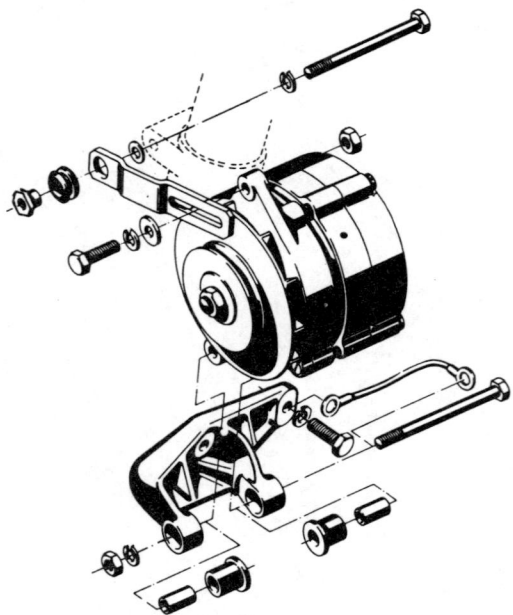

FIG 12:1   Typical alternator mounting details

These figures assume electrolyte temperature of 60°F or 16°C. If the temperature of the electrolyte exceeds this, add 0.002 to the readings for each 5°F or 3°C rise. Subtract 0.002 for any corresponding drop below 60°F or 16°C.

If the battery is in a low state of charge, take the car for a long daylight run or put the battery on a charger at 5 amps, with the vents in place, until it gases freely. Do not use a naked light near the battery as the gas is inflammable. If the battery is to stand unused for long periods give a refreshing charge every month. It will be ruined if it is left uncharged.

12:3   The alternator

The alternator provides current for the various items of electrical equipment and to charge the battery, the unit operating at all engine speeds. The current produced is alternate, this being rectified to direct current supply by diodes mounted in the alternator casing. Alternator drive is by belt from the crankshaft pulley. Very little maintenance is needed, apart from the occasional check on belt tension as described in **Chapter 4, Section 4:4**, and on the condition and tighteness of the wiring connections. Keep the outside of the unit free from dirt, particularly around the ventilation holes in the cover.

The alternator must never be run with the battery disconnected, nor must the battery cables be reversed at any time. Test connections must be carefully made, and the battery and alternator must be completely disconnected before any electric welding is carried out on any part of the car. The engine must never be started with a battery charger still connected to the battery. These warnings must be observed otherwise extensive damage to the alternator components, particularly the diodes, will result.

The alternator is designed and constructed to give many years of trouble-free service. If, however, a fault should develop in the unit, it should be checked and serviced by a fully equipped service station or a new or reconditioned unit obtained and fitted. Typical alternator mounting details are shown in **FIG 12:1**.

Alternator testing:

A simple check on alternator charging can be carried out after dark by switching on the headlamps and starting the engine. If the alternator is charging, the headlamps will brighten considerably as the system voltage rises from the nominal battery voltage to the higher figure produced by the alternator.

If the alternator is not charging, check the wiring and connections in the charging circuit. If these are in order, a fault in the alternator unit is indicated and it should be checked and repaired by a service station.

Alternator removal:

Disconnect the battery, then disconnect the wiring from the alternator. Slacken the alternator lower mounting bolt and the bolt securing the alternator to the upper slotted link (see **FIG 12:1**). Push the alternator towards the engine and detach the drive belt, then remove the mounting bolts and remove the unit from the car.

Refit the alternator in the reverse order of removal, setting drive belt tension as described in **Chapter 4, Section 4:4**, on completion.

12:4   Starter motor testing

Check that the battery is in good condition and fully charged and that its connections are clean and tight. Switch on the headlamps and operate the starter switch. Current is reaching the starter if the lights dim when the starter is operated, in which case it will be necessary to remove the starter for servicing. If the lights do not dim significantly, switch them off and operate the starter switch while listening for a clicking sound at the starter motor, which will indicate that the starter solenoid is operating.

If no sound can be heard at the starter when the switch is operated, check the wiring and connections between the battery and the starter switch, and between the switch and the solenoid. If the solenoid can be heard operating when the starter switch is operated, check the wiring and connections between the battery and the main starter motor terminal, taking care not to accidentally earth the main battery to starter motor lead which is live at all times. If the wiring is not the cause of the trouble, the fault is internal and the starter motor must be removed and serviced.

12:5   Bosch starter motor

The starter is a brush type series wound motor equipped with an over-running clutch and operated by a solenoid. The armature shaft is supported in metal bushes which require no routine servicing.

When the starter is operated from the switch, the engagement lever moves the pinion into mesh with the engine ring gear. When the pinion meshes with the ring gear teeth, the solenoid contact closes the circuit and the starter motor operates to turn the engine. When

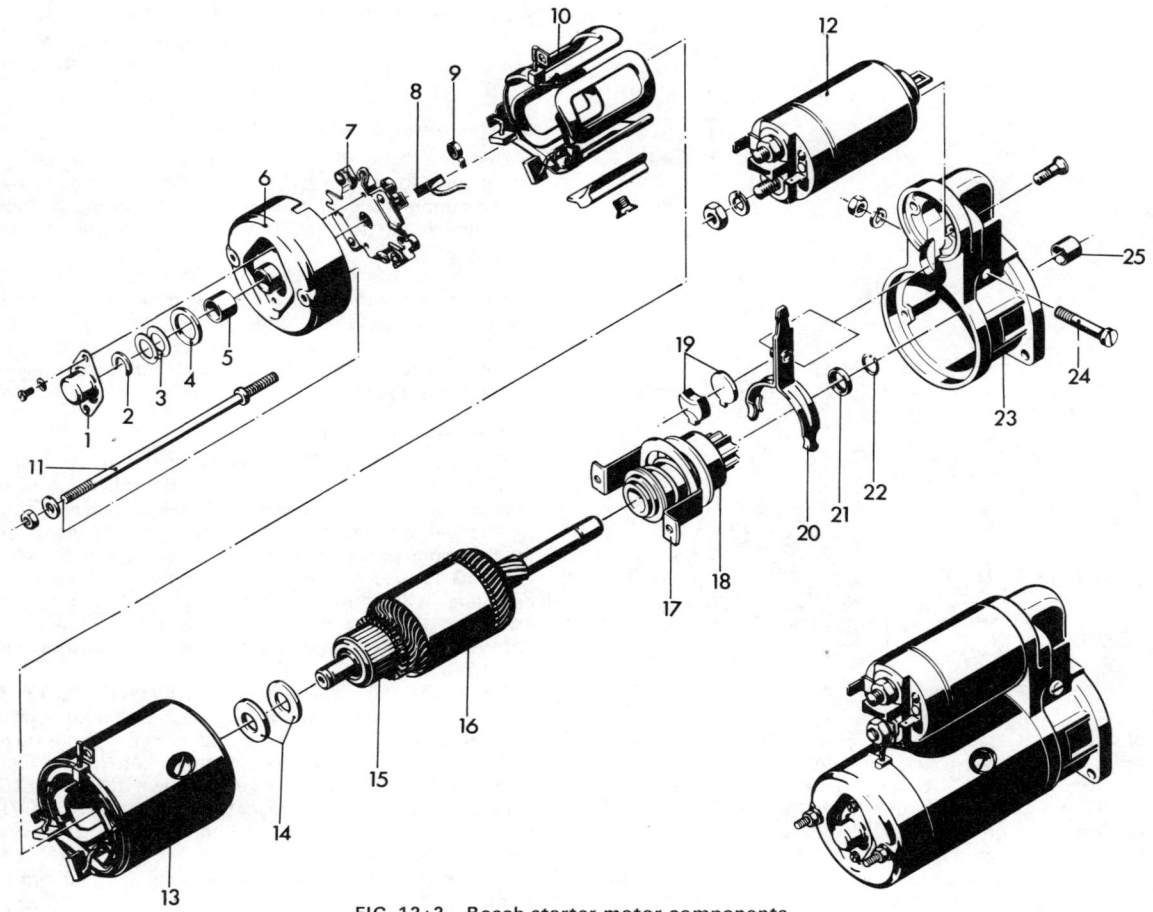

FIG 12:2   Bosch starter motor components

Key to Fig 12:2   1 Bearing   2 Retainer   3 Shims   4 Sealing ring   5 Bush   6 Commutator end bracket   7 Brush plate
8 Brush   9 Brush spring   10 Field coils   11 Through bolt   12 Solenoid   13 Starter body   14 Thrust washers
15 Commutator   16 Armature   17 Brake friction plate   18 Drive pinion assembly   19 Blanking plates   20 Engagement
lever   21 Thrust collar   22 Jump ring   23 Drive end bracket   24 Pivot bolt   25 Bush

the engine starts, the speed of the rotating ring gear causes the pinion to overrun the clutch and armature. The pinion continues in engagement until the switch is released when the engagement lever returns it to the rest position under spring pressure.

Starter removal and installation:

Disconnect the leads from the terminals on the starter motor, then remove the bolt securing the support bracket to cylinder block. Remove starter flange securing bolts and remove the starter.

Install the starter in the reverse order of removal, making sure that the two nuts securing the bracket to the starter are slack. Do not tighten these nuts until the bolts securing the starter flange and the bolts securing the bracket to the cylinder block have been tightened. Connect the black/red wire to the terminal marked 50 on the solenoid and the black wire to the terminal marked 16.

Starter dismantling:

FIG 12:2 shows Bosch starter motor components. Disconnect the positive lead from solenoid 12, then remove bearing cap 1. Remove U-shaped retainer 2 from the armature shaft, then remove shims 3 and rubber sealing ring 4. Remove the nuts from through bolts 11 then detach commutator end bracket 6.

Before removing brush holder plate, use a suitable spring scale to check brush spring pressure as shown in **FIG 12:3**. This should be between 11.12 and 13.10N (40 to 47oz). Lift each brush spring in turn to remove the brushes from their holders, then remove brush plate 7 (see **FIG 12:2**) and remove the two thrust washers 14.

Remove the two screws securing the solenoid to the drive end bracket, then withdraw the solenoid and unhook solenoid plunger link from top of engagement lever (see **FIG 12:4**). Withdraw the starter body shown at 13 in **FIG 12:2**, then remove the rubber and metal

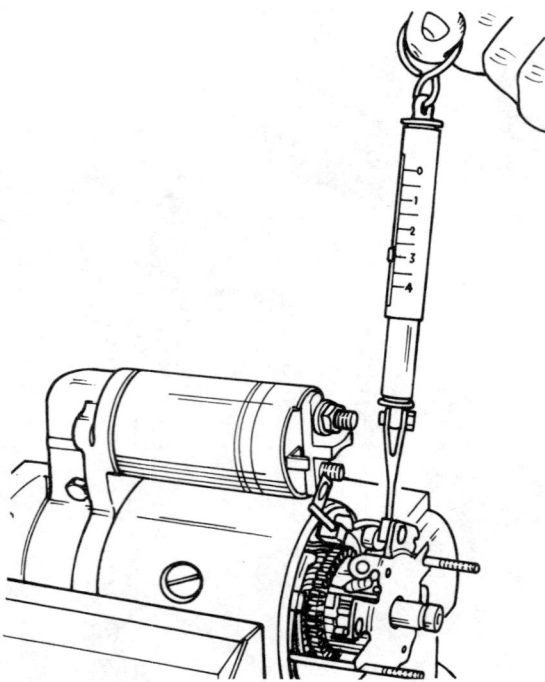

FIG 12:3   Checking brush spring pressure

blanking plates as shown in **FIG 12:5**. Lock two nuts against each other on the outer end of the through bolts as shown in **FIG 12:6**, then use a spanner to turn the inner nut to unscrew the through bolts from the drive end bracket. Through bolt removal will also release the brake friction plate shown at 17 in **FIG 12:2**.

Remove engagement lever pivot bolt 24 (see **FIG 12:2**), then remove armature 16 together with engagement lever 20.

Service the starter motor components as described in **Section 12:7**.

Reassemble the starter motor in the reverse order of dismantling, noting the following points:

Insert the metal and rubber blanking plates in the drive end bracket before installing the starter body. Make sure that the steel washer followed by the fibre washer are located on the armature shaft before installing the brush holder plate.

FIG 12:4   Solenoid removal

12:6 Delco-Remy starter motor

The Delco-Remy starter motor is similar in design and operation to the Bosch unit described in **Section 12:5**.

Starter removal and installation:

Disconnect the wires from the starter motor terminals, noting their positions for correct refitting. Remove the bolt securing the support bracket to the cylinder block then remove the bolts from the starter flange and remove the starter.

Install the starter in the reverse order of removal, making sure that the two nuts securing the bracket to the starter are slack. Do not tighten these nuts until the bolts securing starter flange and bolt securing bracket to cylinder block have been tightened. Reconnect the wires to the starter terminals.

Starter dismantling:

FIG 12:7 shows Delco-Remy starter motor components. With the starter mounted vertically in a vice, remove the screws securing field coil connecting strip to solenoid, as shown in **FIG 12:8**. Using a spanner on the hexagons provided, unscrew the two through bolts 5 (see **FIG 12:7**), then remove commutator end bracket 6 complete with through bolts. Remove starter body assembly 12. As the starter body is withdrawn, take care not to lose brush springs and insulating sleeves shown in **FIG 12:9**.

Collect the anti-noise washer shown at 8 in **FIG 12:7**. Remove the two screws then detach solenoid 1 and plunger spring 2. Disengage the armature and drive pinion assembly from the engagement lever, then withdraw from drive end bracket as shown in **FIG 12:10**. Take care not to lose stop collar 18 (see **FIG 12:7**). If necessary, remove pivot bolt 3 and detach engagement lever and plunger assembly 4.

Service the starter motor components as described in **Section 12:7**.

Reassembly:

Reassemble the starter motor in the reverse order of dismantling, noting the following points:

Smear the armature shaft journals with a recommended grade of grease. When installing the solenoid, coat the area around the bottom of the solenoid flange with a suitable sealing compound. Before installing the starter body, retain the brushes in their holders using four pieces of wire shaped as shown in **FIG 12:11**. Remove the pieces of wire to release the brushes when the body is fully installed. Ensure that the thin insulators are correctly fitted around the brush holders as shown in the illustration (see also **FIG 12:7**). The locating dowel on the starter body must align with the hole in drive end bracket as shown in **FIG 12:12**. Check that the anti-noise washer shown at 8 in **FIG 12:7** is correctly located before installing the commutator end bracket and through bolts. Make sure that the through bolts pass through the insulating sleeves which are arrowed in **FIG 12:9**.

12:7 Starter motor servicing

Cleaning:

Blow away all loose dust and dirt with an air line. Use a small brush to clean out crevices. Petrol or

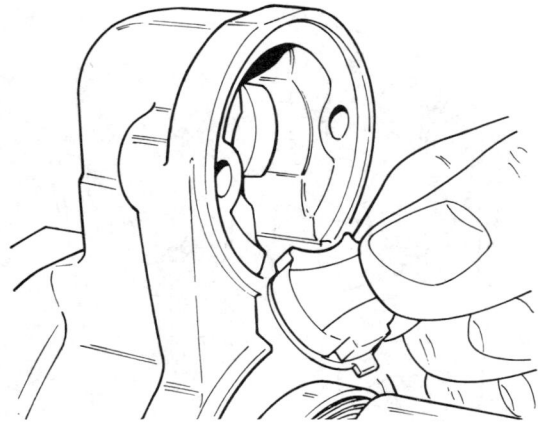

FIG 12:5   Removing blanking plates

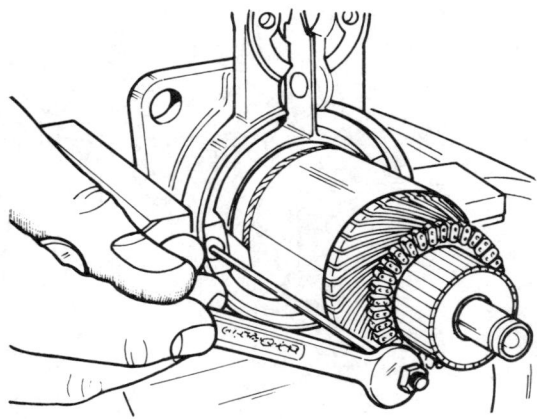

FIG 12:6   Through bolt removal

methylated spirits may be used to help in cleaning the metal parts, but the field coils, armature and drive pinion assembly must under no circumstances be soaked with solvent.

Brush gear:

Check the brushes for wear or contamination. Clean the brushes and holders with a petrol moistened cloth and check that the brushes move freely in the holders.

If a brush sticks, ease the sides of the brush by polishing with a smooth file. Brushes must be renewed if any brush has worn to a length of 13mm (0.51in) for Bosch units, or 9.5mm (0.38in) for Delco-Remy units. Renew any brush spring that is damaged, distorted or weakened.

On Delco-Remy units, brush assemblies are renewed complete. On Bosch units, the old brushes must be unsoldered and new brushes soldered in position. Hold the brush lead close to the work with pliers when soldering, to prevent solder from running down the lead.

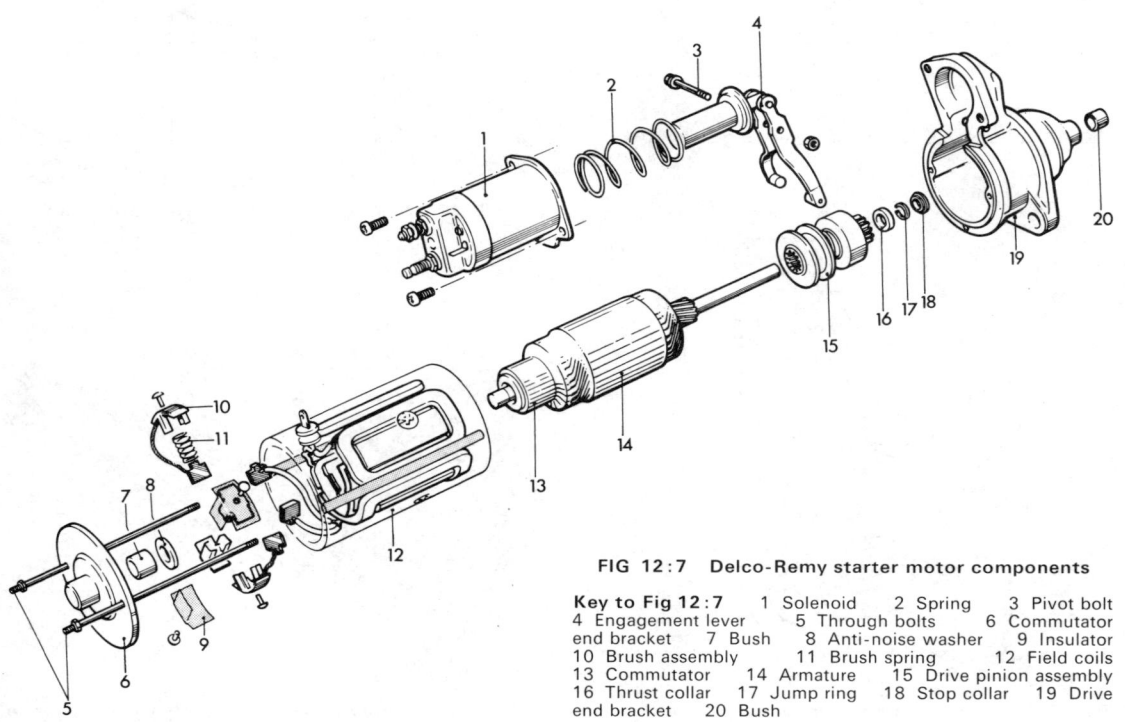

FIG 12:7   Delco-Remy starter motor components

Key to Fig 12:7   1 Solenoid   2 Spring   3 Pivot bolt
4 Engagement lever   5 Through bolts   6 Commutator
end bracket   7 Bush   8 Anti-noise washer   9 Insulator
10 Brush assembly   11 Brush spring   12 Field coils
13 Commutator   14 Armature   15 Drive pinion assembly
16 Thrust collar   17 Jump ring   18 Stop collar   19 Drive
end bracket   20 Bush

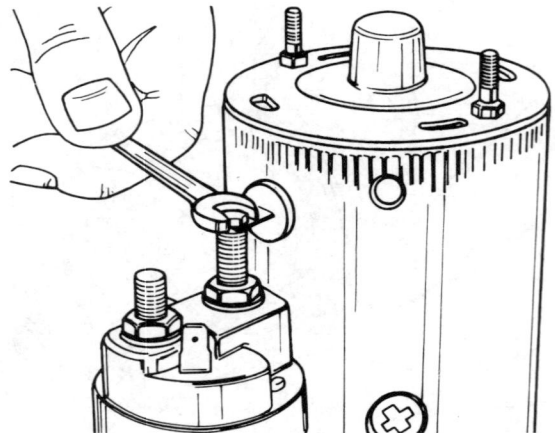

FIG 12:8   Removing connecting strip securing screw

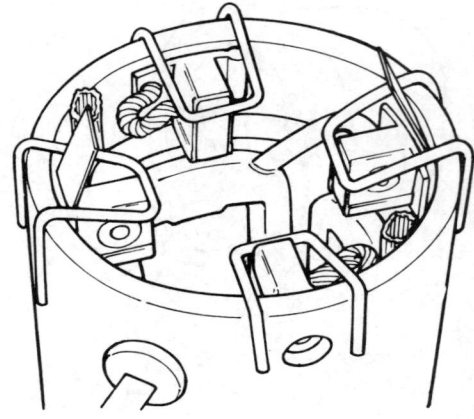

FIG 12:11   Retaining brushes in holders

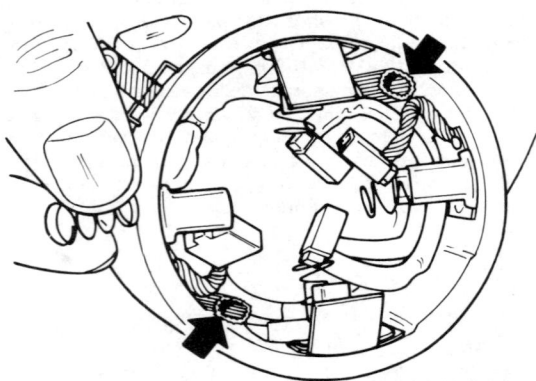

FIG 12:9   Brush springs and insulating sleeves

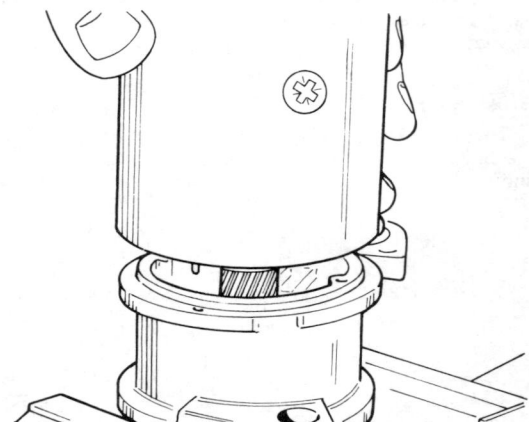

FIG 12:12   Aligning starter body locating dowel

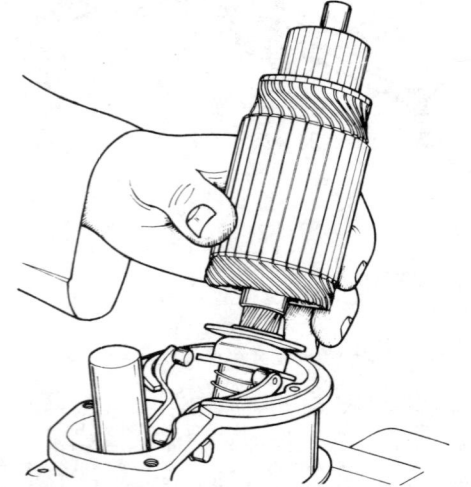

FIG 12:10   Removing armature and drive pinion

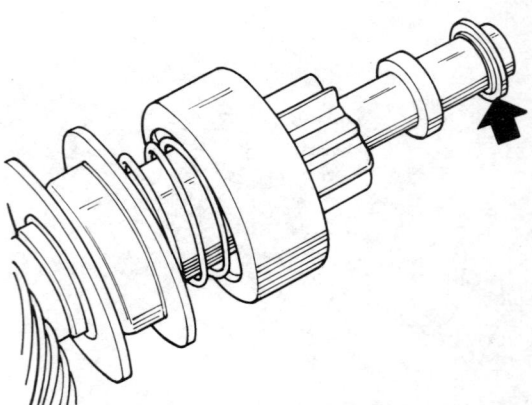

FIG 12:13   Stop collar on Delco-Remy starter drive

The commutator:

The commutator on which the carbon brushes operate should have a smooth polished surface which is dark in appearance. Wiping over with a piece of cloth moistened with methylated spirits or petrol is usually sufficient to clean the surface. Light burn marks or scores can be polished off with fine grade glasspaper (do not use emerycloth as this leaves particles embedded in the copper). Deeper damage may be skimmed off in a lathe, at high speed and using a very sharp tool. A diamond tipped tool should be used for a light final cut. Note that commutator diameter must not be reduced below 32.8mm (1.29in) for Bosch units, or 37mm (1.46in) for Delco-Remy units.

On Bosch units, the mica between the commutator segments must be undercut to a depth of 0.5mm (0.02in) over the full width. Do not undercut the mica between segments on Delco-Remy units.

On completion, give a light, final polish with fine glasspaper, then clean away all dust from the commutator.

The armature:

Check the armature for charred insulation, loose segments or laminations and for scored laminations. Shortcircuited windings may be suspected if individual commutator segments are badly burned. If the armature is damaged in any way it should be renewed. If an electrical fault in the armature is suspected, have it tested on special equipment at a service station.

Field coils:

The field coils and pole pieces are held in place by special screws. To ensure correct installation and alignment, it is recommended that field coil checking and servicing be carried out at a service station.

The field coils can be checked for continuity using a test lamp and battery. A better method is to check resistance using an ohmmeter. The resistance can also be checked using a 12-volt battery and ammeter (voltage divided by current equals resistance).

Drive pinion assembly:

The starter drive pinion and clutch assembly must not be washed in solvents, as this would wash away the internal lubricant. Cleaning should be confined to wiping away dirt with a cloth. Light damage to the pinion teeth which engage the engine ring gear can be cleaned off with a fine file or oilstone, but deeper damage necessitates the renewal of the complete drive assembly. Check that the clutch takes up the drive instantaneously but slips freely in the opposite direction. The complete pinion and clutch assembly must be renewed if the clutch is defective. The drive pinion assembly can be removed in the following manner:

On Delco-Remy units, remove the stop collar arrowed in **FIG 12:13**. On all models, drive thrust collar 1 (see **FIG 12:14**) down the shaft then remove jump ring 2. Remove the thrust collar, then pull the pinion and clutch assembly from the shaft. On Bosch units, this will also release the brake friction plate.

Refit the drive pinion in the reverse order of removal, making sure that the brake friction plate is installed first

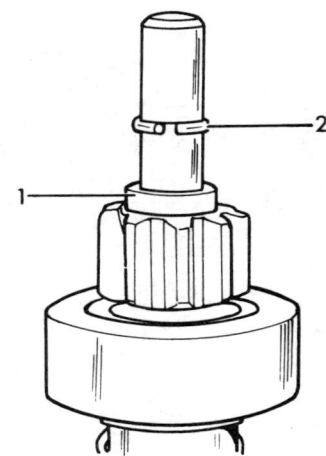

FIG 12:14   Thrust collar 1 and jump ring 2

FIG 12:15   Fitting thrust collar over jump ring

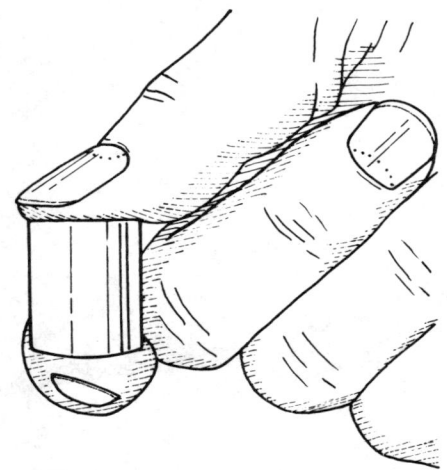

FIG 12:16   Forcing lubricant through an armature shaft bush

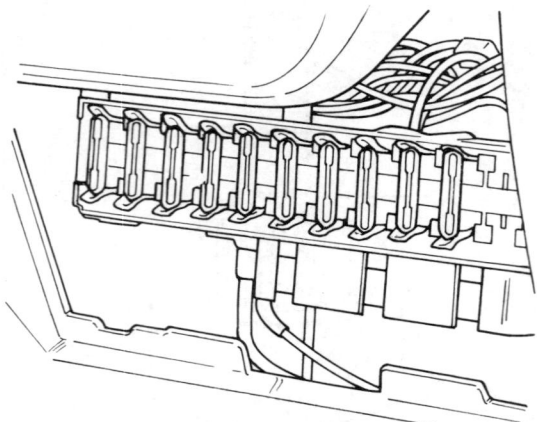

FIG 12:17 Installation of fuse box showing the 10-fuse type

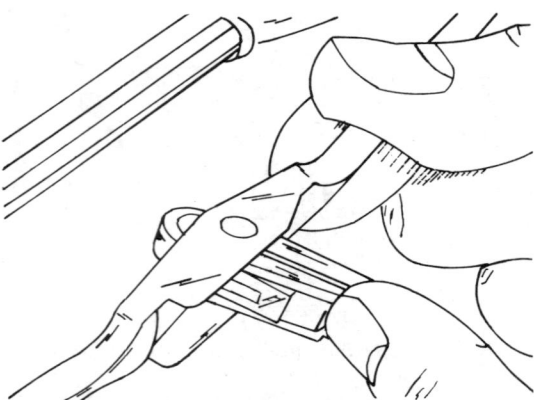

FIG 12:18 Wiper blade removal

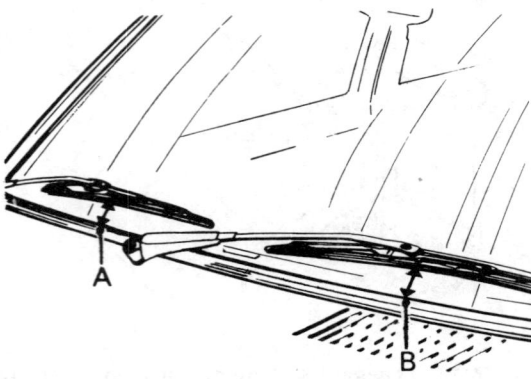

FIG 12:19 Parked position of wipers

on Bosch units. Fit a new jump ring if the original is damaged or distorted. Fit the thrust collar with open side towards shaft end, pushing it past the shaft groove, then prise the jump ring into the groove. Force the thrust collar over the jump ring to secure, as shown in **FIG 12:15**.

Bearings:

The porous bearing bushes shown at 5 and 25 in **FIG 12:2** or at 7 and 20 in **FIG 12:7** should be renewed if worn or damaged. If suitable mandrels and press equipment is not available, have the work carried out at a service station.

Using a suitable mandrel, press the old bush from the commutator end bracket or drive end bracket. New bushes must be proerly lubricated before installation. To do this, place a forefinger over one end and fill the bush with engine oil. Place the thumb over the other end and apply pressure until oil seeps through the bush wall (see **FIG 12:16**). Fit the bush using a shouldered mandrel having a polished pilot of the correct diameter.

Solenoid:

No attempt should be made to service a faulty solenoid unit. Any mechanical or electrical faults will dictate renewal of the assembly.

Check the engagement lever for wear or damage and renew if necessary. Minimum diameter for the engagement lever pegs on Delco-Remy units is 5mm (0.20in). If less than this figure, renew the engagement lever.

12:8 Fuses

The fuses which protect the main electrical circuits are mounted in a fuse box situated beneath the instrument panel and provided with a snap-on cover. The fuses are numbered from left to right (see **FIG 12:17**). Two 5amp, one or three 16amp and seven 8amp continuously rated fuses are provided. The continuous rating expresses the normal load carried by the fuse, according to Continental rating method. The equivalent UK rating is expressed as the level at which the fuse is designed to blow, therefore, for example, the 8amp continuously rated fuse will blow at 16amps.

If a fuse blows, briefly check the circuit that it protects and install a new fuse. Check each circuit in turn and if the new fuse does not blow, it is likely that the old one had weakened with age. If the new fuse blows, carefully check the circuit that was live at the time and do not fit another fuse until the fault has been found and repaired. A fuse that blows intermittently will make it more difficult to correct the fault, but try shaking the wiring loom, as the fault is likely to be caused by chafed insulation making intermittent contact.

Never fit a fuse of higher rating than that specified, and never use anything as a substitute for a fuse of the correct type. The fuse is designed to be the weak link in the circuit and if a higher rated fuse or an incorrect substitute is installed the wiring may fail instead.

12:9 Windscreen wipers and washers

The windshield wipers are operated by a two-speed electric motor incorporating a self-parking switch. The

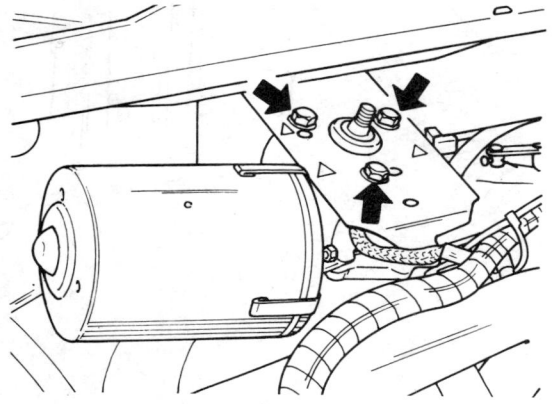

FIG 12:20 Wiper motor removal

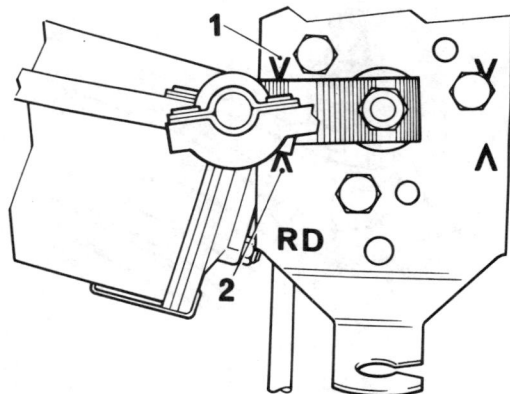

FIG 12:21 Connecting crank to wiper motor

motor, links and pivot housings are assembled to a mounting bracket as a complete unit. The windscreen washer system incorporates an electrically operated pump.

Wiper blade removal:

To remove a wiper blade, depress the catch and withdraw the blade towards the wiper arm pivot, as shown in **FIG 12:18**. Refit in the reverse order, making sure the catch is fully engaged.

Wiper arm removal:

Use a screwdriver to lever the plastic cap from the wiper spindle. Remove the fixing nut, then prise the arm

from the spindle using a screwdriver. Refit in the reverse order, making sure that the arm is correctly located in the parked position. Dimension **A** should be 45mm (1.8in) and dimension **B** 50mm (2.0in), as shown in **FIG 12:19**.

Wiper motor removal:

The wiper motor can be removed leaving the linkage and mounting bracket in the vehicle. Refer to **FIG 12:20**. Disconnect the crank from motor cross-shaft and remove the three bolts arrowed. Disconnect the wiring connector from the motor, then lift the unit from the vehicle. It is recommended that a faulty motor should be taken to a service station for attention or replacement and not dismantled by the owner.

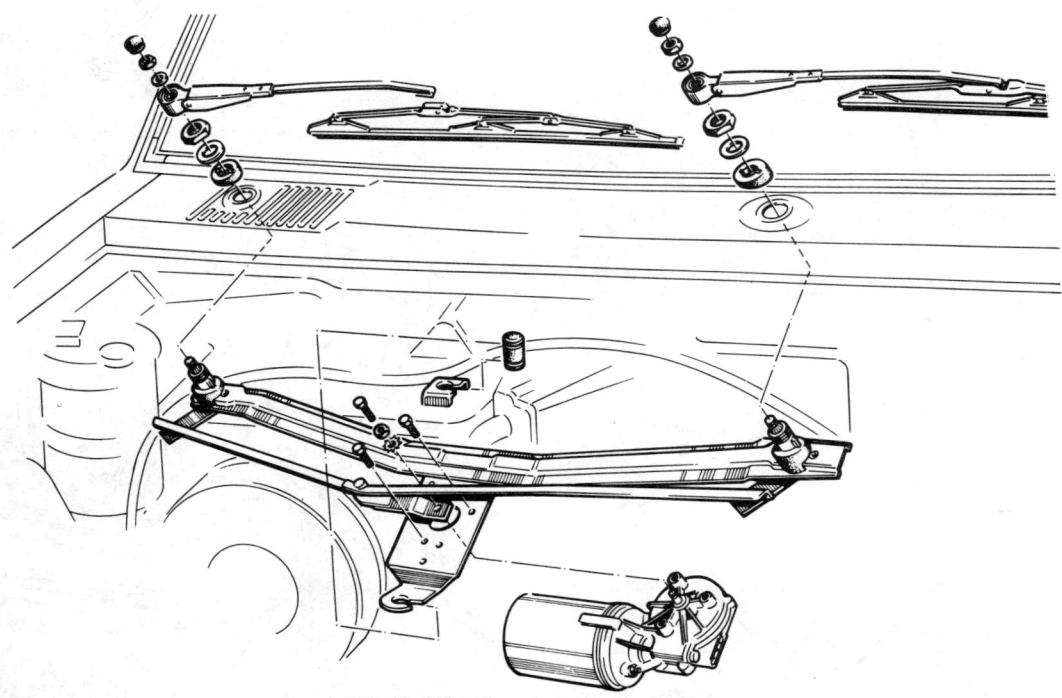

FIG 12:22 Wiper linkage components

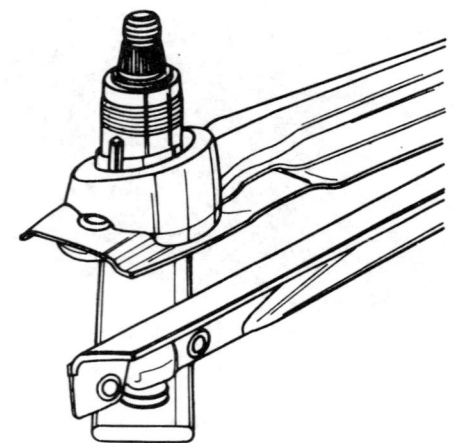

FIG 12:23   Rubber seal installation

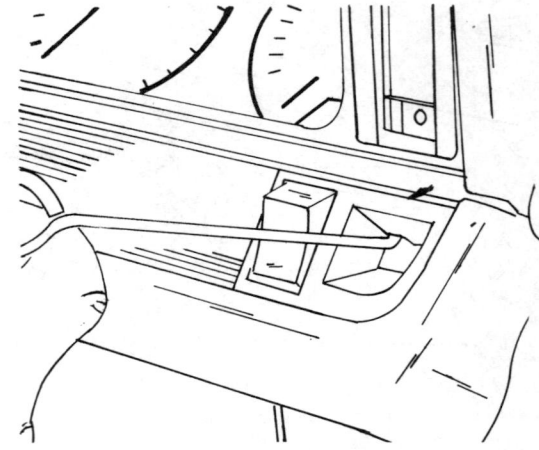

FIG 12:26   Removing switch from panel

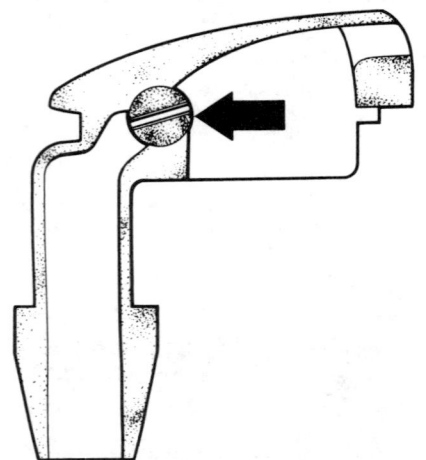

FIG 12:24   Washer jet location

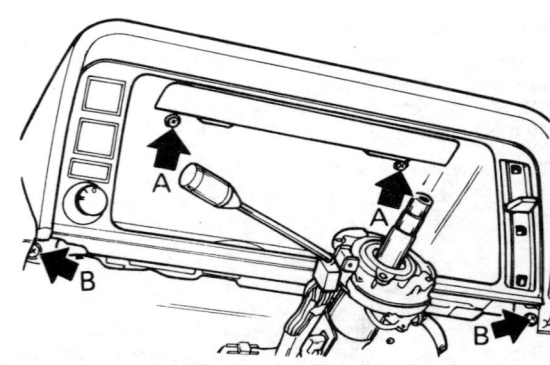

FIG 12:27   Instrument cowl retaining screws

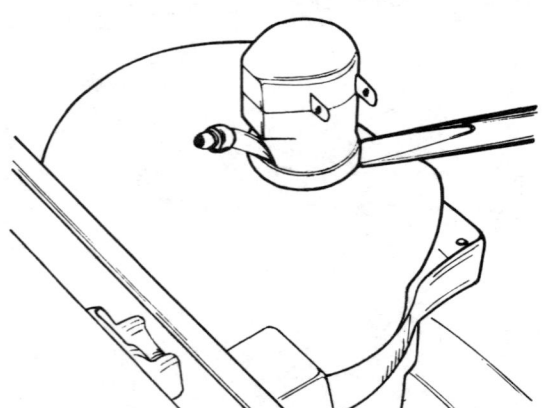

FIG 12:25   Washer pump removal

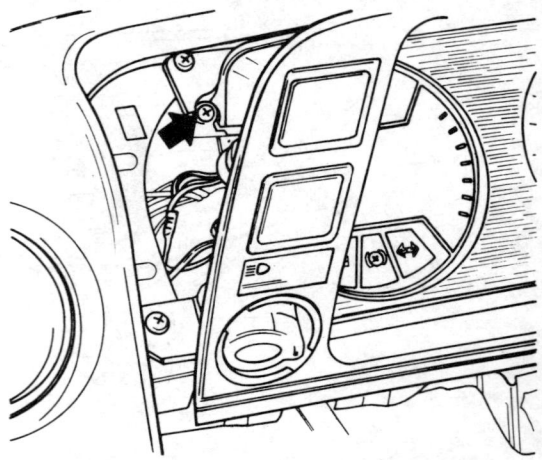

FIG 12:28   Instrument panel retaining screw

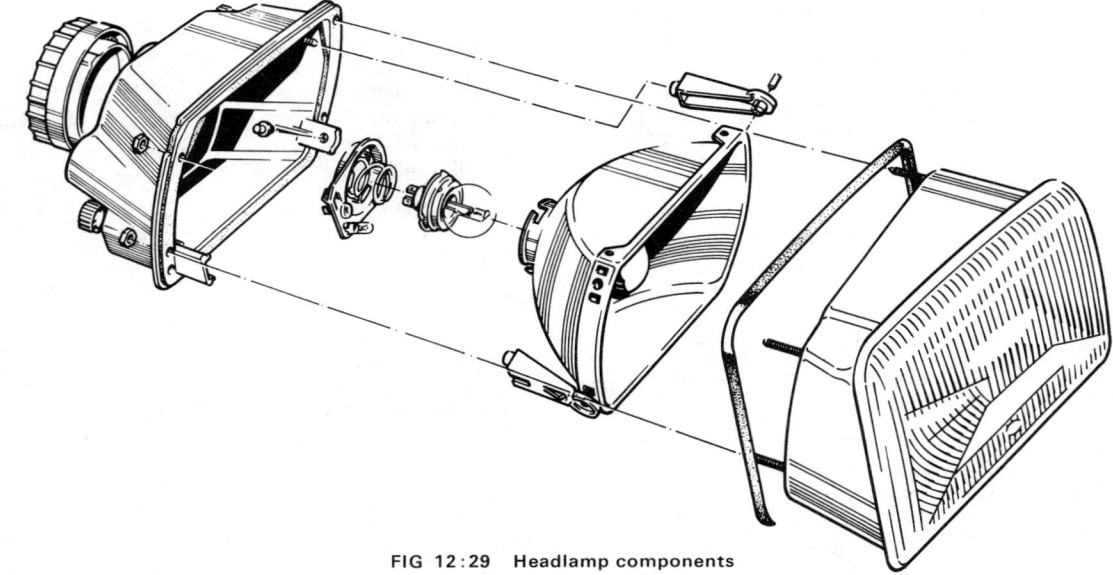

FIG 12:29 Headlamp components

Make sure that the motor is in the parked position before refitting. Connect the wiring connector, install the wiper motor and tighten the three retaining bolts. Connect the crank to the motor as shown in **FIG 12:21**, so that the crank lines up between arrows 1 and 2.

Wiper linkage removal:

The wiper linkage, shown in **FIG 12:22**, is accessible from inside the engine compartment. Remove the wiper arms as described previously, then remove the nuts and rubber spacers from pivot housings. To enable the links to clear the shroud panel when withdrawing the assembly, the crank must be disconnected from the wiper motor. Remove the earth cable screw, then prise off the rubber retainer and disconnect the wiper motor plug connector. Withdraw the wiper linkage from the engine compartment.

The links and pivots, together with their bushes and the motor crank, are serviced as a unit with the mounting bracket.

Refit the linkage in the reverse order of removal, making sure that the rubber seals are correctly positioned on the pivot housing as shown in **FIG 12:23**. Make sure that the motor is in the parked position, then install the crank so that it lines up between the arrows 1 and 2 shown in **FIG 12:21**.

Windscreen washers:

The electrically operated washer system incorporates two jets mounted on the bonnet and an electric pump mounted in the top of the supply reservoir. The jets are spherical and situated on the inner face of the housing, as shown in **FIG 12:24**. If a jet is blocked, it can be cleared by carefully passing a thin piece of wire through it. A jet can be adjusted for direction, if necessary, by inserting a pin into the jet and rotating it in the desired direction.

The windscreen washer pump is serviced as an assembly only, so if it is damaged or faulty it must be renewed complete. To remove the pump, disconnect the wiring and the water hose, then lever the unit from the reservoir using a screwdriver as shown in **FIG 12:25**. Refit the pump in the reverse order.

12:10 Instrument panel
Removal:

Remove the backlight demister switch and the heater fan switch, pulling them from their mountings with a piece of hooked wire as shown in **FIG 12:26**. Disconnect the wiring connectors to detach the switches. Remove the screw on each side which is exposed by switch removal, then remove the switch panel by easing out one end first.

Reach behind the instrument panel and remove the two screws **A** shown in **FIG 12:27**, then remove the two screws **B**. The instrument panel cowl can now be withdrawn after pulling away from the two clips at the top. Remove both heater control knobs by pulling them from the levers. Remove the two screws, one each side, securing instrument panel and lens (see **FIG 12:28**).

Disconnect the plugs from lighting switch and instrument lamp printed circuit, then lift away the instrument panel and lens. Disconnect the speedometer cable if the panel is to be removed completely. The instruments and warning lamps are accessible from the front of the panel.

Refit the instrument panel and lens in the reverse order of removal, making sure that the plug for instrument lamp printed circuit is clipped to the panel and lens assembly before installing the cowl.

12:11 Headlamps

The pre-focus type headlamps have a rectangular light unit fitted with a twin filament bulb which is integral with the holder and retained in the light unit by a coil spring and retaining plate (see **FIG 12:29**). Two

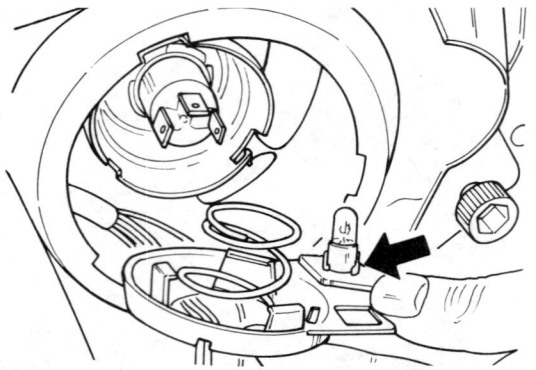

FIG 12:30 Bulb holder, showing sidelamp bulb (arrowed)

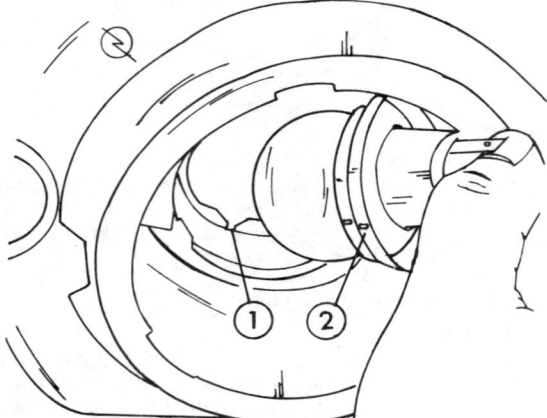

FIG 12:31 Headlamp bulb installation

knurled trim screws are provided for adjusting headlamp beam alignment and the lamp assembly is secured to the front end panel by four studs and nuts.

Bulb renewal:

Access to the bulb assembly is from the inside of the engine compartment. Remove the protective plastic cover from the rear of the lamp unit by rotating it anticlockwise. Push the retaining plate in towards the reflector and turn anticlockwise to release the headlamp bulb (see **FIG 12:30**). The side lamp bulb, which is arrowed, can also be withdrawn if necessary.

Install the bulb in the reverse order of removal, making sure that projection 2 (see **FIG 12:31**) in the holder engages slot 1 in the reflector.

Beam setting:

Headlamp beam setting is carried out by turning the knurled trim screws provided at the rear of the headlamp housing. This work is best carried out by a service station having special optical equipment, in order to achieve accurate results. When the work is carried out, the car must be normally loaded, the tyres inflated to the recommended pressures and the headlamps switched to dipped beam.

12:12 Fault diagnosis

(a) Battery discharged

1 Terminal connections loose or dirty
2 Shorts in lighting circuits
3 Alternator not charging
4 Regulator faulty
5 Battery internally defective

(b) Insufficient charge rate

1 Check 1 and 4 in (a)
2 Drive belt slipping
3 Alternator defective

(c) Battery will not hold charge

1 Low electrolyte level
2 Battery plates sulphated
3 Electrolyte leakage from cracked case
4 Battery plate separators defective

(d) Battery overcharged

1 Regulator faulty

(e) Alternator output low or nil

1 Drive belt broken or slipping
2 Regulator faulty
3 Brushes sticking, springs weak or broken
4 Faulty internal windings
5 Defective diode

(f) Starter motor lacks power or will not turn

1 Battery discharged, loose cable connections
2 Starter switch or solenoid faulty
3 Brushes worn or sticking, leads detached or shorting
4 Commutator dirty or worn
5 Starter shaft bent
6 Engine abnormally stiff

(g) Starter runs but does not turn engine

1 Pinion engagement mechanism faulty
2 Broken teeth on pinion or engine ring gear
3 Battery low

(h) Starter rough or noisy

1 Mounting bolts loose
2 Pinion engagement mechanism faulty
3 Damaged pinion or engine ring gear teeth

(j) Noisy starter when engine is running

1 Pinion return mechanism faulty
2 Mounting bolts loose

(k) Starter motor inoperative

1 Check 1, 2 and 3 in (f)
2 Armature or field coils faulty

(l) Lamps inoperative or erratic

1 Battery low, bulbs burned out
2 Faulty earthing of lamps or battery
3 Lighting switch faulty, loose or broken connections

(m) Wiper motor sluggish, taking high current

1 Wiper motor internally defective
2 Linkage worn or binding

CHAPTER 13

THE BODYWORK

13:1 Bodywork finish

Large scale repairs to body panels are best left to expert panel beaters. Even small dents can be tricky, as too much hammering will stretch the metal and make things worse instead of better. If panel beating is to be attempted, use a dolly on the opposite side of the panel. The head of a large hammer will suffice for small dents, but for large dents a heavy block of metal will be necessary. Use light hammer blows to reshape the panel, pressing the dolly against the opposite side of the panel to absorb the blows. If this method is used to reduce the depth of dents, final smoothing with a suitable filler will be easier, although it may be better to avoid hammering minor dents and just use the filler.

Clean the area to be filled, making sure that it is free from paint, rust and grease, then roughen the area with emerycloth or a file to ensure a good bond. Use a proprietary glassfibre filler paste mixed according to the instructions and press it into the dent with a putty knife. Allow the filler to stand proud of the surrounding area to allow for rubbing down after hardening. Use a file and emerycloth or a disc sander to blend the repaired area to the surrounding bodywork, using finer grade abrasives as the work nears completion. Apply a coat of primer surfacer and, when it is dry, rub down with 'Wet-or-Dry'

paper lubricated with soapy water, finishing with 400 grade. Apply more primer and repeat the operation until the surface is perfectly smooth. Take time in achieving the best finish possible at this stage as it will control the final effect.

The touching-up of paintwork can be carried out with self-spraying cans of paint, these being available in a wide range of colours. Use a piece of newspaper or board as a test panel to practice on first, so that the action of the spray will be familiar when it is used on the panel. Before spraying the panel, remove all traces of wax polish. Mask off large areas such as windows with newspaper and masking tape. Small areas such as trim strips or door handles can be wrapped with masking tape or carefully coated with grease or petroleum jelly. Apply the touching-up paint, spraying with short bursts and keeping the spray moving. Do not attempt to cover the area in one coat, applying several successive coats with a few minutes drying time between each. If too much paint is applied at one time, runs will develop. If so, do not try to remove the run by wiping but wait until it is dry and rub down as before.

After the final coat has been applied, allow a few hours of drying time before blending the new finish to the old with fine cutting compound and a cloth, buffing

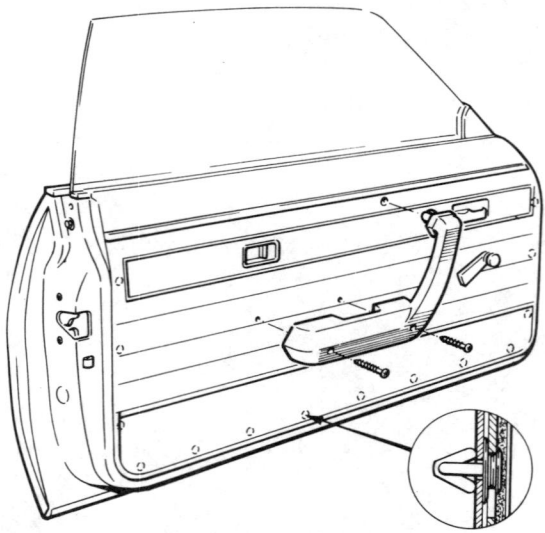

FIG 13:1　Door trim pad attachments

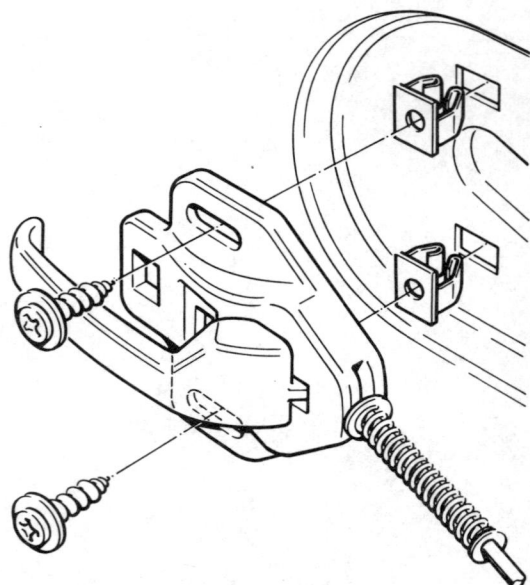

FIG 13:4　Door lock remote control mechanism

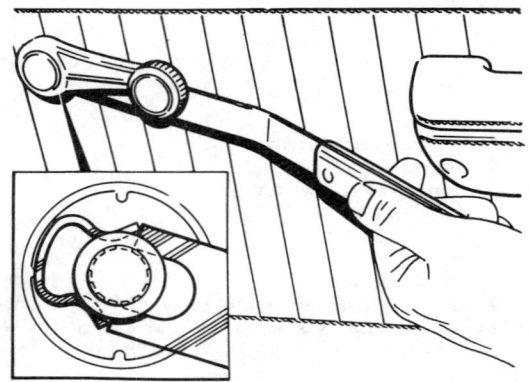

FIG 13:2　Removing the regulator handle spring retainer

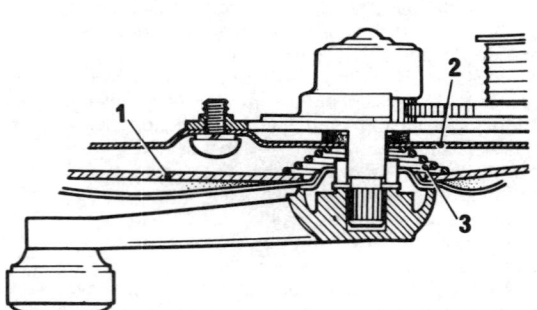

FIG 13:3　Regulator handle installation

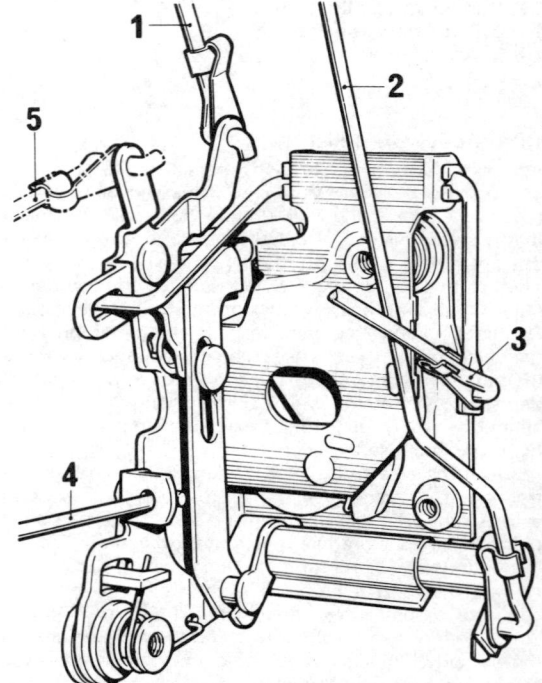

FIG 13:5　Front door lock components

with a light circular motion. Leave the paint to harden for a period of weeks rather than days before applying wax polish.

13:2 Door components

Removal of the complete door assembly from the car bodywork requires the use of special tools to extract the split hinge pins, so this work is best left to a service station. However, removal and servicing of door components can be carried out without the need for door removal as described in this section.

Trim pad removal:

Take out the two screws and detach the armrest (see **FIG 13:1**). On Coupé models, the extended arm on the armrest can be released from the door inner panel after pulling back the capping and rotating the armrest upwards.

On Saloon models, use a thin blade to prise off the remote control handle escutcheon, which is retained by pegs which clip into holes in the remote control casing. On Coupé models, the escutcheon chrome finisher is integral with the trim pad and need not be removed separately.

Use a suitable tool such as that shown in **FIG 13:2** to press the spring retainer from the groove in the window regulator handle boss. Remove the regulator handle.

Use a thin bladed tool fitted between the trim pad and door panel to lever the spring clips from position and release the pad. To prevent damage to the pad, make sure that the tool is positioned as close as possible to each fastener as it is levered from position.

If access to door internal components is required, the plastic water deflector sheet must be carefully peeled from the door inner panel.

Refit the trim pad in the reverse order of removal. To install the water deflector, apply recommended adhesive to edges of deflector and mating surfaces of door inner panel, allow the adhesive to become tacky, then press the deflector into place carefully smoothing out wrinkles. If a good seal is not obtained, water may enter and saturate the trim pad. When installing the trim pad, refer to **FIG 13:3** and make sure that spring 3 is located around the window regulator spindle and between the trim pad 1 and door inner panel 2. The large conical end of the spring must be against the trim pad.

Door locks:

For access to door lock components, first remove the trim pad as described previously. The remote control mechanism is attached to the door inner panel by two screws and connected to the lock by a rod, as shown in **FIG 13:4**. The slotted mounting holes in the mechanism allow it to be moved for adjustment of the control linkage. Before finally tightening the attaching screws, move the control assembly forward to eliminate free movement in the linkage without applying any load on the locking mechanism. Lubricate the friction surfaces of the control and rod with high melting point grease.

The front door lock and catch are operated by a series of rods, as shown in **FIG 13:5**. The remote control rod 4 operates the catch release from inside the car. The locking mechanism is connected to the internal lock button on

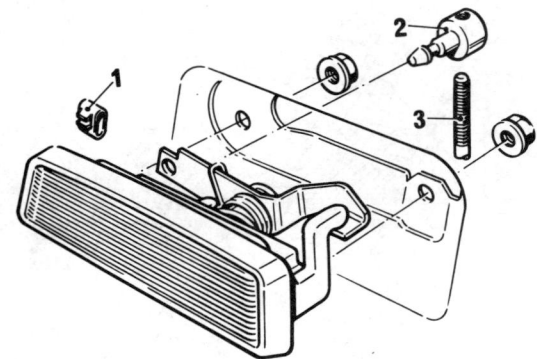

FIG 13:6   Door outside handle assembly

Saloon models by rod 1, or to the internal sliding lock on Coupé models by rod 5. The outside handle is connected to the catch release by rod 2. Rod 3 operates the locking mechanism from the outside key lock.

To remove front door lock assembly, first remove the trim pad as described previously. The door window glass must be raised fully. Refer to **FIG 13:6** and remove the nuts securing the outside handle then prise the adjusting nut 2 from clip 1. Remove the outside handle from the door panel. Refer to **FIG 13:7** and remove clip 1 from the outside key lock, gaining access through the aperture in the door inner panel. Prise rod 3 from the lock lever and detach the key lock assembly.

Refit the door lock assembly in the reverse order of removal. Friction surfaces of lock and rods should be smeared with high melting point grease before installing

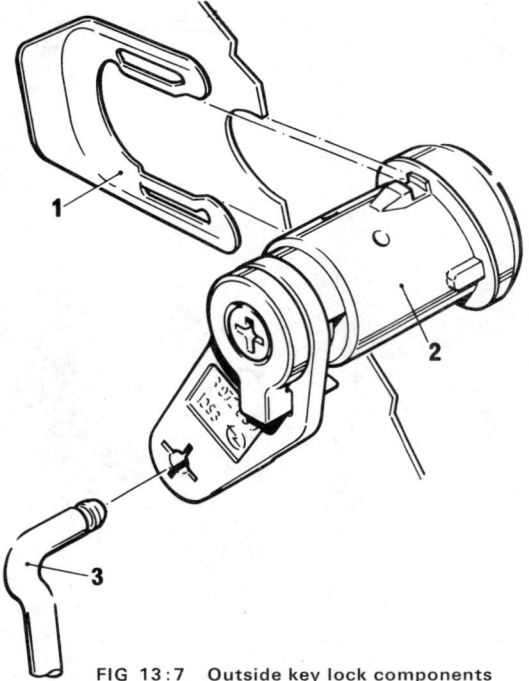

FIG 13:7   Outside key lock components

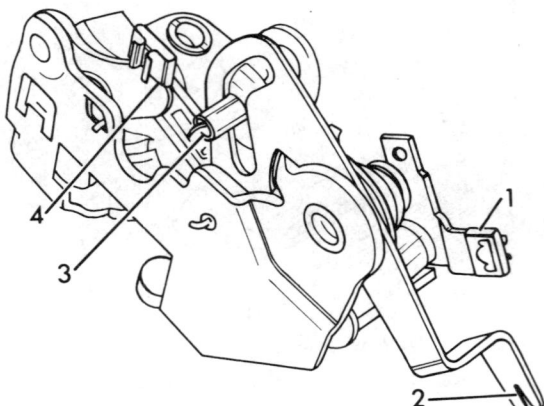

FIG 13:8 Rear door lock components

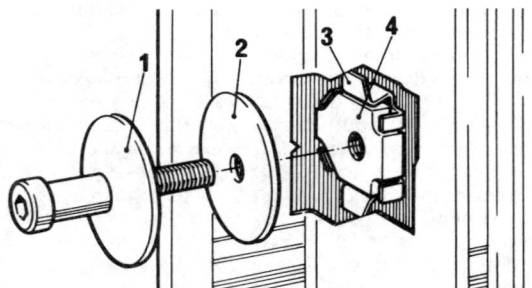

FIG 13:9 Door lock striker

the lock in the door. When fitting the lock barrel to the key lock, lubricate with dry graphite. Do not use ordinary oil which could result in damage to locks caused by grit or fluff adhering to the components. When installing the outside handle, refer to **FIG 13:6** and adjust nut 2 on release rod 3 so that free movement is eliminated without applying a load on the locking mechanism and handle.

The rear door lock and catch is similar to the front but operated by three rods (see **FIG 13:8**). Lock button rod is connected to lever 4 via a bellcrank. Lever 1 is connected by an adjustable rod to the outside handle and the remote control rod is connected to clip 3. A child-safety catch 2 is incorporated in the lock mechanism. When this catch is moved towards the rear of the door, the remote control mechanism is isolated and the inside lock button rendered inoperative. The door must then be opened from the outside.

The lock can be withdrawn through aperture in door inner panel after disconnecting all three rods from lock. Lubricate all friction surfaces of lock and rod ends with high melting point grease before installation. The rear door outside handle is similar to that previously described for front doors, except that the lock assembly must be removed to gain access to the outside handle securing nuts.

Door lock strikers:

Door lock striker components are shown in **FIG 13:9**. The anchor plate 4 is held to the door lock pillar by a bracket 3. Sufficient movement of the plate is provided to permit sideways and up and down adjustment of the striker. Fore and aft adjustment of the striker 1 is obtained by packing washers 2. A special hexagon key will be needed to remove or tighten the striker bolt. The point of

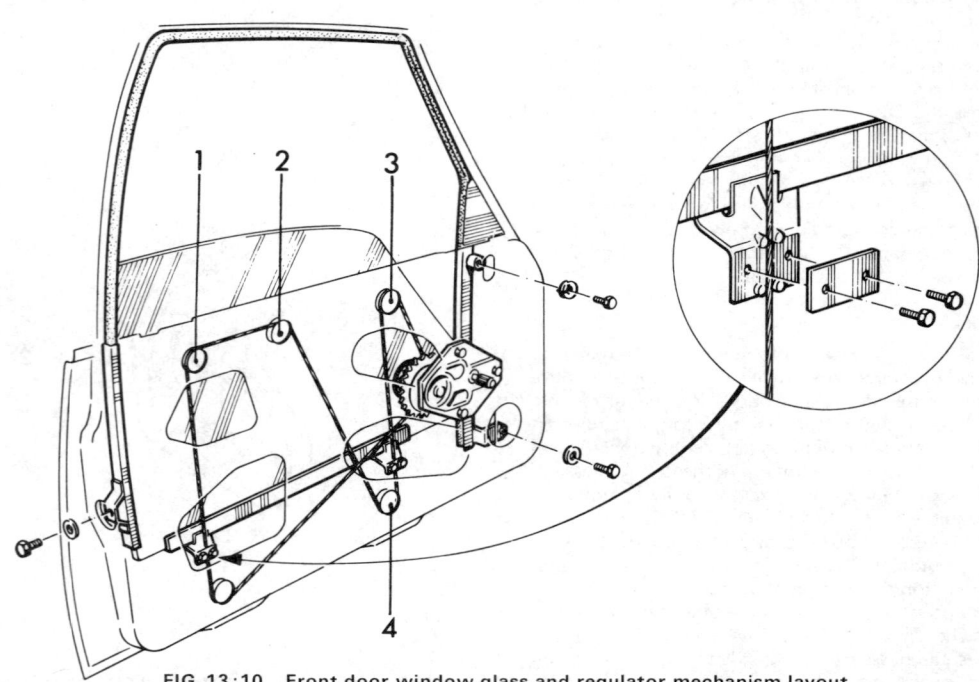

FIG 13:10 Front door window glass and regulator mechanism layout

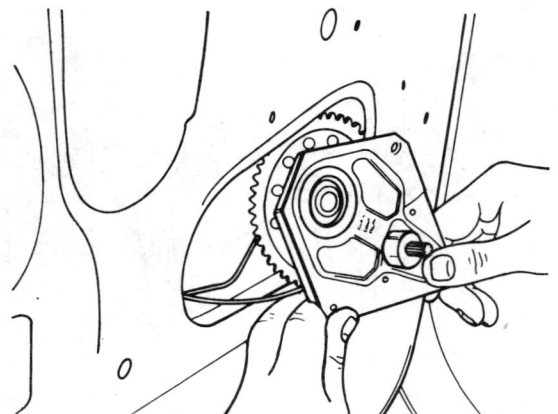

FIG 13:11 Front door window regulator removal, saloon models

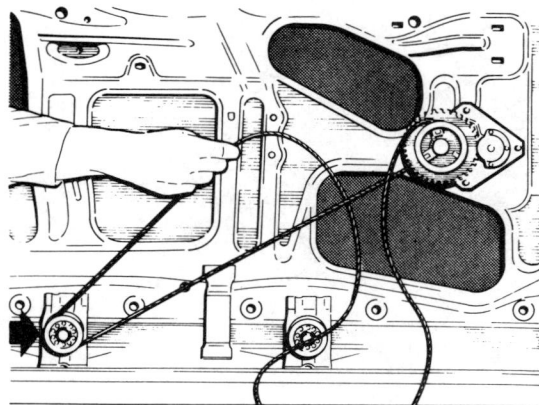

FIG 13:13 Fitting inner cable around rear lower roller

contact of the door lock fork bolt on the striker can be determined by pressing plasticine on to the waisted portion of the striker. Close and open the door and check the indentation made in the plasticine. The contact point should be approximately in the centre of the striker. If not, adjust by fitting packing washers of different thickness. When installing the striker, tighten to 54Nm (40lb ft).

Window glass and regulator:

Front doors, Saloon models:

Removal:

The door window glass and regulator mechanism (see **FIG 13:10**) on two-door models and the front doors of four-door models are similar. The window glass is controlled by a continuous cable which runs on five roller guides and is operated by a grooved drum regulator. Glass support channel is attached to cable by two clamps.

Remove the trim pad as described previously, then lower the window until the clamp bolts are aligned with the apertures in the inner door panel. Slacken the bolts to release the clamps. Lift the glass and withdraw through the inside of door upper frame.

The regulator and cable assembly can be removed after withdrawing door window glass, slackening nut securing cable tension roller and removing three screws retaining regulator to door inner panel (see **FIG 13:11**). Regulators are handed and identified by the letters Re for righthand and L1 for lefthand, situated on the inside face of the drum.

Refitting:

Install regulator to door inner panel ensuring that the rubber sealing ring arrowed in **FIG 13:12** is located

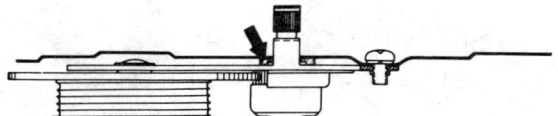

FIG 13:12 Rubber sealing ring location

between panel and regulator spindle. To install the cable, position regulator drum so that inner cable is pointing towards rear lower roller, which is arrowed in **FIG 13:13**, then wrap inner cable around roller.

Maintaining tension on the cable, wind the cable on to the drum by rotating the regulator handle anticlockwise on righthand door, or clockwise on lefthand door, until four grooves on the drum are full of cable and the outer cable is vertical (see **FIG 13:14**). Keep the outer cable clear of the drum while winding the inner cable, so that the outer cable does not wrap itself around the drum. Now refer to **FIG 13:10** and wrap cable around rear upper roller 1, adjustable roller 2, front lower roller 4 and finally around front upper roller 3, ensuring cable does not become kinked. Tension cable using firm hand pressure on adjustable roller then tighten the nut to secure.

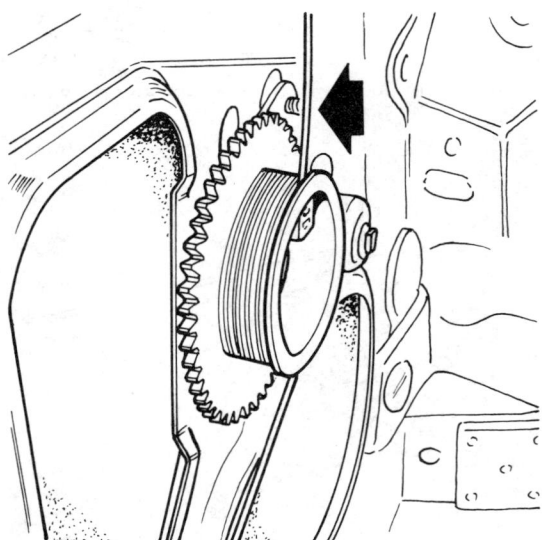

FIG 13:14 Inner cable wound four turns around regulator drum with outer cable (arrowed) vertical

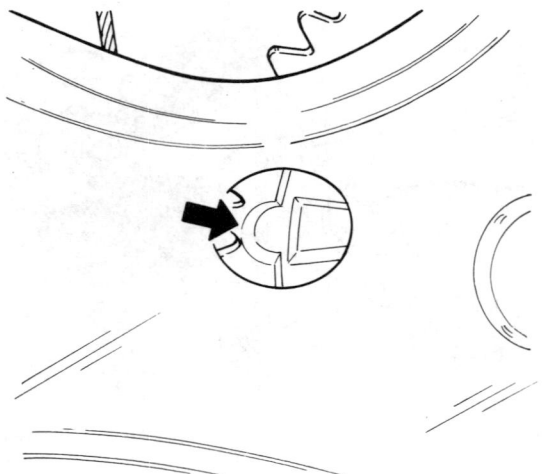

FIG 13:15 Indicator mark on regulator drum

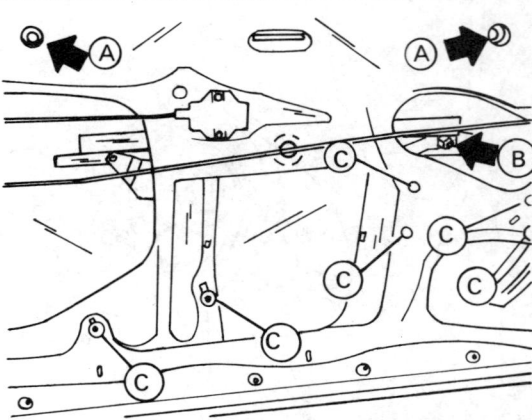

FIG 13:18 Regulator removal, coupé models

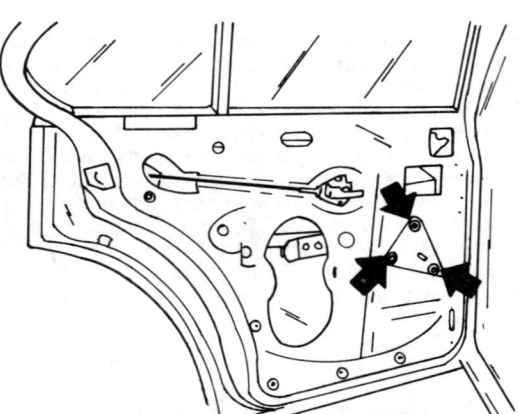

FIG 13:16 Rear door window regulator removal

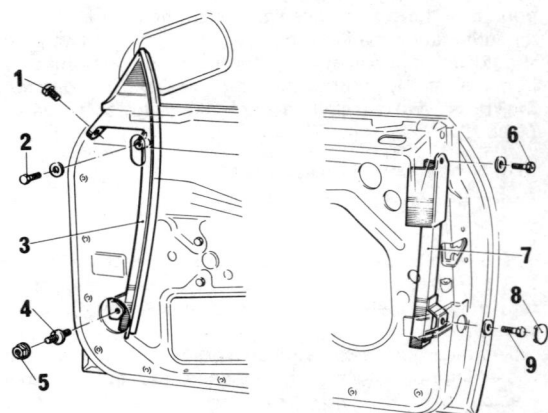

FIG 13:19 Glass run channels, coupé models

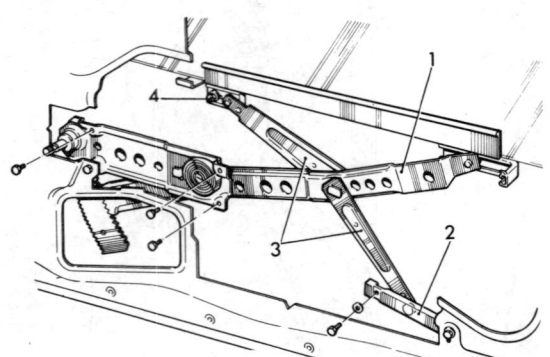

FIG 13:17 Window regulator mechanism, coupé models

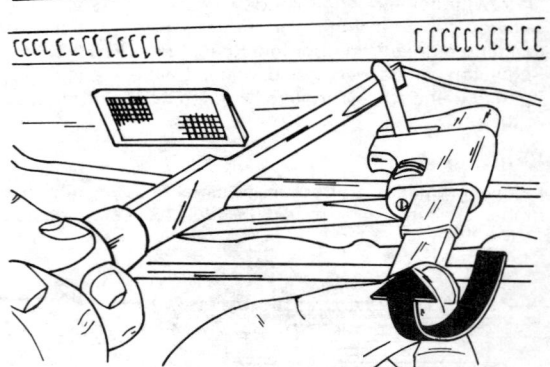

FIG 13:20 Torque rod removal

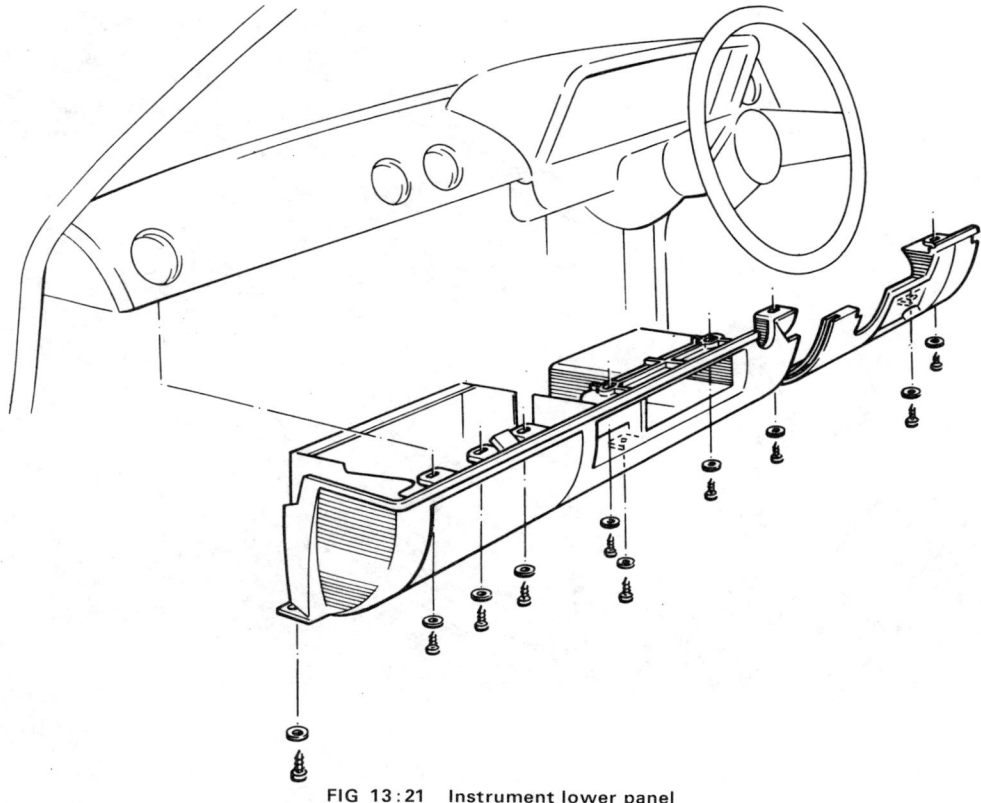

FIG 13:21   Instrument lower panel

From the position shown in **FIG 13:14**, rotate the window regulator handle clockwise on righthand door or anticlockwise on lefthand door until the indicator mark on regulator drum (arrowed in **FIG 13:15**), appears through the hole in the door inner panel for the fourth time. With the cable set to this position, install glass to door, positioned squarely into the rear run channel. Bolt cable to glass support channel through apertures in door inner panel with glass approximately 76mm (3in) down from the fully up position. Reposition the window glass if necessary by slackening the cable clamps and adjusting accordingly. Lubricate the cable rollers with gear oil and the regulator and cable with high melting point grease. Refit the remaining components in the reverse order of removal.

Rear doors, Saloon models:

Removal:

Remove the trim pad as described previously. The window regulator can be withdrawn through the aperture in door inner panel after removing the three screws arrowed in **FIG 13:16**. Before the window glass can be withdrawn, it is necessary to remove rear run channel which is secured by two screws on the upper window frame and one bolt on the door inner panel. The glass can then be withdrawn through the inside of door upper frame. If necessary, the rear fixed glass can then be

withdrawn by sliding it towards the front of the door, after removing the two screws to door upper frame and single bolt to door inner panel.

Refitting:

Refitting is a reversal of the removal procedure.

Coupé models:

Removal:

The Coupé door window regulator incorporates two balance arms 3 (see **FIG 13:17**) riveted together but pivoting on main arm 1. This ensures equal lift at front and rear of glass. The lower balance arm engages an adjustable support channel 2 which is attached to the door inner panel by two bolts. To remove the regulator assembly, remove the trim pad as described previously, then refer to **FIG 13:18** and remove two bolts **A** securing upper stops, one bolt **B** securing upper balance arm to glass support channel and six bolts **C** retaining regulator and balance arm support channel to door inner panel. Withdraw the assembly through the aperture in door inner panel. The window glass can then be withdrawn, rear end first, after disengaging the glass from the run channels.

Refitting:

Carefully refit the window glass, making sure that it slides smoothly in the run channels which are shown in

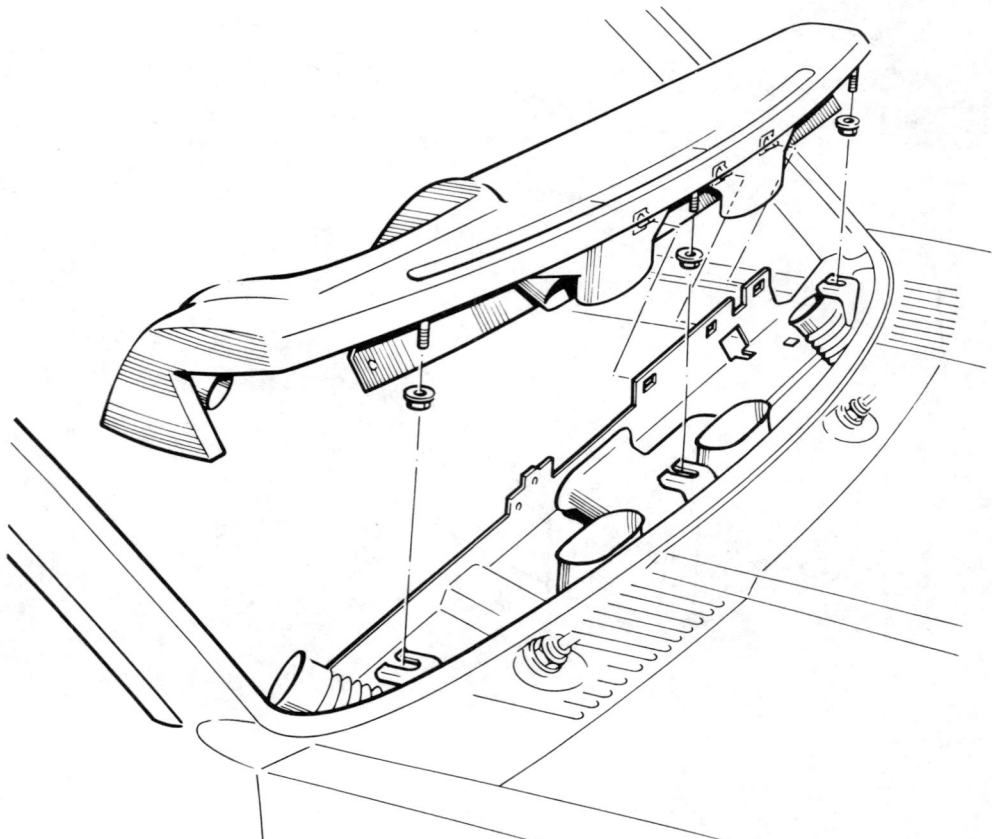

FIG 13:22   Instrument panel cover

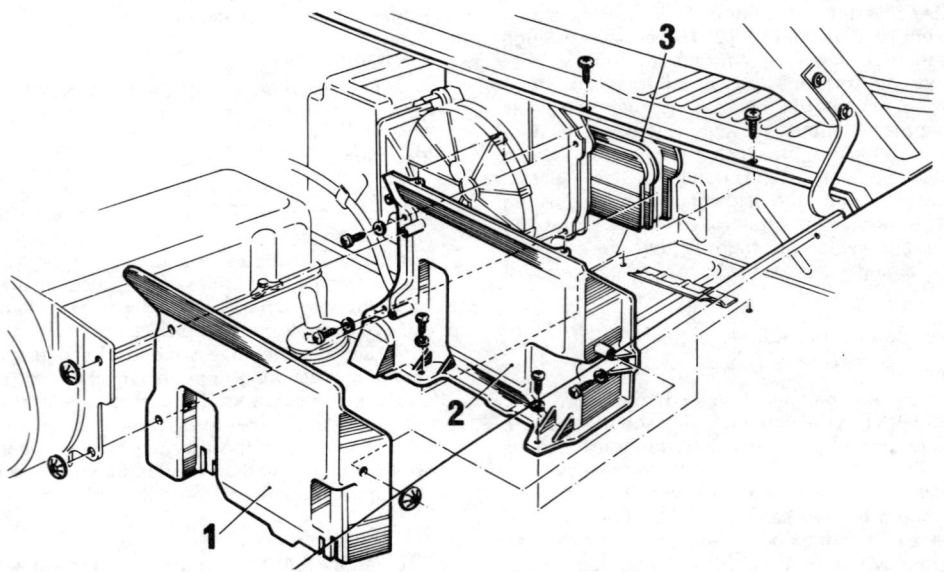

FIG 13:23   Insulator 1, closing panel 2 and deflector 3

FIG 13:19. The front channel 3 can be aligned by means of an adjusting screw 4 and locknut 5. The channel is also secured at the upper end by a bolt 2 and screw 1. The rear channel 7 is secured at the lower end by a bolt 9, which is accessible after removing plug 8 in the door shut. The upper end is secured to the door inner panel by one bolt 6.

After installing window glass, adjust height of glass by moving upper stops shown at **A** in **FIG 13:18** so that top of glass locates just below lip of door weather strip. With window raised fully against upper stops, adjust lower balance arm support channel shown at 2 in **FIG 13:17** so that glass remains square and does not tilt when lowered. Sideways adjustment of glass is provided for by a slotted hole at the upper balance arm mounting 4.

13:3 The bonnet

The bonnet hinges are welded to brackets at the upper dash panel and bolted to the bonnet panel. Slotted holes in the hinge arms allow for adjustment of bonnet position in the body aperture. Adjustable rubber buffers mounted on the front panel control bonnet front end height. The bonnet is secured in the closed position by a spring lock and separate safety catch, and is unlocked from inside the car by means of a cable control.

If the bonnet is difficult to close after adjusting the front end height, or if up and down movement can be felt after closing the bonnet, the dovetailed spring-bolt can be adjusted. To do this, slacken the locknut at the bonnet panel and use a screwdriver in the conical end of the bolt to turn it in the required direction. When the adjustment is correct firmly tighten the locknut.

A nut and lockwasher secures the bonnet lock release outer cable to the mounting bracket inside the car. The release cable can be disconnected from the lock spring after releasing the outer cable securing clip from the front end panel and removing the lock assembly which is attached by two bolts.

13:4 Luggage compartment lid

The luggage compartment lid is hinged at the front by torque rod type hinges, which provide a counterbalance to hold the lid in the open position. The lid is secured in the closed position by a latch engaging a striker mounted on the rear end panel. If the lid does not close properly, slacken the single bolt securing the striker and move the striker up or down as necessary then firmly retighten the bolt. The lid should close under firm hand pressure.

The key lock is secured to the trunk lid by a spring retainer. After removing the latch, use a screwdriver to prise the clip from the lock. The lock barrel can be withdrawn after removing the retaining ring securing it to the lock housing and inserting the key to align the lock internal components. When installing the lock barrel, lubricate with dry graphite. Do not use ordinary grease or oil as this can result in damage due to grit or fluff adhering to the components. A short length of rubber hose can be used to install the spring clip over the lock when it is repositioned in the panel. Place the clip on the end of the hose and push on to the lock. The clip must be installed with the raised release tag pointing towards the hinged end of the lid. Lubricate friction surfaces of lock, latch and striker with high melting point grease.

To remove a torque rod, refer to **FIG 13:20**. Disengage hooked anchor end from centre of rear shelf panel using an adjustable wrench to twist the rod and a screwdriver to prise the hooked end from the hole. The other end of the torque rod can then be withdrawn from the hole in the hinge arm and the rod removed from the vehicle. Install the rod in the reverse order of removal, lubricating friction surfaces with high melting point grease.

If the lid is not properly centralised in the body aperture, the position can be adjusted by slackening the hinge mounting bolts, moving the panel within the limits of the slotted mounting holes, then firmly retightening the bolts.

13:5 The facia

The lower instrument panel comprises two sections, the longer section being secured to the support by eight screws and the shorter section by means of two screws (see **FIG 13:21**). When removing the lower panel assembly, the shorter section must be removed first in order to gain access to the screw at the adjacent end of the longer section. Three of the screws securing the longer panel are located inside the glove box. When installing the longer section, make sure that the panel is located on top of the support bracket in the centre.

The instrument panel cover is secured to three brackets by studs and nuts, and three clips which engage holes in the front of the instrument panel support (see **FIG 13:22**). In addition, two screws securing instrument cowl also pass through metal frame of the panel cover. Each of the windscreen demist jets are attached to the panel cover by two studs and nuts. The two side demist vents and fresh air vents are bonded to the panel cover. To remove the panel cover, first remove the lower panel assembly as described previously. Remove the instrument panel assembly as described in **Chapter 12**. After removing three nuts securing panel cover, ease cover towards rear of vehicle to disengage the three spring clips, then detach demist jets and air vents from the ducts and lift away the cover. Refit in the reverse order of removal.

13:6 Heating and ventilation

Ventilation of the car interior with cool air is by face level adjustable vents in the centre of the instrument panel, supplied from an air intake in the shroud panel. Additional ventilation is provided by a ventilator assembly incorporating a heater radiator and fan, mounted in the scuttle. Air is extracted through grilles in the rear quarter panels of Saloon models or in the centre support pillar on Coupé models.

Instrument panel vents:

The fresh air outlets can be withdrawn from the instrument panel padding after rotating until the flap pivots are vertical. If necessary, use a thin bladed tool to carefully prise the vent out of position. For access to the instrument panel vent duct it is necessary to remove the switch panel and instrument lower panels (see **Section 13:5**). On installation, ensure duct is correctly located over instrument panel outlets and scuttle panel deflector.

Access to the ventilator intake closing panel 2 (see **FIG 13:23**) is gained by removing moulded noise

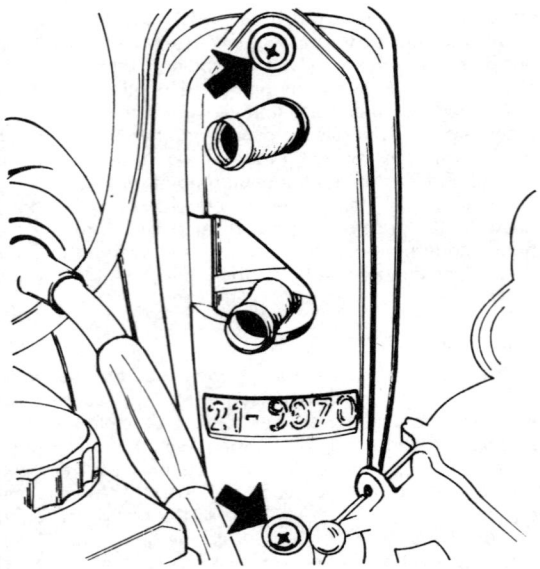

FIG 13:24 Heater radiator removal

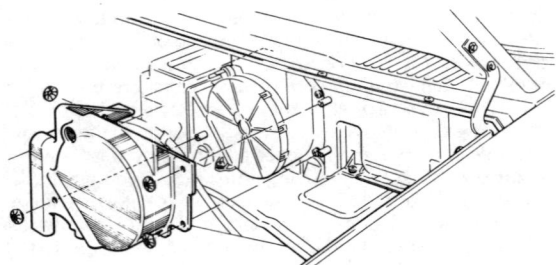

FIG 13:25 Ventilator fan noise insulator

insulator 1 which is secured by three spring clips. Access to the scuttle panel deflector 3 is gained after removing the intake closing panel, which is secured to the scuttle and shroud panel by seven screws.

Heater radiator:

The heater radiator is mounted in the heater casing and may be withdrawn after disconnecting and plugging the coolant hoses then removing the two attaching screws arrowed in **FIG 13:24**. It is also necessary to release the throttle linkage bracket from the inlet manifold to provide clearance for radiator withdrawal. When refitting the heater radiator, make sure that the foam sealing strips are securely attached to the radiator and apply recommended sealer to the joint face of the radiator retainer. On completion, top up the cooling system as described in **Chapter 4**, after running the engine up to normal operating temperature.

Ventilator fan:

The two-speed fan motor is mounted in the ventilator assembly and secured by one screw. Access to the fan and motor cover is gained after removing the moulded noise insulator which is secured to the heater casing by four spring clips (see **FIG 13:25**). The fan cover can be removed after releasing the retaining clips around the edge. After removing the single retaining screw, the ventilator fan and motor assembly can be lifted from the two retaining lugs. The motor and fan are serviced only as a complete assembly, so if defective must be renewed complete. When refitting, apply recommended sealer to fan cover joint faces.

Adjusting controls:

Access to the heater controls for cable removal is gained after removing switch panel and instrument panel frame (see **Chapter 12**).

Adjustment of cables should be made with control levers in the upward position and the distribution and temperature control flap levers set in the fully rearward position. When installing retaining clips, ensure that outer cables do not restrict flap lever movement.

APPENDIX

TECHNICAL DATA

HINTS ON MAINTENANCE AND OVERHAUL

GLOSSARY OF TERMS

INDEX

Inches	Decimals	Milli-metres	Inches to Millimetres		Millimetres to Inches	
			Inches	mm	mm	Inches
1/64	.015625	.3969	.001	.0254	.01	.00039
1/32	.03125	.7937	.002	.0508	.02	.00079
3/64	.046875	1.1906	.003	.0762	.03	.00118
1/16	.0625	1.5875	.004	.1016	.04	.00157
5/64	.078125	1.9844	.005	.1270	.05	.00197
3/32	.09375	2.3812	.006	.1524	.06	.00236
7/64	.109375	2.7781	.007	.1778	.07	.00276
1/8	.125	3.1750	.008	.2032	.08	.00315
9/64	.140625	3.5719	.009	.2286	.09	.00354
5/32	.15625	3.9687	.01	.254	.1	.00394
11/64	.171875	4.3656	.02	.508	.2	.00787
3/16	.1875	4.7625	.03	.762	.3	.01181
13/64	.203125	5·1594	.04	1.016	.4	.01575
7/32	.21875	5.5562	.05	1.270	.5	.01969
15/64	.234375	5.9531	.06	1.524	.6	.02362
1/4	.25	6.3500	.07	1.778	.7	.02756
17/64	.265625	6.7469	.08	2.032	.8	.03150
9/32	.28125	7.1437	.09	2.286	.9	.03543
19/64	.296875	7.5406	.1	2.54	1	.03937
5/16	.3125	7.9375	.2	5.08	2	.07874
21/64	.328125	8.3344	.3	7.62	3	.11811
11/32	.34375	8.7312	.4	10.16	4	.15748
23/64	.359375	9.1281	.5	12.70	5	.19685
3/8	.375	9.5250	.6	15.24	6	.23622
25/64	.390625	9.9219	.7	17.78	7	.27559
13/32	.40625	10.3187	.8	20.32	8	.31496
27/64	.421875	10.7156	.9	22.86	9	.35433
7/16	.4375	11.1125	1	25.4	10	.39370
29/64	.453125	11.5094	2	50.8	11	.43307
15/32	.46875	11.9062	3	76.2	12	.47244
31/64	.484375	12.3031	4	101.6	13	.51181
1/2	.5	12.7000	5	127.0	14	.55118
33/64	.515625	13.0969	6	152.4	15	.59055
17/32	.53125	13.4937	7	177.8	16	.62992
35/64	.546875	13.8906	8	203.2	17	.66929
9/16	.5625	14.2875	9	228.6	18	.70866
37/64	.578125	14.6844	10	254.0	19	.74803
19/32	.59375	15.0812	11	279.4	20	.78740
39/64	.609375	15.4781	12	304.8	21	.82677
5/8	.625	15.8750	13	330.2	22	.86614
41/64	.640625	16.2719	14	355.6	23	.90551
21/32	.65625	16.6687	15	381.0	24	.94488
43/64	.671875	17.0656	16	406.4	25	.98425
11/16	.6875	17.4625	17	431.8	26	1.02362
45/64	.703125	17.8594	18	457.2	27	1.06299
23/32	.71875	18.2562	19	482.6	28	1.10236
47/64	.734375	18.6531	20	508.0	29	1.14173
3/4	.75	19.0500	21	533.4	30	1.18110
49/64	.765625	19.4469	22	558.8	31	1.22047
25/32	.78125	19.8437	23	584.2	32	1.25984
51/64	.796875	20.2406	24	609.6	33	1.29921
13/16	.8125	20.6375	25	635.0	34	1.33858
53/64	.828125	21.0344	26	660.4	35	1.37795
27/32	.84375	21.4312	27	685.8	36	1.41732
55/64	.859375	21.8281	28	711.2	37	1.4567
7/8	.875	22.2250	29	736.6	38	1.4961
57/64	.890625	22.6219	30	762.0	39	1.5354
29/32	.90625	23.0187	31	787.4	40	1.5748
59/64	.921875	23.4156	32	812.8	41	1.6142
15/16	.9375	23.8125	33	838.2	42	1.6535
61/64	.953125	24.2094	34	863.6	43	1.6929
31/32	.96875	24.6062	35	889.0	44	1.7323
63/64	.984375	25.0031	36	914.4	45	1.7717

UNITS	Pints to Litres	Gallons to Litres	Litres to Pints	Litres to Gallons	Miles to Kilometres	Kilometres to Miles	Lbs. per sq. In. to Kg. per sq. Cm.	Kg. per sq. Cm. to Lbs. per sq. In.
1	.57	4.55	1.76	.22	1.61	.62	.07	14.22
2	1.14	9.09	3.52	.44	3.22	1.24	.14	28.50
3	1.70	13.64	5.28	.66	4.83	1.86	.21	42.67
4	2.27	18.18	7.04	.88	6.44	2.49	.28	56.89
5	2.84	22.73	8.80	1.10	8.05	3.11	.35	71.12
6	3.41	27.28	10.56	1.32	9.66	3.73	.42	85.34
7	3.98	31.82	12.32	1.54	11.27	4.35	.49	99.56
8	4.55	36.37	14.08	1.76	12.88	4.97	.56	113.79
9		40.91	15.84	1.98	14.48	5.59	.63	128.00
10		45.46	17.60	2.20	16.09	6.21	.70	142.23
20				4.40	32.19	12.43	1.41	284.47
30				6.60	48.28	18.64	2.11	426.70
40				8.80	64.37	24.85		
50					80.47	31.07		
60					96.56	37.28		
70					112.65	43.50		
80					128.75	49.71		
90					144.84	55.92		
100					160.93	62.14		

UNITS	Lb ft to kgm	Kgm to lb ft	UNITS	Lb ft to kgm	Kgm to lb ft
1	.138	7.233	7	.967	50.631
2	.276	14.466	8	1.106	57.864
3	.414	21.699	9	1.244	65.097
4	.553	28.932	10	1.382	72.330
5	.691	36.165	20	2.765	144.660
6	.829	43.398	30	4.147	216.990

TECHNICAL DATA

ENGINE

Bore and stroke:
   16 and 16S engine .. .. 85.0 × 69.8
   19S engine .. .. 93.0 × 69.8

Capacity:
   16 and 16S engine 1584cc
   19S engine 1897cc

Compression ratio:
   16 engine 8.0:1
   16S and 19S engine 8.8:1

Firing order 1–3–4–2

Cylinder head:
   Permissible face distortion:
     Longitudinally 0.05 (0.002)
     Transversely 0.02 (0.001)
   Valve seating angle .. .. .. 45°
   Valve seat width:
     Inlet .. .. 1.3 to 1.6 (0.05 to 0.06)
     Exhaust .. .. .. , .. 1.6 to 1.9 (0.06 to 0.07)

Valves:
   Stem diameter, standard:
     Inlet .. .. 8.977 to 8.990 (0.3534 to 0.3539)
     Exhaust .. .. 8.967 to 8.980 (0.3530 to 0.3535)
   Stem clearance in guide:
     Inlet .. .. 0.035 to 0.073 (0.0014 to 0.0029)
     Exhaust .. .. 0.045 to 0.083 (0.0018 to 0.0033)
   Seat angle .. .. 44°

Valve springs:
   Free length:
     Inlet 56.8 (2.24)
     Exhaust (16 and 16S) 49.0 (1.93)
     Exhaust (19S) 52.0 (2.05)
   Assembled length:
     Inlet 40.0 (1.57)
     Exhaust (16 and 16S) 34.5 (1.36)
     Exhaust (19S) 35.5 (1.40)
   Spring load at 40mm (1.57in):
     Inlet .. .. 390 to 439N (88 to 99lbf)
     Exhaust (16 and 16S) .. .. .. 243 to 290N (55 to 65lbf)
     Exhaust (19S) .. .. .. 286 to 328N (64 to 74lbf)

Valve tappets:
   Diameter .. .. 21.392 to 21.405 (0.8422 to 0.8427)
   Clearance in guide .. .. .. 0.032 to 0.070 (0.0013 to 0.0028)

Valve clearance:
   Inlet and exhaust (hot) 0.3 (0.012)

Camshaft and bearings:
   Journal diameter, 16 and 16S:
     First (front) .. .. 48.935 to 48.950 (1.9266 to 1.9272)
     Second .. .. 48.685 to 48.700 (1.9167 to 1.9173)
     Third .. .. 48.435 to 48.450 (1.9069 to 1.9075)
   Journal diameter, 19S:
     First (front) .. .. 48.935 to 48.950 (1.9266 to 1.9272)
     Second .. .. 48.685 to 48.700 (1.9167 to 1.9173)
     Third .. .. 48.560 to 48.575 (1.9118 to 1.9124)
     Fourth .. .. 48.435 to 48.450 (1.9069 to 1.9075)

Clearance in bearings	..	..	..	..	0.070 to 0.110 (0.0028 to 0.0043)
End float ..	..	..	..	..	0.10 to 0.20 (0.004 to 0.008)
Cam peak to base (max.)		..	..	..	40.28 (1.586)

Cylinder block:
  Bore diameter:
    16 and 16S engine 85.00 (3.346)
    19S engine , ... 93.00 (3.661)
  Permissible face distortion:
    Longitudinally 0.05 (0.002)
    Transversely 0.02 (0.001)

Piston ring gap in cylinder bore:
  16 and 16S engine:
    Top and centre rings .. .. .. 0.30 to 0.45 (0.012 to 0.018)
  19S engine:
    Top ring .. .. 0.35 to 0.45 (0.014 to 0.018)
    Centre ring .. .. 0.30 to 0.45 (0.012 to 0.018)

Thickness (top to bottom face):
  Top and centre ring .. .. .. 1.978 to 1.990 (0.0779 to 0.0780)

Clearance in groove:
  Top ring .. .. 0.060 to 0.087 (0.0024 to 0.0034)
  Centre ring .. .. 0.035 to 0.062 (0.0014 to 0.0024)

Gudgeon pins:
  Clearance at 20°C .. .. .. 0.009 to 0.014 (0.00035 to 0.00053)

Piston clearance in bore .. .. 0.02 to 0.04 (0.001 to 0.002)

Crankshaft and bearings:
  Crankpin diameter .. .. 51.971 to 51.990 (2.0461 to 2.0468)
  Crankpin clearance in bearing .. 0.015 to 0.061 (0.0006 to 0.0024)
  Crankpin journal width .. .. 25.00 to 25.08 (0.984 to 0.987)
  Crankpin fillet radius .. .. 1.5 to 1.7 (0.059 to 0.067)
  Crank throw .. .. .. 34.84 to 34.96 (1.372 to 1.376)
  Main journal diameter .. .. 57.987 to 58.003 (2.2829 to 2.2836)
  Main journal clearance .. .. 0.023 to 0.064 (0.0009 to 0.0025)
  Main journal fillet radius .. .. 1.5 to 1.7 (0.059 to 0.067)
  Crankshaft end float .. .. 0.043 to 0.156 (0.0017 to 0.0061)

Oil pump driving spindle diameter:
  Standard .. .. 12.444 to 12.455 (0.4899 to 0.4903)
  Oversize .. .. 12.644 to 12.655 (0.4977 to 0.4983)
  Clearance in pump body .. .. 0.009 to 0.038 (0.0004 to 0.0015)

Driven impeller bore diameter:
  Standard .. .. 12.404 to 12.424 (0.4883 to 0.4891)
  Oversize .. .. 12.604 to 12.624 (0.4962 to 0.4970)

Oil pump backlash between teeth .. .. 0.10 to 0.20 (0.004 to 0.009)

Oil pressure relief valve spring:
  Free length 35.0 (1.38)
  Spring load at 22mm (0.87in) .. .. 39.0 to 42.5N (8lb 13ozf to 9lb 9ozf)

FUEL SYSTEM

Fuel pump pressure .. .. 0.17 to 0.24 bar ($2\frac{1}{2}$ to $3\frac{1}{2}$lb/sq in)

Carburetter:
  Engine type:
    16 .. .. Solex 35 PDSI
    16S .. .. Solex 32/32 DIDTA
    19S .. .. Zenith 35/40 INAT

Single choke type: *Solex 35 PDSI*
  Float needle valve 1.75
  Sealing ring 2.0
  Venturi 26

Mixture outlet	2.4	
Main jet	X127	
Air correction jet	80	
Idling jet	50	
Injector tube	50	
Return bore (pump)	0.2	
Enrichment	75	
Idle speed	800 to 850rev/min	

		Solex		
Twin choke type:		32/32 DIDTA		Zenith 35/40 INAT
Float needle valve	2.0			2.0
Float needle valve washer	1.0			1.0
Venturi:	Primary	Secondary	Primary	Secondary
Diameter	26	26	26	32
Mixture outlet	2.8	3.2	3.1	3.1
Main jet	X135	X145	X135	X165
Air correction jet	140	125	120	140
Emulsion tube	—	—	9S	4K
Idling jet	50	—	45	—
Progression jet	—	60	—	120
Progression air jet	—	—	—	1.0
Enrichment:				
Main tube system	80	—	40	—
Tube in cover	100	—	—	—
Additional idling fuel jet	—	—	55	—
Additional idling mixture jet	—	—	50	—
Idle speed	800 to 850rev/min both types			

IGNITION SYSTEM

Distributor:

Contact breaker gap	0.50 (0.020)
Contact arm spring tension:	
Delco-Remy	4.7 to 5.8N (17 to 21ozf)
Bosch	5.0 to 6.3N (18 to 22.6ozf)
Cam dwell angle	47° to 53°
Ignition timing	5° BTDC

Spark plugs:

Type	AC 42 FS or Bosch W200T35
Gap	0.75 (0.030)

COOLING SYSTEM

Fan belt tension:

Measured either with a tension gauge or by belt deflection when hard thumb pressure is applied midway between alternator and water pump pulleys

New belt	450N (99lbf) tension gauge reading or 5mm (0.20in) deflection
Used belt	300N (66lbf) tension gauge reading or 8mm (0.32in) deflection

Thermostat:

Opening temperature	87°F

Radiator:

Leak test pressure	1.4 bar (20lbf/sq in)
Cap valve opening pressure	0.94 to 1.21 bar (13.5 to 17.5lbf/sq in)

CLUTCH

Fork setting dimension	109 (4.29)
Pedal shaft:	
Diameter	14.96 to 15.00 (0.589 to 0.591)
Clearance in bush	0.05 to 0.16 (0.002 to 0.006)

TRANSMISSION

Ratios, manual:	
First	3.428
Second	2.156
Third	1.366
Fourth	1.0
Reverse	3.317
Ratios, automatic:	
First	2.40
Second	1.48
Third	1.0
Reverse	1.92
Automatic transmission fluid	ATF type DEXRON suffix B

PROPELLER SHAFT

Sliding sleeve diameter:	
Manual	32.95 to 32.97 (1.297 to 1.298)
Automatic	38.15 to 38.17 (1.502 to 1.503)
Sleeve clearance in rear cover:	
Manual	0.07 to 0.12 (0.003 to 0.005)
Automatic	0.05 to 0.12 (0.002 to 0.005)

FRONT AXLE AND WHEELS

Steering geometry:
With vehicle standing level within 15mm (0.20in) side for side at the front and rear

Front wheel alignment	30' to 50' toe-in, equivalent to 2.8 to 4.8 (0.11 to 0.19) at the wheel rims
Camber angle	0° 20' positive to 1° 10' negative *
Caster angle	3° positive to 5° 30' positive *
Toe-out on turns	Outside wheel 18° 25' to 19° 55' from straightahead with inside wheel at 20°

To be within 1° side for side

Wheels:

Permissible lateral run-out, checked on vertical inside face of flange	1.0 (0.04) maximum
Permissible radial run-out, checked on tyre seat face of flange	0.8 (0.03) maximum

BRAKES

Pedal shaft and bush:	
Shaft diameter	14.96 to 15.00 (0.589 to 0.591)
Clearance in bush	0.04 to 0.16 (0.002 to 0.006)
Brake drums:	
Permissible diameter after refacing ..	231 (9.09)
Permissible braking surface run-out, checked on axle	0.1 (0.004)

Disc brake pads:
    Friction material thickness   ..   ..   ..   1.5 (0.06) minimum
Brake disc:
    Permissible run-out 0.22 (0.009)
    Permissible thickness after refacing 11.7 (0.46)

ELECTRICAL SYSTEM

Battery:
    Delco-Remy or Varta   ..   ..   44amps hour at 20 hour rate
Bosch alternator:
    Voltage 12
    Output 45amps
    Rotor resistance ($\pm$ 5%) 4.2ohms
    Stator resistance ($\pm$ 5%) 0.19ohms
    Brush length .. .. 5 (0.2) minimum protrusion
    Slip rings:
        Permissible eccentricity .. .. 0.03 (0.0012) maximum
        Minimum diameter 31.5 (1.24)
    Regulator:
        Type .. .. ADN 1/4 V
        Voltage setting .. .. .. 13.9 to 14.8 volts
Delco-Remy alternator:
    Voltage 12
    Output 45amps
    Rotor resistance ($\pm$ 5%) 2.8ohms
    Stator resistance ($\pm$ 5%) 0.24ohms
    Brush length .. .. 10 (0.4) minimum
    Brush spring pressure .. .. 2.2 to 3.6N (8 to 13ozf)
    Slip rings:
        Permissible eccentricity .. .. 0.07 (0.003) maximum
        Minimum diameter 21.95 (0.864)
Bosch starter:
    Brush length .. .. 13 (0.51) minimum
    Brush spring pressure .. .. 11.12 to 13.10N (40 to 47ozf)
    Commutator:
        Diameter after skimming .. .. 32.8 (1.29) minimum
        Permissible eccentricity .. .. 0.03 (0.0012) maximum
    Armature end float .. .. .. 0.01 to 0.30 (0.0004 to 0.0120)
    Free running current .. .. .. 35 to 55amps at 6000 to 8000rev/
                min at 11.5 volts
    Lock torque .. .. 12.3Nm (9lb ft) at 320 to 410amps
Delco-Remy starter:
    Brush length .. .. 9.5 (0.38) minimum
    Brush spring pressure .. .. 10.6 to 17.8N (38 to 64ozf) at 6mm
                (0.25in)
    Commutator:
        Diameter after skimming .. .. 37 (1.46) minimum
        Permissible eccentricity .. .. 0.05 (0.002) maximum
    Thickness of engagement lever pegs .. .. 5 (0.20) minimum
    Free running current .. .. .. 43 to 51amps at 7400 to 9000rev/
                min at 10.6 volts
    Lock torque .. .. 11.2Nm (8lb ft) at 325amps
Wiper motor:
    Light running current consumption:
        High speed 5amps
        Low speed 2.5amps
    Wiper arm spring tension 6.5N (23ozf)

CAPACITIES

Engine oil sump:
    Dry engine   ..   ..   4.1 litres (7.2 pints)
    Refill with new filter   ..   ..   3.8 litres (6.7 pints)
    Refill   ..   ..   3.5 litres (6.2 pints)

Cooling system:
    19S engine and heater   ..   ..   ..   7.0 litres (12.0 pints)
    16S engine and heater:
        Manual transmission   ..   ..   ..   6.5 litres (11.4 pints)
        Automatic transmission   ..   ..   7.2 litres (12.7 pints)

Transmission   ..   ..   1.1 litres (1.9 pints)
Rear axle   ..   ..   1.1 litres (1.9 pints)

TORQUE WRENCH SETTINGS

Figures in Nm (lb ft) unless otherwise stated

Engine and clutch:
Connecting rod bolts	50 (37)
Crankshaft main bearing bolts	100 (74)
Flywheel/flexplate bolts	60 (44)
Cylinder head bolts	100 (74)
Head to timing case bolts	20 (15)
Clutch to flywheel bolts	20 (15)
Converter to flexplate bolts	55 (41)
Rocker studs	40 (30)
Clutch housing to crankcase bolts	45 (32)

Manual transmission:
Transmission to clutch housing bolts	40 (29)
Transmission rear cover to casing bolts	28 (20)
Rear engine mounting to rear cover	45 (32)
Rear mounting crossmember to underbody	40 (29)

Propeller shaft:
U-bolt nuts	12 (9)

Rear suspension:
Panhard rod to body mounting bolt	98 (72)
Panhard rod to axle nut	110 (81)
Suspension arm bolts	67 (50)
Pinion housing crossmember to underbody	40 (30)
Lower shock absorber nuts	43 (32)

Front suspension, steering and wheels:
Upper arm fulcrum bolts	55 (41)
Lower arm fulcrum bolts	75 (55)
Lower arm outrigger fulcrum bolts	75 (55)
Upper ball joint retaining nuts	40 (30)
Stabiliser bar mounting nuts	20 (15)
Lower shock absorber bolts	45 (33)
Axle upper mounting retaining bolts	75 (55)
Axle upper mounting nuts	60 (44)
Crossmember brace rear mounting bolts	80 (59)
Wheel nuts	90 (66)
Steering wheel nut	15 (11)
Column upper support bracket nuts	15 (11)
Column lower mount bolt	Shear-type (see text)
Steering coupling pinch bolt	20 (15)
Pinion shaft retaining nut	15 (11)
Rack pre-load adjusting screw locknut	60 (44)
Tie rod inner ball joint to rack	100 (74)
Tie rod outer ball joint to steering knuckle	40 (30)
Steering gear mounting bolts	45 (33)

Brakes:
Brake caliper to steering knuckle bolts	95 (70)
Brake disc to hub bolts	40 (30)
Rear brake flange plate nuts	60 (44)
Master cylinder to servo nuts	18 (13)

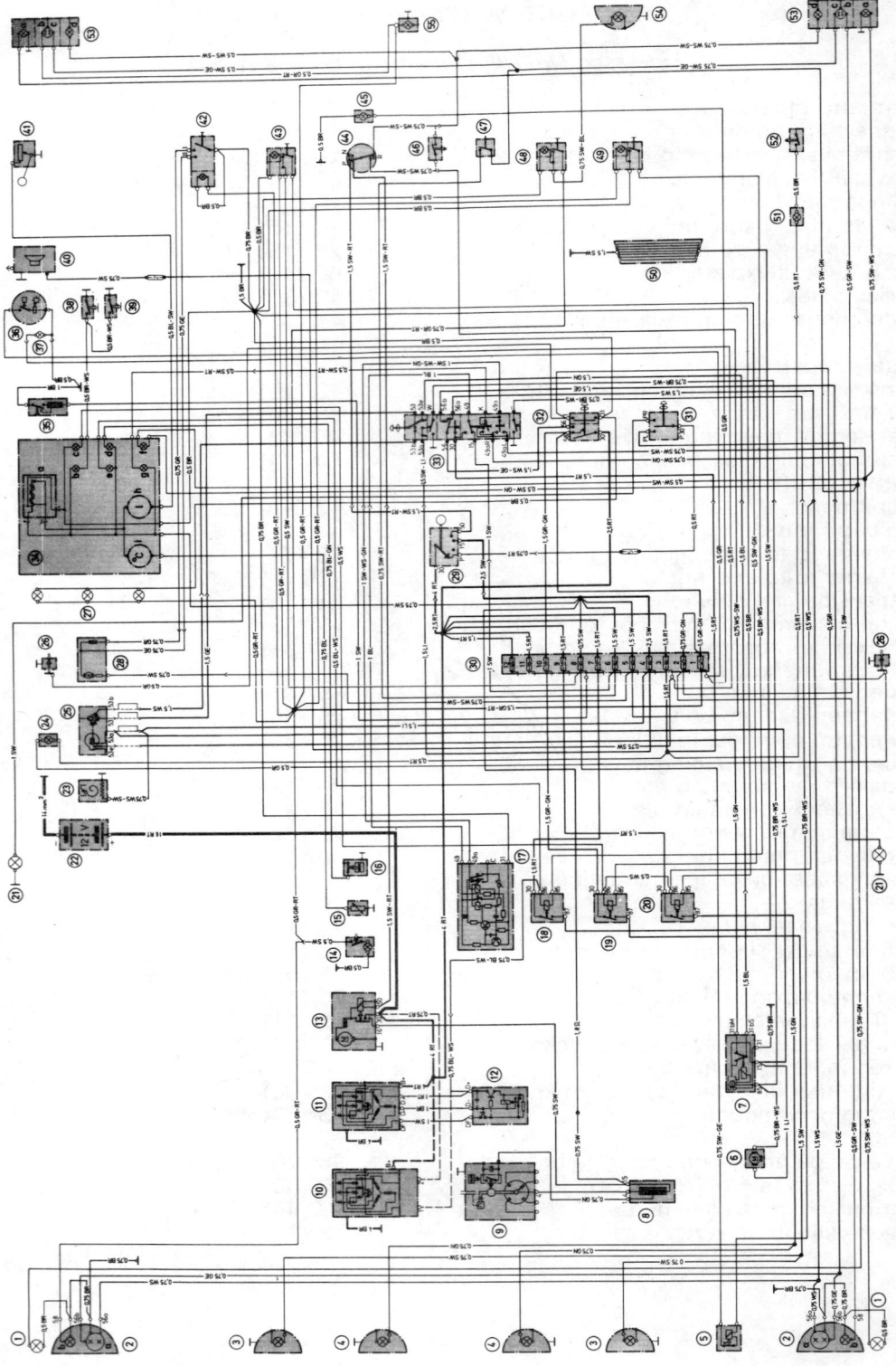

FIG 14:1   Wiring diagram for Saloon and Coupé models

Key to Fig 14:1 1 Front indicators 2a Headlamps 2b Sidelights 3 Fog lamps 4 Driving lamps 5 Horn 6 Washer pump 7 Washer relay 8 Coil 9 Distributor 10 Delco-Remy alternator 11 Bosch alternator 12 Bosch regulator 13 Starter 14 Engine compartment lamp 15 Temperature sender 16 Oil pressure switch 17 Flasher unit 18 Heated rear window relay 19 Fog lamp relay 20 Driving lamp relay 21 Parking lamps 22 Battery 23 Automatic choke 24 Interior lamp 25 Wiper motor 26 Door switches 27 Ignition switch 28 Fan motor 29 Ignition switch 30 Fuse box 31 Parking lamp switch 32 Light switch 33 Combination switch 34a Voltage stabiliser 34b Handbrake and clutch wear indicator 34c Main beam warning 34d Oil pressure warning 34e Alternator warning 34f Indicator repeater 34g Hazard warning indicator 34h Fuel gauge 34i Temperature gauge 35 Cigar lighter 36 Clock 37 Clock, cigar lighter and glove compartment lamp 38 Clutch warning switch 39 Handbrake warning switch 40 Radio 41 Fuel gauge sender 42 Fan motor switch 43 Fog lamp switch 44 Starter inhibitor switch 45 Selector lever lamp 46 Reverse lamp switch 47 Stop lamp switch 48 Rear fog lamp switch 49 Heated rear window switch 50 Heated rear window 51 Boot lamp 52 Boot lamp switch 53a Indicator 53b Tail light 53c Stop light 53d Reversing light 54 Rear fog lamp 55 Number plate lamp

Items 44 and 45 for models with automatic transmission. The diagram includes optional equipment not fitted to all models.

Wiring colour code: **BL** Blue **BR** Brown **GE** Yellow **GN** Green **GR** Grey **LI** Purple **RT** Red **SW** Black **WS** White

The figure on each wire before the colour code indicates the cross-sectional area of the wire in sq mm.

NOTES

HINTS ON MAINTENANCE AND OVERHAUL

There are few things more rewarding than the restoration of a vehicle's original peak of efficiency and smooth performance.

The following notes are intended to help the owner to reach that state of perfection. Providing that he possesses the basic manual skills he should have no difficulty in performing most of the operations detailed in this manual. It must be stressed, however, that where recommended in the manual, highly-skilled operations ought to be entrusted to experts, who have the necessary equipment, to carry out the work satisfactorily.

Quality of workmanship:

The hazardous driving conditions on the roads to-day demand that vehicles should be as nearly perfect, mechanically, as possible. It is therefore most important that amateur work be carried out with care, bearing in mind the often inadequate working conditions, and also the inferior tools which may have to be used. It is easy to counsel perfection in all things, and we recognise that it may be setting an impossibly high standard. We do, however, suggest that every care should be taken to ensure that a vehicle is as safe to take on the road as it is humanly possible to make it.

Safe working conditions:

Even though a vehicle may be stationary, it is still potentially dangerous if certain sensible precautions are not taken when working on it while it is supported on jacks or blocks. It is indeed preferable not to use jacks alone, but to supplement them with carefully placed blocks, so that there will be plenty of support if the car rolls off the jacks during a strenuous manoeuvre. Axle stands are an excellent way of providing a rigid base which is not readily disturbed. Piles of bricks are a dangerous substitute. Be careful not to get under heavy loads on lifting tackle, the load could fall. It is preferable not to work alone when lifting an engine, or when working underneath a vehicle which is supported well off the ground. To be trapped, particularly under the vehicle, may have unpleasant results if help is not quickly forthcoming. Make some provision, however humble, to deal with fires. Always disconnect a battery if there is a likelihood of electrical shorts. These may start a fire if there is leaking fuel about. This applies particularly to leads which can carry a heavy current, like those in the starter circuit. While on the subject of electricity, we must also stress the danger of using equipment which is run off the mains and which has no earth or has faulty wiring or connections. So many workshops have damp floors, and electrical shocks are of such a nature that it is sometimes impossible to let go of a live lead or piece of equipment due to the muscular spasms which take place.

Work demanding special care:

This involves the servicing of braking, steering and suspension systems. On the road, failure of the braking system may be disastrous. Make quite sure that there can be no possibility of failure through the bursting of rusty brake pipes or rotten hoses, nor to a sudden loss of pressure due to defective seals or valves.

Problems:

The chief problems which may face an operator are:
1 External dirt.
2 Difficulty in undoing tight fixings.
3 Dismantling unfamiliar mechanisms.
4 Deciding in what respect parts are defective.
5 Confusion about the correct order for reassembly.
6 Adjusting running clearance.
7 Road testing.
8 Final tuning.

Practical suggestions to solve the problems:

1 Preliminary cleaning of large parts—engines, transmissions, steering, suspensions, etc,—should be carried out before removal from the car. Where road dirt and mud alone are present, wash clean with a high-pressure water jet, brushing to remove stubborn adhesions, and allow to drain and dry. Where oil or grease is also present, wash down with a proprietary compound (Gunk, Teepol etc,) applying with a stiff brush—an old paint brush is suitable—into all crevices. Cover the distributor and ignition coils with a polythene bag and then apply a strong water jet to clear the loosened deposits. Allow to drain and dry. The assemblies will then be sufficiently clean to remove and transfer to the bench for the next stage.

On the bench, further cleaning can be carried out, first wiping the parts as free as possible from grease with old newspaper. Avoid using rag or cotton waste which can leave clogging fibres behind. Any remaining grease can be removed with a brush dipped in paraffin. If necessary, traces of paraffin can be removed by carbon tetrachloride. Avoid using paraffin or petrol in large quantities for cleaning in enclosed areas, such as garages, on account of the high fire risk.

When all exteriors have been cleaned, and not before, dismantling can be commenced. This ensures that dirt will not enter into interiors and orifices revealed by dismantling. In the next phases, where components have to be cleaned, use carbon tetrachloride in preference to petrol and keep the containers covered except when in use. After the components have been cleaned, plug small holes with tapered hard wood plugs cut to size and blank off larger orifices with grease-proof paper and masking tape. Do not use soft wood plugs or matchsticks as they may break.

2 It is not advisable to hammer on the end of a screw thread, but if it must be done, first screw on a nut to protect the thread, and use a lead hammer. This applies particularly to the removal of tapered cotters. Nuts and bolts seem to 'grow' together, especially in exhaust systems. If penetrating oil does not work, try the judicious application of heat, but be careful of starting a fire. Asbestos sheet or cloth is useful to isolate heat.

Tight bushes or pieces of tail-pipe rusted into a silencer can be removed by splitting them with an open-ended hacksaw. Tight screws can sometimes be started by a tap from a hammer on the end of a suitable screwdriver. Many tight fittings will yield to the judicious use of a hammer, but it must be a soft-faced hammer if damage is to be avoided, use a heavy block on the opposite side to absorb shock. Any parts of the steering system which have been damaged should be renewed, as attempts to repair them may lead to cracking and subsequent failure, and steering ball joints should be disconnected using a recommended tool to prevent damage.

3 It often happens that an owner is baffled when trying to dismantle an unfamiliar piece of equipment. So many modern devices are pressed together or assembled by spinning-over flanges, that they must be sawn apart. The intention is that the whole assembly must be renewed. However, parts which appear to be in one piece to the naked eye, may reveal close-fitting joint lines when inspected with a magnifying glass, and, this may provide the necessary clue to dismantling. Lefthanded screw threads are used where rotational forces would tend to unscrew a righthanded screw thread.

Be very careful when dismantling mechanisms which may come apart suddenly. Work in an enclosed space where the parts will be contained, and drape a piece of cloth over the device if springs are likely to fly in all directions. Mark everything which might be reassembled in the wrong position, scratched symbols may be used on unstressed parts, or a sequence of tiny dots from a centre punch can be useful. Stressed parts should never be scratched or centre-popped as this may lead to cracking under working conditions. Store parts which look alike in the correct order for reassembly. Never rely upon memory to assist in the assembly of complicated mechanisms, especially when they will be dismantled for a long time, but make notes, and drawings to supplement the diagrams in the manual, and put labels on detached wires. Rust stains may indicate unlubricated wear. This can sometimes be seen round the outside edge of a bearing cup in a universal joint. Look for bright rubbing marks on parts which normally should not make heavy contact. These might prove that something is bent or running out of truth. For example, there might be bright marks on one side of a piston, at the top near the ring grooves, and others at the bottom of the skirt on the other side. This could well be the clue to a bent connecting rod. Suspected cracks can be proved by heating the component in a light oil to approximately 100°C, removing, drying off, and dusting with french chalk, if a crack is present the oil retained in the crack will stain the french chalk.

4 In determining wear, and the degree, against the permissible limits set in the manual, accurate measurement can only be achieved by the use of a micrometer. In many cases, the wear is given to the fourth place of decimals; that is in ten-thousandths of an inch. This can be read by the vernier scale on the barrel of a good micrometer. Bore diameters are more difficult to determine. If, however, the matching shaft is accurately measured, the degree of play in the bore can be felt as a guide to its suitability. In other cases, the shank of a twist drill of known diameter is a handy check.

Many methods have been devised for determining the clearance between bearing surfaces. To-day, the best and simplest is by the use of Plastigage, obtainable from most garages. A thin plastic thread is laid between the two surfaces and the bearing is tightened, flattening the thread. On removal, the width of the thread is compared with a scale supplied with the thread and the clearance is read off directly. Sometimes joint faces leak persistently, even after gasket renewal. The fault will then be traceable to distortion, dirt or burrs. Studs which are screwed into soft metal frequently raise burrs at the point of entry. A quick cure for this is to chamfer the edge of the hole in the part which fits over the stud.

5 **Always check a replacement part with the original one before it is fitted.**

If parts are not marked, and the order for reassembly is not known, a little detective work will help. Look for marks which are due to wear to see if they can be mated. Joint faces may not be identical due to manufacturing errors, and parts which overlap may be stained, giving a clue to the correct position. Most fixings leave identifying marks especially if they were painted over on assembly. It is then easier to decide whether a nut, for instance, has a plain, a spring, or a shakeproof washer under it. All running surfaces become 'bedded' together after long spells of work and tiny imperfections on one part will be found to have left corresponding marks on the other. This is particularly true of shafts and bearings and even a score on a cylinder wall will show on the piston.

6 Checking end float or rocker clearances by feeler gauge may not always give accurate results because of wear. For instance, the rocker tip which bears on a valve stem may be deeply pitted, in which case the feeler will simply be bridging a depression. Thrust washers may also wear depressions in opposing faces to make accurate measurement difficult. End float is then easier to check by using a dial gauge. It is common practice to adjust end play in bearing assemblies, like front hubs with taper rollers, by doing up the axle nut until the hub becomes stiff to turn and then backing it off a little. Do not use this method with ballbearing hubs as the assembly is often preloaded by tightening the axle nut to its fullest extent. If the splitpin hole will not line up, file the base of the nut a little.

Steering assemblies often wear in the straight-ahead position. If any part is adjusted, make sure that it remains free when moved from lock to lock. Do not be surprised if an assembly like a steering gearbox, which is known to be carefully adjusted outside the car, becomes stiff when it is bolted in place. This will be due to distortion of the case by the pull of the mounting bolts, particularly if the mounting points are not all touching together. This problem may be met in other equipment and is cured by careful attention to the alignment of mounting points.

When a spanner is stamped with a size and A/F it means that the dimension is the width between the jaws and has no connection with ANF, which is the designation for the American National Fine thread. Coarse threads like Whitworth are rarely used on cars to-day except for studs which screw into soft aluminium or cast iron. For this reason it might be found that the top end of a cylinder head stud has a fine thread and the lower end a coarse thread to screw into the cylinder block. If the car has mainly UNF threads then it is likely that any coarse threads will be UNC, which are not the same as Whitworth. Small sizes have the same number of threads in Whitworth and UNC, but in the $\frac{1}{2}$ inch size for example, there are twelve threads to the inch in the former and thirteen in the latter.

7 After a major overhaul, particularly if a great deal of work has been done on the braking, steering and suspension systems, it is advisable to approach the problem of testing with care. If the braking system has been overhauled, apply heavy pressure to the brake pedal and get a second operator to check every possible source of leakage. The brakes may work extremely well, but a leak could cause complete failure after a few miles.

Do not fit the hub caps until every wheel nut has been checked for tightness, and make sure the tyre pressures are correct. Check the levels of coolant, lubricants and hydraulic fluids. Being satisfied that all is well, take the car on the road and test the brakes at once. Check the steering and the action of the handbrake. Do all this at moderate speeds on quiet roads, and make sure there is no other vehicle behind you when you try a rapid stop.

Finally, remember that many parts settle down after a time, so check for tightness of all fixings after the car has been on the road for a hundred miles or so.

8 It is useless to tune an engine which has not reached its normal running temperature. In the same way, the tune of an engine which is stiff after a rebore will be different when the engine is again running free. Remember too, that rocker clearances on pushrod operated valve gear will change when the cylinder head nuts are tightened after an initial period of running with a new head gasket.

Trouble may not always be due to what seems the obvious cause. Ignition, carburation and mechanical condition are interdependent and spitting back through the carburetter, which might be attributed to a weak mixture, can be caused by a sticking inlet valve.

For one final hint on tuning, never adjust more than one thing at a time or it will be impossible to tell which adjustment produced the desired result.

NOTES

GLOSSARY OF TERMS

Allen key   Cranked wrench of hexagonal section for use with socket head screws.

Alternator   Electrical generator producing alternating current. Rectified to direct current for battery charging.

Ambient temperature   Surrounding atmospheric temperature.

Annulus   Used in engineering to indicate the outer ring gear of an epicyclic gear train.

Armature   The shaft carrying the windings, which rotates in the magnetic field of a generator or starter motor. That part of a solenoid or relay which is activated by the magnetic field.

Axial   In line with, or pertaining to, an axis.

Backlash   Play in meshing gears.

Balance lever   A bar where force applied at the centre is equally divided between connections at the ends.

Banjo axle   Axle casing with large diameter housing for the crownwheel and differential.

Bendix pinion   A self-engaging and self-disengaging drive on a starter motor shaft.

Bevel pinion   A conical shaped gearwheel, designed to mesh with a similar gear with an axis usually at 90 deg. to its own.

bhp   Brake horse power, measured on a dynamometer.

bmep   Brake mean effective pressure. Average pressure on a piston during the working stroke.

Brake cylinder   Cylinder with hydraulically operated piston(s) acting on brake shoes or pad(s).

Brake regulator   Control valve fitted in hydraulic braking system which limits brake pressure to rear brakes during heavy braking to prevent rear wheel locking.

Camber   Angle at which a wheel is tilted from the vertical.

Capacitor   Modern term for an electrical condenser. Part of distributor assembly, connected across contact breaker points, acts as an interference suppressor.

Castellated   Top face of a nut, slotted across the flats, to take a locking splitpin.

Castor   Angle at which the kingpin or swivel pin is tilted when viewed from the side.

cc   Cubic centimetres. Engine capacity is arrived at by multiplying the area of the bore in sq cm by the stroke in cm by the number of cylinders.

Clevis   U-shaped forked connector used with a clevis pin, usually at handbrake connections.

Collet   A type of collar, usually split and located in a groove in a shaft, and held in place by a retainer. The arrangement used to retain the spring(s) on a valve stem in most cases.

Commutator   Rotating segmented current distributor between armature windings and brushes in generator or motor.

Compression ratio   The ratio, or quantitative relation, of the total volume (piston at bottom of stroke) to the unswept volume (piston at top of stroke) in an engine cylinder.

Condenser   See capacitor.

Core plug   Plug for blanking off a manufacturing hole in a casting.

Crownwheel   Large bevel gear in rear axle, driven by a bevel pinion attached to the propeller shaft. Sometimes called a 'ring gear'.

'C'-spanner   Like a 'C' with a handle. For use on screwed collars without flats, but with slots or holes.

Damper   Modern term for shock-absorber, used in vehicle suspension systems to damp out spring oscillations.

Depression   The lowering of atmospheric pressure as in the inlet manifold and carburetter.

Dowel   Close tolerance pin, peg, tube, or bolt, which accurately locates mating parts.

Drag link   Rod connecting steering box drop arm (pitman arm) to nearest front wheel steering arm in certain types of steering systems.

Dry liner   Thinwall tube pressed into cylinder bore

Dry sump   Lubrication system where all oil is scavenged from the sump, and returned to a separate tank.

Dynamo   See Generator.

Electrode   Terminal, part of an electrical component, such as the points or 'Electrodes' of a sparking plug.

Electrolyte   In lead-acid car batteries a solution of sulphuric acid and distilled water.

End float   The axial movement between associated parts, end play.

EP   Extreme pressure. In lubricants, special grades for heavily loaded bearing surfaces, such as gear teeth in a gearbox, or crownwheel and pinion in a rear axle.

Fade	Of brakes. Reduced efficiency due to overheating.
Field coils	Windings on the polepieces of motors and generators.
Fillets	Narrow finishing strips usually applied to interior bodywork.
First motion shaft	Input shaft from clutch to gearbox.
Fullflow filter	Filters in which all the oil is pumped to the engine. If the element becomes clogged, a bypass valve operates to pass unfiltered oil to the engine.
FWD	Front wheel drive.
Gear pump	Two meshing gears in a close fitting casing. Oil is carried from the inlet round the outside of both gears in the spaces between the gear teeth and casing to the outlet, the meshing gear teeth prevent oil passing back to the inlet, and the oil is forced through the outlet port.
Generator	Modern term for 'Dynamo'. When rotated produces electrical current.
Grommet	A ring of protective or sealing material. Can be used to protect pipes or leads passing through bulkheads.
Grubscrew	Fully threaded headless screw with screwdriver slot. Used for locking, or alignment purposes.
Gudgeon pin	Shaft which connects a piston to its connecting rod. Sometimes called 'wrist pin', or 'piston pin'.
Halfshaft	One of a pair transmitting drive from the differential.
Helical	In spiral form. The teeth of helical gears are cut at a spiral angle to the side faces of the gearwheel.
Hot spot	Hot area that assists vapourisation of fuel on its way to cylinders. Often provided by close contact between inlet and exhaust manifolds.
HT	High Tension. Applied to electrical current produced by the ignition coil for the sparking plugs.
Hydrometer	A device for checking specific gravity of liquids. Used to check specific gravity of electrolyte.
Hypoid bevel gears	A form of bevel gear used in the rear axle drive gears. The bevel pinion meshes below the centre line of the crownwheel, giving a lower propeller shaft line.
Idler	A device for passing on movement. A free running gear between driving and driven gears. A lever transmitting track rod movement to a side rod in steering gear.
Impeller	A centrifugal pumping element. Used in water pumps to stimulate flow.
Journals	Those parts of a shaft that are in contact with the bearings.
Kingpin	The main vertical pin which carries the front wheel spindle, and permits steering movement. May be called 'steering pin' or 'swivel pin'.
Layshaft	The shaft which carries the laygear in the gearbox. The laygear is driven by the first motion shaft and drives the third motion shaft according to the gear selected. Sometimes called the 'countershaft' or 'second motion shaft.'
lb ft	A measure of twist or torque. A pull of 10 lb at a radius of 1 ft is a torque of 10 lb ft.
lb/sq in	Pounds per square inch.
Little-end	The small, or piston end of a connecting rod. Sometimes called the 'small-end'.
LT	Low Tension. The current output from the battery.
Mandrel	Accurately manufactured bar or rod used for test or centring purposes.
Manifold	A pipe, duct, or chamber, with several branches.
Needle rollers	Bearing rollers with a length many times their diameter.
Oil bath	Reservoir which lubricates parts by immersion. In air filters, a separate oil supply for wetting a wire mesh element to hold the dust.
Oil wetted	In air filters, a wire mesh element lightly oiled to trap and hold airborne dust.
Overlap	Period during which inlet and exhaust valves are open together.
Panhard rod	Bar connected between fixed point on chassis and another on axle to control sideways movement.
Pawl	Pivoted catch which engages in the teeth of a ratchet to permit movement in one direction only.
Peg spanner	Tool with pegs, or pins, to engage in holes or slots in the part to be turned.
Pendant pedals	Pedals with levers that are pivoted at the top end.
Phillips screwdriver	A cross-point screwdriver for use with the cross-slotted heads of Phillips screws.
Pinion	A small gear, usually in relation to another gear.
Piston-type damper	Shock absorber in which damping is controlled by a piston working in a closed oil-filled cylinder.
Preloading	Preset static pressure on ball or roller bearings not due to working loads.
Radial	Radiating from a centre, like the spokes of a wheel.

Radius rod	Pivoted arm confining movement of a part to an arc of fixed radius.
Ratchet	Toothed wheel or rack which can move in one direction only, movement in the other being prevented by a pawl.
Ring gear	A gear tooth ring attached to outer periphery of flywheel. Starter pinion engages with it during starting.
Runout	Amount by which rotating part is out of true.
Semi-floating axle	Outer end of rear axle halfshaft is carried on bearing inside axle casing. Wheel hub is secured to end of shaft.
Servo	A hydraulic or pneumatic system for assisting, or, augmenting a physical effort. See 'Vacuum Servo'.
Setscrew	One which is threaded for the full length of the shank.
Shackle	A coupling link, used in the form of two parallel pins connected by side plates to secure the end of the master suspension spring and absorb the effects of deflection.
Shell bearing	Thinwalled steel shell lined with anti-friction metal. Usually semi-circular and used in pairs for main and big-end bearings.
Shock absorber	See 'Damper'.
Silentbloc	Rubber bush bonded to inner and outer metal sleeves.
Socket-head screw	Screw with hexagonal socket for an Allen key.
Solenoid	A coil of wire creating a magnetic field when electric current passes through it. Used with a soft iron core to operate contacts or a mechanical device.
Spur gear	A gear with teeth cut axially across the periphery.
Stub axle	Short axle fixed at one end only.
Tachometer	An instrument for accurate measurement of rotating speed. Usually indicates in revolutions per minute.

TDC	Top Dead Centre. The highest point reached by a piston in a cylinder, with the crank and connecting rod in line.
Thermostat	Automatic device for regulating temperature. Used in vehicle coolant systems to open a valve which restricts circulation at low temperature.
Third motion shaft	Output shaft of gearbox.
Threequarter floating axle	Outer end of rear axle halfshaft flanged and bolted to wheel hub, which runs on bearing mounted on outside of axle casing. Vehicle weight is not carried by the axle shaft.
Thrust bearing or washer	Used to reduce friction in rotating parts subject to axial loads.
Torque	Turning or twisting effort. See 'lb ft'.
Track rod	The bar(s) across the vehicle which connect the steering arms and maintain the front wheels in their correct alignment.
UJ	Universal joint. A coupling between shafts which permits angular movement.
UNF	Unified National Fine screw thread.
Vacuum servo	Device used in brake system, using difference between atmospheric pressure and inlet manifold depression to operate a piston which acts to augment brake pressure as required. See 'Servo'.
Venturi	A restriction or 'choke' in a tube, as in a carburetter, used to increase velocity to obtain a reduction in pressure.
Vernier	A sliding scale for obtaining fractional readings of the graduations of an adjacent scale.
Welch plug	A domed thin metal disc which is partially flattened to lock in a recess. Used to plug core holes in castings.
Wet liner	Removable cylinder barrel, sealed against coolant leakage, where the coolant is in direct contact with the outer surface.
Wet sump	A reservoir attached to the crankcase to hold the lubricating oil.

NOTES

INDEX

NOTES

NOTES

NOTES

NOTES